Applied Innovation and Technology Management

Series Editors

Tugrul U Daim, Department of Engineering & Technology Management
Portland State University
Portland, OR, USA

Marina Dabić, Faculty of Economics & Business
University of Zagreb
Zagreb, Croatia

Technology is not just limited to technology companies. Managing innovation and technology is no longer a luxury and needs to be understood by all sectors around the world and by both technical and non-technical managers. This book series explores existing and emerging technologies that address current challenges within innovation and technology managements. Each title is developed to provide a set of frameworks, tools and methods that can be adopted by researchers, managers and student in engineering, innovation and technology fields. Research, policy and practice-based books in the series cover topics such as roadmapping, portfolio management, technology forecasting, R&D management, health technologies, bio technologies, transportation management, smart cities, and open innovation, among many others.

Giuseppina Passiante
Editor

Digital Innovation Management

People, Process, Platforms and Policy

Springer

Editor
Giuseppina Passiante
Aldo Romano Building
University of Salento
LECCE, Lecce, Italy

ISSN 2662-9402 ISSN 2662-9410 (electronic)
Applied Innovation and Technology Management
ISBN 978-3-031-80425-0 ISBN 978-3-031-80426-7 (eBook)
https://doi.org/10.1007/978-3-031-80426-7

This Springer imprint is published by the registered company Springer Nature Switzerland AG
The registered company address is: Gewerbestrasse 11, 6330 Cham, Switzerland

Introduction

Digital technologies have radically changed the nature and structure of products and services, offering new value-creation and value-appropriation pathways. Digital innovation is also reconfiguring the organisations' value chains and value systems, allowing them to become faster, more flexible and able to rapidly address unexpected challenges and emerging opportunities.

The exponential diffusion of digital technologies is transforming the rules of 'traditional' markets and industries, and the consolidated ways in which companies operate in the global competitive scenario. A 'digital-at-the-core' business model, a new way of creating value through technologies, dominates today as the key competitive framework to support those organisations which, regardless of size, location and industry, aim to compete in the digital economy. However, the 'digital-at-the-core' business model is successful only if it is supported by fast learning rates and the capacity of organisations to leverage and integrate effectively an array of fast-evolving market and technology knowledge assets available at local and global level.

From a societal perspective, the diffusion of digital technologies has introduced significant changes in people's lifestyle and behaviour, thus forcing companies and public administrations to accelerate their digital transformation processes. The penetration of technologies within organisations, industries and societies is thus contributing to the affirmation of a socio-technical phenomenon and composite trend which is termed *digital innovation*. Consequently, we can refer to *digital innovation management* as the set of practices, processes and principles that underlie the effective orchestration of digital innovation, and which are aimed to develop close, trust-based relationships among organisations and their stakeholders aiming to achieve business results while guaranteeing socio-environmental sustainability.

Virtuous interdependences among organisations and individuals are also influenced by institutions, which are called to create and sustain effective patterns of social interaction within a territory. All such actors are closely interconnected, and contribute to create innovative industrial clusters able to increase the innovation rate of regional economies.

These 'creative environments' have been characterised as *digital innovation ecosystems*, i.e. integrated and digitally enabled systems of research, innovation and education that promote and foster dynamic synergies among research institutions, financial organisations, entrepreneurs and experts working in continuous interaction to generate new knowledge, competencies and innovation. An example of such ecosystems is the smart city, where investments in Information and Communication Technologies (ICTs), technological infrastructure and digital services are aimed to ensure sustainable economic development and a high quality of life, changing the spatiality of territories by integrating geographical contiguity with relational proximity.

The paradigm of digital innovation includes four integrated dimensions, which are adopted in this book as building blocks of the emerging socio-technical scenario: (1) *People*, i.e. the individual agents and core engine of technology-based transformation; (2) *Process*, i.e. the modality, mechanism and space through which the innovation actually happens; (3) *Platform*, i.e. the integrated system of solutions and tools driving the transformation; and (4) *Policy*, i.e. the institutional layer that supports and sustains socio-technical transformation. Around such four dimensions, the structure of the book is articulated in ten chapters, which offer relevant glimpses into the emerging stream of research on digital innovation and digital innovation management.

In the **Opening Remarks**, the first chapter by Passiante et al. highlights the current challenges of innovative management in the digital economy. In the **People** section, Secundo et al. aim to investigate dynamic capabilities for a digitally transformed era whereas Ndou et al. focus on crucial competencies and skills for a digital journey within the public administration sector.

In the **Process** section, Margherita et al. analyse digital innovation in the human resource management to generate people-centred organisations whereas Elia et al. highlight the results of an experiment of digital innovation in the reverse-logistics process.

In the **Platform** section, Solazzo et al. analyse the role of digital technologies for energy management and in particular for supporting renewable energy communities, whereas Lorenzo et al. focus on artificial intelligence platforms that enable conversational chatbots and Girardo et al. emphasise the smart city as a model of digital innovation for urban development.

In the **Policy** section, Mele et al. focus on digital innovation ecosystems for sustainable growth, whereas Petti et al. discuss the main issues of digital transformation in international education.

Finally, since digital innovation is a multi-stakeholder process, each chapter is co-authored by academicians and professionals working in private companies or public institutions, in the aim to provide readers with an integrated perspective of such complex phenomenon.

Contents

1 An Innovative Management in the Digital Economy: The CNR Case Study 1
Giuseppina Passiante and Gianpiero Ruggiero

2 Orchestrating Open Innovation Ecosystems Based on Digital Technologies: The Lutech Case Study 21
Giustina Secundo, Domenica Barile, Antonello Garzoni, and Giuseppe Ieva

3 Competencies and Skills for Public Administration: A Digital Journey 41
Valentina Ndou and Giusi Miccoli

4 Digital Human Resource Management: Innovative Methods to Build a People-Centred Organisation in the Healthcare Industry 61
Alessandro Margherita, Hila Chalutz-Ben Gal, and Guy Topaz

5 Digital Factory 5.0: Experimenting Digital Innovation in the Reverse Logistics Process 81
Gianluca Elia, Gianpaolo Ghiani, Emanuele Manni, Francesco Nucci, Stefano Giuri, and Alberto Paglialunga

6 Digital Technologies for Sustainable Development: Opportunities and Challenges in the Renewable Energy Communities Paradigm 103
Gianluca Solazzo, Gianluca Elia, Giuseppina Passiante, and Palmalisa Marra

7 Artificial Intelligence Platforms Enabling Conversational Chatbots: The Case of Tiledesk.com 119
Gianluca Lorenzo, Gianluca Elia, and Andrea Sponziello

8 The Smart City as a Model of Digital Innovation for Urban Development 139
Gianmarco Girardo, Alessandro Bartolini, and Giuseppina Passiante

9 Digital Innovation Ecosystems for the Sustainable Growth: Analysis of the Italian Circular Economy Platform and Networks . . 157
Gioconda Mele, Pasquale Del Vecchio, and Marco De Maggio

10 Digital Transformation in International Education 185
Claudio Petti, Antonella Longo, and Antonio Ficarella

Chapter 1
An Innovative Management in the Digital Economy: The CNR Case Study

Giuseppina Passiante and Gianpiero Ruggiero

Abstract Virtuous linkages and interdependences among organizations, companies, and individuals that share and exchange knowledge are also influenced by institutions that are called to create and sustain virtuous and regular patterns of social interactions within a territory. These functions could represent the "mission" of a local development agency that acts as an "Intelligent Agency" supporting the combination of localization forces and digitalization forces. The Italian National Research Council (CNR) is the largest public research institution in Italy, the only one under the Ministry of University and Research performing multidisciplinary activities.

CNR intends to support the foundations of knowledge through continuous interactions and contaminations, in a process that involves the sharing of ideas and programs, but also of crucial research infrastructures at a national and international level to carry out high-level projects, and of training opportunities and discussions for envisioning new research horizons.

This chapter presents the reorganization of the CNR, which presents important food for thought for stimulating and supporting two specific forms of intervention: (i) implementation of specific education and training programs based on new training frameworks; and (ii) activation of systematic consultation between internal actors and the network of stakeholders.

Keywords Digital economy · Knowledge exchange · Innovation agency · Organizational model · Digital transformation

G. Passiante (✉)
Department of Engineering for Innovation, University of Salento, Lecce, Italy
e-mail: giuseppina.passiante@unisalento.it

G. Ruggiero
Research Support and Grant Office, CNR—National Research Council, Rome, Italy
e-mail: gianpiero.ruggiero@cnr.it

G. Passiante (ed.), *Digital Innovation Management*, Applied Innovation and Technology Management, https://doi.org/10.1007/978-3-031-80426-7_1

1.1 Introduction

The significant phenomena of the digital economy have been studied by scholars, as well as by economic and institutional operators (Gerwe & Silva, 2020; Brynjolfsson & Collis, 2019). Predominantly, digital technologies have led to an exponential growth of knowledge: indeed, these technologies formed the infrastructure for the circulation and mobility of knowledge and, more generally, of intangible assets. Consequently, the following stylized facts emerge (Popkova et al., 2022):

- The synergistic interaction between the digital economy and the knowledge economy that is increasingly reinforced by the large-scale development of new digital technologies.
- The increasing productivity in transforming knowledge into new products, new services, and in the growth of their innovative capacities.

More in general, a wide array of theoretical approaches emphasizes the role of linkages and interdependences among organizations that create digital knowledge networks of production, suitable for developing innovations (Romer, 1990; Grillitsch, Asheim and Trippl, 2014; Clarke, 2001). These linkages and interdependences are dynamic interconnections with a specific division of labor, a particular extent and nature of links that develop among customers, suppliers, and competitors. Organizations operating in turbulent times can also benefit from banding together to enhance their resilience and find or create new opportunities. A network-based approach to setting strategy offers a safe and creative space to explore alternatives, understand different opinions, reinterpret identities, and work together effectively (Ujwary-Gil & Potoczek, 2023).

Digital technologies create value along three related pathways (The World Economic Forum, 2023):

- Transform business: digital transformation plans to boost a sustained, long-term value for the company.
- Support stakeholders: digital technologies respond to the needs and priorities of a far-reaching set of stakeholders, including employees, consumers, governments, and society.
- Change systems: digital technologies create new collaborations and value-creation processes across ecosystems, thus enabling a systemic change.

Five important business dimensions are characterizing the evolution of a company experiencing the digital transformation (The World Economic Forum, 2023):

- New value from digital transformation: companies are using digital technologies to go beyond linear value chains and industry boundaries toward the creation of shared value in broader digital ecosystems.
- Accelerating to "digital-at-the-core" business models: instead of extending traditional models with digital channels, companies are orchestrating new digitally enabled ecosystems.

- Operating models and supply chains are becoming intelligent, cyber-resilient, agile, and free from functional silos, with humans working with artificial intelligence across the company, to match its organizational structure to the technology transition.
- Decisions based on historical data and traditional forecasting models are evolving toward "at the edge" decisions made by front-line employees to deliver personalized services and forge new collaborations.
- Companies use data and analytics to de-risk revenue and cost profiles, plan for new growth areas, rethink how to finance innovation, consider the financial impact of economic uncertainty, share efforts with ecosystem partners, and deliver environmental, social, and governance (ESG) outcomes.

For digital innovation to deliver real growth and value to any organization, three key conditions are required: (1) teams must be empowered to move fast and experiment to discover what works in the marketplace; (2) boards must be empowered to oversee and advise portfolios of teams, allocating resources where most needed; and (3) both must follow regular processes for green-lighting new ventures, funding them iteratively, and shutting them down to free up resources for the next emerging opportunity (Rogers, 2023).

To support digital operating models, most companies are engaged also in a rapid upskilling, to prepare for closer collaboration between humans and smart digital technologies.

The remainder of the chapter is organized as follows. The next two sections introduce the key issues on academic and public institutions in the digital economy, which are reshaping their knowledge networks. Section 1.4 presents the experience of the National Research Council (CNR), as an agency supporting knowledge networks for innovation within the national industrial system. Section 1.5 highlights the CNR Relaunch Plan to monitor the impact of these activities and encourage the exploitation of the results to create a methodology and an organizational structure that can capitalize on these experiences. Section 1.6 concludes the chapter by highlighting some issues to be solved in the innovation management of the CNR.

1.2 Academic Institutions in the Digital Economy

The new economic and competitive landscape needs new competencies that require new theoretical approaches and new learning strategies and processes mainly based on scanning across different disciplines and industry domains. However, most universities and business schools are functionally structured organizations with each department responsible for their courses (Terjesen, 2022). There is little encouragement for cross-functionally teaching or research (D'Souza et al., 2022). In the terminology of Schumpeterian firms' analysis, the "creative destruction process" does not concern only the traditional industry, the traditional technological assets, the traditional competitive positioning strategies, and the traditional regulatory approach. The "creative destruction process" also involves the universities and business schools and calls for radical innovation in their knowledge organization, learning strategies, and processes (Miller, 2010).

Academic institutions in the digital economy develop research activities to activate and "microcosm of real settings" (Passiante & Andriani, 2000), where talented people can learn how to learn together, enhancing their collective intelligence, competence, and capacity to imagine research questions and pilot projects oriented to generate innovation in the digital economy for exploring different uses of ICT/digital media capacity in every field and innovative ways. Universities are uniquely placed to provide answers to key challenges—digital literacy, inclusion, take up of digital technologies by SMEs, and retention of emerging talent. The "microcosm of real settings" engine is provided by the basic and applied research activities, which boost the creation and exploitation of experiential knowledge (often tacit, related to specific events, experiences, trials, observations), emerging knowledge (explicit knowledge designed to meet the needs of a specific situation), and formalized knowledge (explicit knowledge generalized and structured to educate) (Ives et al., 2000). The basic and applied research activities are strictly interrelated: indeed, it is presumed that theory and practice foster each other in a synergic manner. The goal of basic research is to predict the transformation induced by structural changes in the digital economy; the outcomes of basic research are necessary to identify new opportunities coming from such transformations. The outcomes facilitate the development of applied research—such as pilot research projects—aimed at experimenting with new organization cases that are based on the new opportunities that emerged during the basic research activities. Basic research is also focused on the assessment of the real opportunities for SMEs to increase their competitiveness by adopting pilot project outcomes. In-progress and final assessment of pilot projects can also provide feedback to enrich the value of the knowledge base generated by basic research activities, possibly validating or updating their contents.

The "microcosm of real settings" strategic resources may be synthesized in the following points:

- Core competencies, including both the scientific community mainly concentrated in the economic-management engineering scientific field and students involved in masters, PhD, undergraduate, and executive learning programs, coming from all over the world.
- "Academic and industrial partners network" made up of all the organizations currently involved in the microcosm, such as prestigious research centers, universities, and institutions at the global level.

These issues are topical in the scientific and institutional debate, and present elements of significant coherence with the strategic and funding lines of both the HORIZON 2020 program and the new HORIZON Europe program, as well as the PNRR, the PON R&C, and the development and innovation programs of the Ionian-Adriatic Macro Region.

1.3 Government Institutions in the Digital Economy

In the digital economy, there is a need for government institutions that play a guiding and a stimulating role for local systems, that are rooted in the community to which they belong, making them able to operate at their best, and that operate according to logic "mission-driven," results-oriented, focused on the needs of individuals and organizations (Tapscott, 1995; Finger & Brand, 1999).

This strategic vision has to be focused on a system-wide transformation, and a solid integration of decisions and activities within and between public sector organizations. Moreover, it has to ensure that the relations with citizens and businesses are promoted through collaborations around public policies and services for both increasing economic productivity and improving societal well-being. Indeed, a successful digital transformation can allow public sectors to operate more efficiently and effectively in the digital environment, as well as to deliver public services that are less complex and more helpful (Greenway et al., 2019).

However, fully realizing this digital transformation requires a paradigm shift toward a digital government, as highlighted by the OECD Recommendation of the Council on Digital Government Strategies. This digital transformation of the public sector is a complex and vast process, where a synergistic combination of technological processes and organizational methods can transform government into environments and therefore real factors and actors of local development (OECD, 2014).

As for the entrepreneurial level, digital technologies are determining a radical reconfiguration of the government institutions' value chain and value system, with the final intention to become a fast-moving, flexible, and robust organization, capable of rapid responses to unexpected challenges, events, and opportunities. The final aim is indeed to achieve continuous innovations in serving customers by speeding up internal knowledge flows as well as by developing close, trust-based relationships with customers and suppliers, to spot digital opportunities and to take advantage of them. The ultimate vision of this digital government institution is an intelligent organization—one that is fully automated, connected, and can respond and adapt its operations as knowledge changes.

These linkages and interdependences are dynamic interconnections with a specific division of labor, a particular extent and nature of links that develop among customers, suppliers, and competitors, as well as with a precise role of the local institutions in creating and sustaining some regular patterns of social interactions in a place. All actors are closely interconnected, and their feedback contributes both to creating innovative industrial clusters and increasing the innovation rate of the regional economies where they are located (Rocha et al., 2020).

More in general, a wide array of theoretical approaches emphasizes the role of linkages and interdependences among organizations that create digital knowledge networks of production, suitable for developing innovations (Romer, 1990; Asheim et al., 2017). These linkages and interdependences are dynamic interconnections with a specific division of labor, a particular extent and nature of links that develop among customers, suppliers, and competitors. All actors are closely interconnected, and their feedback contributes both to creating industrial clusters and increasing the innovation rate of the knowledge networks where they are located.

It becomes then necessary a precise role of the institutions in creating and sustaining some regular patterns of social and business interactions within knowledge networks. In this view, it is important to understand the complex and dynamic role of an agency in supporting knowledge networks for digital innovation.

1.4 An Agency Supporting Knowledge Networks for Digital Innovation: The National Research Council of Italy (CNR)

This section presents the experience of the Italian National Research Council (CNR), as an agency supporting knowledge networks for innovation within the national industrial system.

The National Research Council (CNR) mission is to perform research in its Institutes, to promote innovation and competitiveness of the national industrial system, to promote the internationalization of the national research system, to provide technologies and solutions to emerging public and private needs, to advice Government and other public bodies, and to contribute to the qualification of human resources. (Adapted from the Statute of the National Research Council—legislative decree n. 218 of November 25, 2016, issued by the Italian Government).

The scientific network of CNR is organized in departments, research institutes, and research units. Departments are organizational units structured in macro-areas of scientific and technological research institutes that are engaged in a great variety of research topics that face the challenges that are at the heart of the international agenda of the research: healthcare, demographic changes and wellness, food safety and sustainable agriculture, energy and environmental protection, accessibility of resources, and intelligent transport. Thanks to their network spread all over Italia and the great variety of research topics, they also give a relevant contribution to the regional and local innovation. In some projects, the institutes are aggregated into research units, structures offering services, and representing for the territory a scientific and cultural attraction pole. Research units are usually located as a project implementer with a specific timetable (https://www.CNR.it/en/about-us, accessed on October 20, 2023).

The CNR, with over 8500 employees of which 65% are researchers and technologists, and an annual budget that exceeds 1 billion euros, is the largest Italian research body and the one with the greatest interdisciplinary vocation, a modality, the latter, which is also specifically indicated among the statutory objectives. In the digital economy, a high responsiveness and operational streamlining as well as an increased interdisciplinary vision are required. The long-term goal is to create a non-hierarchical but organized environment to support research activities, foster scientific careers, and develop infrastructures accessible to qualified research groups.

The digital economy has generated several complexities deriving from both institutional and contextual factors. It may generate then threats and as well as opportunities for an agency in supporting knowledge networks for digital innovation.

Moving from the analysis of the CNR 3-year plan, we illustrate how CNR has grasped these opportunities through its process of reorganization by leveraging digital technologies (https://www.CNR.it/en/programming-documents, accessed on May 14, 2024).

Furthermore, some details are presented, based on the discussions we had with the OIV members from 2010 to 2016 (OIV is the internal body for evaluation).

Here, the objective is not based solely on opening or closing institutes and/or departments—a "periodic maintenance" necessary for the consolidation and development of the scientific network—but also responding in a timely and efficient manner to emerging demands of society, also solicited by the Ministry of University and Research or by the Presidency of the Council. The objective is therefore not based solely on opening or closing institutes and/or departments—a "periodic maintenance" necessary for the consolidation and development of the scientific network—but also responding in a timely and efficient manner to emerging demands of society.

The concept of "attractor" can be defined as a macro-theme of a scientific or intellectual nature, as well as an emerging challenge that society has an urgency to face. Examples of attractors are the proposals presented in the context of the PNRR. These proposals arise from a clear strategic direction of the government, which has identified the emerging scientific priorities for the next few years. The scientific network of the CNR has been involved almost entirely, albeit to varying degrees, in the three PNRR calls for proposal on "Innovation Ecosystems," "Research Infrastructures," and "National Centers." The mechanism triggered by the three PNRR calls for proposal is summarized in Fig. 1.1, which shows the example of the proposal presented by the CRN for the "National Center for Biodiversity," to which 17 institutes from 4 different departments contributed.

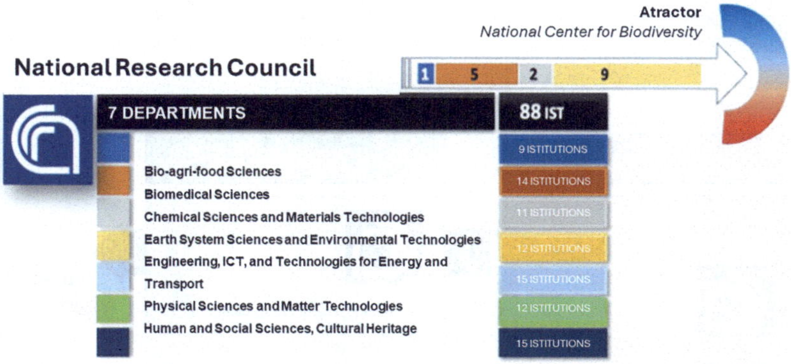

Fig. 1.1 CNR structure. (Adapted from https://www.CNR.it/en/programming-documents, accessed on May 14, 2024)

The attractor offered by the PNRR has induced synergy and coordination between CNR institutes, as shown in Fig. 1.1. In the specific example, the numbers on the arrow indicate the institutes belonging to different departments coordinated to respond to the attractor "National Center of Biodiversity."

Strategic planning has then to be integrated with "light" organizational structures, that is, without administrative autonomy, which are defined as "goal-oriented research units" (URGOs), which may, for example, be inspired by European programs, as shown in Fig. 1.2.

The URGOs aim to

- Promote large frontier and interdisciplinary projects in line with international initiatives (PNRR, Agenda 2030, UN SDGs, Missions & Partnerships, Horizon Europe ERC or EIC, Green Pact, etc.)
- Integrate the skills and interests of institutes and/or research groups through the elaboration of joint action plans capable of dealing with complex and strategic issues for the country in which the organization decides to invest in the medium/long term.
- Involve industrial and institutional stakeholders and the world of nonprofit foundations in the strategic plan of the institution.
- Develop solid partnerships with regional governments, public administrations, and universities, contributing to a balanced distribution of research in the country by promoting multidirectional flows between all institutions.

The URGOs may therefore be open to other research institutions and universities at national and international levels, as well as to collaborations with other public and private entities subject to agreement for the management and exploitation of the intellectual property generated. A system of dedicated budgets has also envisaged to allow the URGOs to be able to use the free funds remaining from competitive research projects or institutional resources, which allows them to offer the necessary breadth and practicability of the activity carried out following the evaluation science of the initiative.

The URGOs, consequently, will play a primary networking role, inspired by the European Coordination and Support Actions (CSA), while for specific strategic

Fig. 1.2 The "goal-oriented research units" (URGOs). (Adapted from https://www.CNR.it/en/programming-documents, accessed on May 14, 2024)

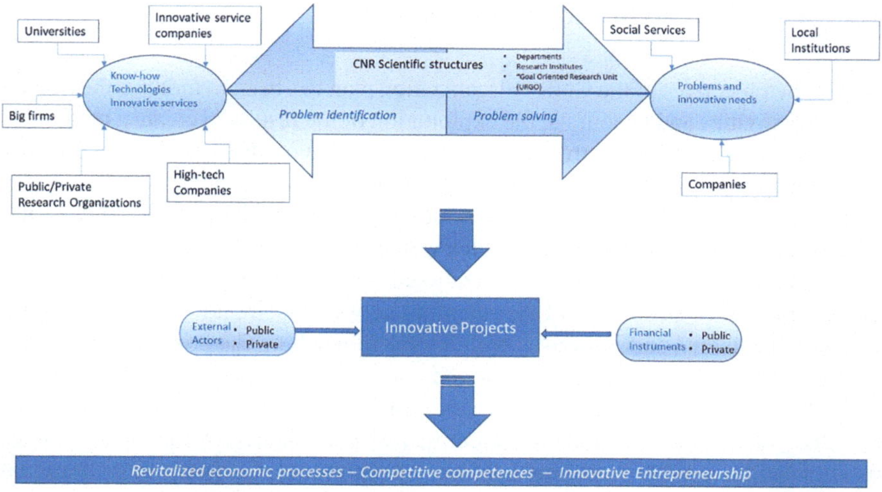

Fig. 1.3 CNR as a catalyst for innovative processes

needs of the country, they can also be activated thanks to a seed grant-type contribution and dedicated financial support.

In this way, CNR becomes a "system of organized cooperation" between a heterogeneous plurality of subjects to promote innovations, as well as a market referent in the access/use of technologies and services of universities, research organizations, local/national/international businesses, local/national government institutions, and financial institutions.

The mission of the CNR is thus to organize all the determinants and enhance the system effect of innovative processes in their technological, economic, sociological, and institutional components. The multiple networks of organizations that govern growth in CNR involve multiple levels of government. Large institutional networks are the emerging form of these multi-scalar interactions. That region planning institutions are comprised of this new composite, termed multi-scalar large institutional networks (MSLIN), has implications for theory, practice, and research because they evolve, learn, and act on emergent phenomena and via emergent processes in extraordinarily complex and dynamic settings in ways radically distinct from individual organizations and institutions. Figure 1.3 provides a representation of the CNR as a catalyst for innovative processes.

Furthermore, the organization provides a considerable number of services aimed at external public administrations and private companies, showing a significant revenue generation capacity and a high degree of interconnection with the social context.

1.5 The CNR Reorganization Plan

One of the objectives of the CNR reorganization plan has been to monitor the impact of these activities and encourage the exploitation of the results to create a methodology and an organizational structure that can capitalize on the experiences, enhancing them and systematizing them for the benefit of trans-nationality.

If, on the one hand, these characteristics represent an element of richness and vitality, on the other, they form a complex web that over time has required a progressive series of management and organizational adjustments that have affected both the administrative structure and the scientific network itself and which still require further adjustments and initiatives with a view to reaching the critical mass necessary to guarantee greater effectiveness and performance of the activities.

In this context today, almost 100 years after its establishment, the CNR is called to rediscover its role as a guide for scientific research inspired by the highest values of knowledge, a guide that must continue to represent, also from an institutional profile, the Italian research far beyond national borders.

In this process of rediscovering the founding institutional values and regenerative transformation, to project itself into scientific progress, in the promotion of scientific and cultural excellence, and in the pursuit of the sustainable development objectives of the United Nations (the 17 SDGs), the CNR cannot start by clearly reaffirming how fundamental research is at the center of one's work, improving one's organizational and management tools and introducing evaluation as a systematic method of decision support. For this reason, it is necessary to create a favorable environment to attract the researchers of tomorrow, without rigid hierarchical structures and sectoral barriers, promoting the encouragement and development of careers to support innovation in a continuous process of social growth and cultural promotion that recognizes the science is a high-impact tool for the pursuit of collective well-being, environmental sustainability, and the highest values of democracy and freedom.

1.5.1 The Reorganization of CNR Scientific Network

Fundamental research, therefore, as a natural vocation of a CNR has to be relocated to the center of the national and international scientific panorama, increasingly a point of reference for universities and research institutions that intend to work on the foundations of knowledge through continuous interactions and contaminations, in a process that involves the sharing not only of ideas and programs, but also of crucial research infrastructures at a national and international level to be able to carry out high-level projects, and of periodic opportunities for training and discussion to guide the horizons of contemporary and future science.

For this project to become reality, there are two protagonists: on the one hand, the researchers and technologists with their future as scientific leaders, supported and supported by the technical-administrative figures who allow the functioning of the infrastructures and the administrative machine; on the other hand, the contemporary science, how it is organized, with the dynamics that characterize it today and its impetus to respond to the emerging challenges of knowledge and contemporary society.

The pressing need to increase scientific productivity, in particular that which is expressed in the highest percentiles of the various ranking systems, the need to identify new research opportunities, to identify with ever greater accuracy what the strategic orientations of the international scientific community are as well as addressing emerging social challenges with innovative tools, requires adequate organizational tools that are able to correctly interpret the times while contributing, at the same time, to the CNR acquiring a well-recognizable identity and international authority.

To meet these needs, it is appropriate to reformulate the research organization and programming model in the CNR, taking inspiration from what the international scientific community offers us and has already chosen as a reference model for its investment policies, starting from the one offered by the European Research Council (ERC). The latter, which is known as the main and most prestigious European agency aimed at financing scientific excellence, bases its activity on evaluation "panels" that are inspired by a division into disciplinary areas that are constantly updated and adapted to the main research trends.

This division is extremely functional both because it involves the use of an updated taxonomy of scientific disciplines and because it allows research activities to be oriented, in aggregate terms, toward emerging challenges while also facilitating comparison and synergy with today's reference scientific institutions that represent excellence on a European and global scale. In the Reorganization and Relaunch Plan of the CNR, the concept of "disciplinary area" (AD) is introduced, understood as a thematic-disciplinary aggregation that essentially follows the subdivision adopted for the ERC panels.

The scientific network of the future CNR will therefore be reorganized in terms of affiliation to the different disciplinary areas. The future structures of the CNR scientific network, including the departments and institutes, will choose the disciplinary scientific fields to which they belong. These connections will be solely of a thematic nature. Each scientific structure of the CNR and the goal-oriented research institutes and units must have a primary affiliation and several secondary affiliations such as to cover the entire disciplinary spectrum of their research activities.

The role of the departments at the CNR is currently defined by Article 12 of the CNR Statute, which in paragraphs 1 and 2 states:

- The activities of the CNR are divided into macro-areas of scientific and technological research, hereinafter "macro-areas,, defined by the board of directors in relation to the mission and research objectives identified by the minister (Paragraph 1).
- The departments are the organizational structures of the macro-areas with promotion, proposal, planning, coordination, and supervision tasks. Institutes

belong to the departments, grouped according to skills and strategic priorities. The departments play a central role in reference and valorization of their respective scientific communities also at a national level (Paragraph 2).

It is then specified in the following paragraphs how the departments are responsible for systematizing skills and supporting the institutes by supporting research activities that emerge in a "bottom-up" mode and coordinating activities within areas characterized by a strong "disciplinary affinity." At the same time, the departments themselves carry out a function of direction and project proposition with typically "top-down" characteristics, entrusting "the institutes belonging to them with the implementation of research programs and projects by assigning them the relevant resources" (Paragraph 4c) or by proposing "to the Board of Directors, through the President, research projects at national, European and international level."

It is precisely this primary role entrusted to the departments of stimulation and coordination as well as strategic planning and management of the institutes that required an in-depth reflection.

A role, that of the departments, which today more than ever needs to be reviewed also in the perspective of the integration of the CNR with European standards and of ever greater participation in international research programs, in particular EU ones. In this new context, freed from the heavy burden of supporting and accelerating project propositions (although not completely alienated from them), future departments will have to focus on the more general aspects of scientific consultancy to support and assist the strategic directions of the CNR, as well as in assuming high representative functions of the organization at national and international tables.

In this profound role review, the future departments will be elevated to a strategic and consultative role and will also be relieved of the current organizational and management burdens of the institutes and projects. This approach eliminates administrative overlaps that today create confusion of roles and simplifies the management machine through the substantial removal of a hierarchical level, allowing a clear and transparent carrying out of the activities that will develop between the central administration, its territorial branches, and the institutes where the research activities are actually managed.

This transformation of the role of the departments will then be accompanied by a gradual reflection on the organization of the thematic areas that will take place through the gradual reduction of the number of departments over the years. The number of departments may be reduced to four, a number designed to aim for a dimensional balance with respect to the ERC panels, each representing broad disciplinary areas combined in such a way as to respect as much as possible the main characteristics of the CNR scientific network.

Once fully operational, therefore, the new departments of the CNR, with renewed strategic coordination functions, role of institutional representation of the institution, and support for the presidency and the board of directors could be the following: (1) physical and chemical sciences; (2) chemical sciences environment and life; (3) engineering and information technologies; and (4) human and social sciences.

The network of CNR institutes is characterized by strong territorial roots and good vitality both at a national and, in part, international level. If, on the one hand, this basic structural element, together with a solid organizational matrix rooted in the department–institute combination, has certainly represented a strong and important basis for the development of research and its articulations, on the other, as often happens in structures well defined, it has not always proven capable of reacting with the necessary flexibility to the knowledge challenges launched by emerging disciplines. The latter, in fact, often requires high responsiveness and operational streamlined-ness as well as an increased interdisciplinary vision, the latter however being a characteristic trait of the CNR. The long-term goal is to create a nonhierarchical but organized organizational environment to support research activities, foster scientific careers, and develop infrastructures, making them accessible to qualified research groups.

The prospective theme is therefore not based solely on opening or closing institutes and/or departments—a theme, in reality, always touched on in relation to a "periodic maintenance" necessary for the consolidation and development of the scientific network—but on combining the current structure with a strong organization and divided into institutes that may not even be rigidly connected to the traditional scientific-disciplinary sectors, with the possibility of responding in a timely and efficient manner to the dynamics of evolution of the scientific areas, to the emerging demands of society and which in some cases can be requested by the Ministry of University and Research or by the Presidency of the Council.

1.5.2 The CNR Administrative and Management Reorganization

The role of the institutes will be crucial as they will maintain management and administrative coordination of their knowledge networks for digital innovation distributed across the territory. This organization will have the task of supporting researchers in administrative management with a strong recovery of scientific productivity and space dedicated to competitive and fundamental research within a context based on two fundamental assumptions:

- Maximum possible freedom in the management of the means of research production, within the budgets deriving from the free resources used for fundamental research and within those coming from competitive funds.
- Maximum responsibility in the proposals for activating projects for the use of budgets and in the scientific reporting of these projects, thus making the overall evaluation of the research activity as a tool for improving and making more efficient the scientific network.

The institutes, within a new space of action freed from excessive constraints determined by "useless bureaucracy," will be called upon to take responsibility for increasing scientific productivity by being accountable for the results produced with the regulatory methods approved by the board of directors regarding the distribution of functional resources, to the results and structure of the scientific network. Always based on these results, freedom of research must be preserved and supported both by the institute directors, guarantors of scientific quality, and by the administrative structure. In this new perspective of stimulus and support, the figure of the directors, of the department, and of the institute will be strengthened and will have to respond with greater scientific responsibilities to the entire community. In order to increase the scientific network's participation tools in strategic decisions, while remaining in compliance with the selection and appointment methods envisaged in the Organization and Operation Regulations, the Relaunch Plan provides for the introduction, alongside the opinion of the institute councils and of the directors, in relation to the selection proposals of the institute and department directors, also the opinion of all the staff belonging to the institutes involved in the requested procedure after the presentation of the strategic lines in the presence of all the relevant staff.

The topic of the reorganization of the National Research Council presents important food for thought, which can only be fully understood with the analysis of the current situation, as is, aided by methodological considerations.

From the general macro-analysis, the challenges that the CNR will be called upon to face will mainly concern.

- Overcoming the concept of geographically centralized administration by favoring a single administration.
- Autonomy in carrying out research activities, strongly connected to the researchers' chart code also present in the statute and which represents a fundamental issue to be protected and defended because it avoids the dangerous drift of centralized administration systems that become an organizational "funnel," which leads entities to reduced activity to the point of paralysis if compared to their size.
- Introduction of management control systems that allow an effective and efficient management of activities, resources, and services across a wide geographical and decentralized scope.
- Capacity in administrative and management terms, and more precisely, the consistency of the administrative apparatus and its sizing with respect to characteristic production, that is, research.

To overcome some problems of the "as is" organizational model, such as the "funnel" effect of the current organization and an excessively generalist framework of skills, it is the establishment of seven administrative structures in areas of the national territory to which new administrative functions to support scientific research, defined as "supervisions," which should be directed by territorial managers.

The superintendents would be entrusted with tasks of a technical, administrative, and logistical nature, with the support of the various administration offices, in relation to the functions of spending planning, rationalization, and efficiency of administrative action in support of the research structures present in the geographical areas of reference under the coordination of the general management.

The new structure would therefore see an administrative structure strengthened and effectively distributed throughout the territory, based on the actual mass administered, directly in support of the institutes where mainly research management activities are carried out, drastically reducing the existence of multiple management levels, in part overlapping and unclear ones that fuel the current "useless bureaucracy."

1.5.3 Performance Management in the CNR Reorganization

Many scholars and academics have read and considered the Italian Legislative Decree 150/2009 as a tool to trigger those management methodologies and techniques typical of performance management in public administrations. The decree to put an end to the application dysfunctions of the system in force up to that moment chose to proceed with a strong legislation of the public personnel evaluation system, removing the evaluation from the integrative bargaining and moving the discipline in the legislative source. The contents of the legislative text immediately appeared as clippings from a real management manual, in some ways too detailed and punctual in establishing some procedures.

Numerous studies have found that the problem of the Italian legislative framework is not the absence of the law, but the serious delay in its application or its merely formal application.

Taking place in a historical period in which the macroeconomic framework was gradually portraying gloomy crisis scenarios, the same reform then had to deal with linear blocks of contracts, turnover, and salary dynamics and, as regards the research sector, with serious financial difficulties, a chronic level of precarious employment and an increase in the average age of employees in the entire sector. In this context, due to cultural delays, internal resistance to change, and sometimes obstructive attitudes of the trade union organizations, in many public, central, and local offices, everything has been done to hinder the application of the regulatory dictate or to get around its constraints.

In the CNR, despite some internal resistance, we have been able to case realize radical organizational changes, especially in some procedures, those most connected to the evaluation processes, which have improved compared to the past. The composition of some economic treatments has undergone changes, oriented more toward the selection and differentiation of reward allowances. Work has been underway for a digital transformation of some performance processes, which for many years have been relegated to the least accessible and transparent procedures. More attention was given to the dynamics of employee engagement and well-being, giving voice to the internal potential in terms of planning.

In this view, the thesis that we intend to support is that innovations in the management of administrations "dictated by decree," complete with a sanctioning system, do not appear, at the moment, that can be applied with success.

1.6 Toward a Conclusion: Some Issues to Be Solved in the Reorganization of CNR

The widespread diffusion of digital technologies in organizations (companies, government institutions, schools, universities, and research centers) has allowed the development of new services, new markets, and new job opportunities.

Digital technologies indeed contribute to organizing, on the one hand, the cooperation between a differentiated plurality of actors and, on the other hand, the network of technological and economic flows, in the local and extra-local areas.

1.6.1 Clear and Practicable Supervision of the Reorganization Processes

A first element of the "structural" weakness of the regulatory system arises from the fact that the evaluation process is mostly managed at the end of the performance management cycle. Therefore, its functioning is affected by the lack of supervision in the other phases of which the cycle is made up. Above all, there is a difficulty in planning strategic and operational objectives and, consequently, the plan's poor ability to identify clear and achievable objectives to assign to structures and individuals. Furthermore, coherence between strategic programming (of individual administrations) and financial programming is not sufficiently guaranteed.

It is quite clear that, if upstream the top bodies do not monitor the planning phase well, to draw up guidelines, plans that are sufficiently precise in their objectives and integrated with each other, realistic with respect to their implementation, downstream the bureaucratic machine it will be difficult for him to recover the deficits of direction and set up his business adequately. While it is possible that much can be adjusted along the way, it is also true that this recovery effort prevents good organization of work and requires the permanent chasing of emergencies and ex post adaptations. Furthermore, the distinction of tasks between the political bodies and the management places different but inseparable responsibilities on the two large components of the PA and, above all, complementary in their functions. One more reason to consider a strong result orientation on the part of the political body as preliminary and essential and the clear transmission of this will to the administrative and bureaucratic system. The performance evaluation must bring together two perspectives: that of those who must guide the strategies of the administrations as a whole and that of those who must guide them day after day on a management level. These two perspectives must be strongly integrated with each other but must not be confused.

As regards the experience in the CNR, the observation that the political level, a fundamental player in the performance management cycle, was not constantly involved in the formulation of guidelines and directions for the drafting of the Performance Plan and of the Transparency Program. Equally problematic was the precise ex ante definition of the strategic objectives to be assigned to the general director, as administrative top management, who never carried out a periodic monitoring action on the general trend and the intermediate results achieved.

1.6.2 Lack of Managerial Autonomy of Managers

Starting from the Brunetta reform—to an even more accentuated extent than what happened previously—the legislator has taken a "dirigiste" approach toward public managers, imposing on them a conspicuous series of legal obligations through which to conduct their activities. The latter appeared, in fact, to be particularly conditioned by legislative provisions that precisely establish the paths to be followed and impose a conspicuous series of obligations, the failure to fulfill which entails the activation of various forms of administrative liability, sometimes particularly burdensome, making the risk arising that the attention of managers mainly focused on compliance with procedures. The scope of responsibility is wider than that of the autonomy granted to managers. This makes it not only more difficult, but also often incorrect, to attribute responsibility solely to managers for the operations of the offices they direct.

Ultimately, the legislator has increasingly "imposed" the methods of carrying out managerial activity through a progressive "administrativization" of public action, which does not allow the adoption of adequate policies for the rationalization and valorization of personnel (including the recognition of prizes for the most deserving) and risks "stiffening" the conduct of public action and "distorting" the privatization of public work that had been sought to be pursued since the early 1990s. In this context, the government's current reform plan aims to introduce more meritocratic and flexible career paths, encouraging greater professionalization and empowerment of management.

1.6.3 Inadequate Measurement Systems

Another risk to avoid is identifying objectives that do not allow the evaluation to be based on valid assumptions. The objectives must therefore be clear, "challenging," and capable of adapting to changing conditions, defined in a shared manner with the subjects evaluated, who must have the possibility of selecting the objectives considered priorities for their activity.

Often the tendency is to reproduce, almost automatically, constant performance over time. It is clear that all this does not take into account the evolution of the needs of the community (which asks for new and better services) and of internal organizational systems where technology, organizational solutions, and preparation of people must be reflected in better and higher-level performances of efficiency and quality. The phenomena of flattening of evaluations on the highest score band are the result of a failure to specify the objectives that frequently, indeed, have been made to coincide with the ordinary functions and institutional tasks that would be assigned to each office by the regulations of the respective administrations.

As regards the experience in the CNR, over the years the OIV has found the presence of all the risks that this topic entails. The assessments carried out in the organization before the entry into force of Legislative Decree 150/2009 (1998–2009 decade), carried out according to the model contained in the then-current resolution 757/1998, were processed directly by the general director alone based on reports in which the main activities carried out with reference to the previous year were described without any reference to the assignment of specific structural or individual objectives.

Immediately after the entry into force of the reform decree, starting from 2010 with the adoption of the first Performance Plans, there was a phenomenon of overlapping of institutional tasks within the new "container" called "objective," a sort of binder of actions that are not yet well defined and internalized. Ordinary and routine activities were assigned to offices with the label of "objective," thus eliminating the challenging and improving character of administrative action. This phenomenon, although in the process of being attenuated, still persists today for some organizational units of the organization and could be completely overcome with a clear distinction between "maintenance objective" and "improvement objective" that the OIV has advanced during the presentation of its proposal for a measurement and evaluation system. Connected to the topic of objectives is that of the use of indicators. In the majority of cases, administrations have resorted to indicators that are too rigid, purely quantitative, generic, and do not concern the reality they intend to evaluate. The analyses carried out by CiVIT and the Civil Service have been highlighted in almost all the administrations.

1.6.4 An Evaluation Flattened at High Levels

Some public bodies give great importance to the results of the evaluation, linking them to a significant change in remuneration, while others do not highlight major links between results and compensation. As we will see later, even at an international level there are differences in recognizing ancillary treatments, which are often absent or provided without a real link to work performance.

An element that emerges from the field analysis is the progressive increase in evaluations with the consequent concentration in the highest bands of the scores assigned by the evaluators, both for management staff and for the rest of the staff. This upward flattening is then combined with a normally limited variability between one score and another, a fact that further accentuates the effect of loss of meaning of the evaluation process, which penalizes the best and risks loosening the "push" especially for that middle segment, which is the most numerous and most susceptible to being incentivized. Another negative effect of the upward leveling consists in progressively raising the expectations of managers, leading them to increasingly demand better economic treatments or to consider bonuses as something "due." By separating the evaluation from the real results, any claim becomes legitimate and for this reason difficult to counter.

As regards the experience in the CNR, the analysis of the historical series of management assessments, carried out in the decade 1998–2009 according to the model contained in Resolution no. 757/1998, shows a flattening of the assessments toward the maximum value (100%) for all management staff. As regards the provision of "productivity" bonuses for nonmanagerial staff at levels IV–VIII, the OIV has found that in the years from 2009 to 2012 the percentages of staff units admitted to benefit from the entire economic amount of the premium was found to be 99.9%.

When you come close to such high percentages for staff admitted to the "bonus," which is paid with a single coefficient that is the same for everyone, you run into that phenomenon known as "sprinkle distribution." When even the economic transitions to the higher salary bands are mainly regulated by automatic advancement mechanisms and only formally depend on the actual work performance performed and, therefore, on the individual contribution, it is evident that they gradually enter the organizational experience as consolidated practices, polluting even the healthiest habits. Finally, great difficulties were encountered even in the simple retrieval of data from which to deduce information regarding the valorization of merit for nonmanagerial personnel. For this reason, it was recommended that the administration guarantee the coordination of subjects, activities, and information systems, with a view to greater integration with management control.

1.6.5 Evaluation Models Based on Bureaucratic Requirements

Finally, the evaluation models are based on rigid and cumbersome rules that apply in an undifferentiated way, regardless of the size and type of activity that public administrations carry out. The failure to recognize the differences existing between the different organizations has meant that it was not considered that the latter perform different functions, with different methods and a different degree of measurability and comparability of the outputs. The risk of conceiving evaluation as a bureaucratic task, to be dismissed almost with annoyance, rather than to be seized as an opportunity for management growth and development, is objectively very widespread. If the evaluation is experienced only as a duty imposed by law, it ends up transforming into a mere procedure completely independent and abstract from the nature and logic of real behavior.

Another risk is that of isolating the evaluation, particularly that of management, from other internal control tools. Strategic control, management control, administrative-accounting control, and management evaluation are in fact tools that not only must be developed adequately, but which must also be made compatible and used in a coordinated manner. Conversely, the evaluation process must not be understood as a bureaucratic requirement, but rather as a management tool to be acquired and internalized. Even if the level of awareness of how important it is to "measure to manage" has made some progress, the bureaucratic culture is still prevalent. This is also because the use of evaluation techniques developed in the "private" sector, without adequate development and adaptation processes for the "public," has demonstrated its substantial ineffectiveness.

References

Asheim, B., Grillitsch, M., & Trippl, M. (2017). Introduction: Combinatorial knowledge bases, regional innovation, and development dynamics. *Economic Geography, 93*(5), 429–435.

Brynjolfsson, E., & Collis, A. (2019). How should we measure the digital economy? *Harvard Business Review, 97*(6), 140–148. https://doi.org/10.1257/aer.20170491

Clarke, T. (2001). The knowledge economy. *Education + Training, 43*(4/5), 189–196. https://doi.org/10.1108/00400910110399184

D'Souza, D. E., Bement, D., & Cory, K. (2022). Cross-functional integration skills: Are business schools delivering what organizations need? *Decision Sciences Journal of Innovative Education, 20*(3), 117–130.

Finger, M., & Brand, S. B. (1999). The concept of the learning organization applied to the transformation of the public sector: Conceptual contributions for theory development. In M. Easterby-Smith, L. Araujo, & J. Burgoyne (Eds.), *Organizational learning and the learning organization: developments in theory and practice* (pp. 130–156). Sage.

Gerwe, O., & Silva, R. (2020). Clarifying the sharing economy: Conceptualization, typology, antecedents, and effects. *Academy of Management Perspectives, 34*(1), 65–96.

Greenway, K., Butt, G., & Walthall, H. (2019). What is a theory-practice gap? An exploration of the concept. *Nurse Education in Practice, 34*, 1–6.

Grillitsch, M., & Trippl, M. (2014). Combining knowledge from different sources, channels and geographical scales. *European Planning Studies, 22*(11), 2305–2325.

Ives, W., Torrey, B., & Gordon, C. (2000). Knowledge sharing is a human behavior. In *Knowledge management: Classic and contemporary work* (pp. 99–129). MIT Press.

Miller, R. C. (2010). Interdisciplinarity: Its meaning and consequences. In *Oxford research encyclopedia of international studies*. Oxford University Press.

OECD. (2014). *Recommendation of the council on digital government strategies* (OECD/LEGAL/0406). OECD. https://legalinstruments.oecd.org/en/instruments/OECDLEGAL-0406

Passiante, G., & Andriani, P. (2000). Modelling the learning environment of virtual knowledge networks: Some empirical evidence. *International Journal of Innovation Management, 4*(01), 1–31.

Popkova, E. G., De Bernardi, P., Tyurina, Y. G., & Sergi, B. S. (2022). A theory of digital technology advancement to address the grand challenges of sustainable development. *Technology in Society, 68*, 101831.

Rocha, H., Kunc, M., & Audretsch, D. B. (2020). Clusters, economic performance, and social cohesion: A system dynamics approach. *Regional Studies, 54*(8), 1098–1091.

Rogers, D. L. (2023). Rethinking governance for digital innovation. *MIT Sloan Management Review, 64*(4), 1–7.

Romer, P. M. (1990). Endogenous technological change. *Journal of Political Economy, 98*(5, Part 2), S71–S102.

Tapscott, D. (1995). The digital economy: Dawn of a new era-Part 1. *Communications Week, 584*(13).

Terjesen, S. (2022). Reducing higher education bureaucracy and reclaiming the entrepreneurial university. In *Questioning the entrepreneurial state* (UNIDO 2013 Emerging trends in global manufacturing industries) (p. 111). Springer.

Ujwary-Gil, A., Florek-Paszkowska, A., & Kozioł, A. (2023). Economic Policy, Business, and Management in the Post-Pandemic Perspective. Institute of Economics Polish Academy of Sciences.

World Economic Forum. (2023). The global competitiveness report. *Insight Report* Annual Report 2022–2023.

Chapter 2
Orchestrating Open Innovation Ecosystems Based on Digital Technologies: The Lutech Case Study

Giustina Secundo, Domenica Barile, Antonello Garzoni, and Giuseppe Ieva

Abstract An innovation ecosystem (IE) that uses internal and external resources can help firms meet innovation timeframes. Open innovation (OI) encourages external partners to accelerate internal innovation processes, promoting bidirectional interactions and collaborations among multiple ecosystem entities. The convergence of IEs and OI has not been an extensively investigated topic. The study aims to fill this gap by concentrating on advancing the notion of open innovation ecosystems (OIEs) in the digital technologies industry. We examine the operations of an OIE through an exploratory-based strategy and a single case study of the large corporation Lutech. To develop, orchestrate and create an IE, Lutech launched the Lutech Campus Ecosystem, a project under the industrial project MILE within the context of the Lutech Campus activities, identified as the group's OI hub. OI strategies, collaboration among firms, institutions and research centres, the engagement of regional innovation system actors and the use of digital technologies are the four interrelated areas under the Lutech OIE. The Lutech example illustrates how a company-led IE may promote collaboration and innovation among various stakeholders. Our research adds to the existing literature on IE powered by OI, providing valuable guidance for creating an effective innovation environment.

Keywords Open innovation · Innovation ecosystem · Open innovation ecosystem · Exploratory case study · Start-up · Big corporation · Lutech

---

G. Secundo (✉) · D. Barile
Department of Engineering, LUM University, Casamassima, Italy
e-mail: secundo@lum.it; barile@lum.it

A. Garzoni
Department of Management, Finance and Technology, LUM University, Casamassima, Italy
e-mail: garzoni@lum.it

G. Ieva
R&D at Lutech SpA, Milan, Italy
e-mail: g.ieva@lutech.it

G. Passiante (ed.), *Digital Innovation Management*, Applied Innovation and Technology Management, https://doi.org/10.1007/978-3-031-80426-7_2

2.1 Introduction

Since Iansiti and Levien (2004) introduced the concept of an *innovation ecosystem* (IE) derived from the *business ecosystem,* it has garnered growing interest from academia and business professionals (de Vasconcelos Gomes et al., 2018; Scaringella & Radziwon, 2018). An IE consists of interconnected and interdependent actors, such as focal enterprises, customers, suppliers and complementary innovators (Adner & Kapoor, 2010; Zahra & Nambisan, 2012). These ecosystems prioritise the creation of value (Ritala et al., 2013). An IE is defined by the presence of numerous actors who share common objectives, together with complementary technologies and competencies (Zhang et al., 2023). The participants and technologies progress together to reach the goals of innovation and value creation (Nambisan & Baron, 2013). An IE that effectively uses all available internal and external resources can help companies shorten their development cycle times and adhere to innovation timelines.

Prior research on IEs has examined prominent corporations like Intel (Adner, 2006; Gawer & Henderson, 2007) and Alipay (Chen et al., 2018). Researchers have widely agreed that ecosystem players use services, tools and technology to improve their innovative performances, as stated by Moore in 1993. Within IE, companies expand their limits by actively controlling the exchange of knowledge to enable two-way flows and speed up their innovation timelines. Open innovation (OI) sustains these firms' processes for engaging with external partners, using different resources to speed up their internal innovation processes and enhance their innovation outcomes (Chesbrough & Bogers, 2014; West & Bogers, 2014). Based on the OI model, the concept of reliance includes both two-way interactions (West & Bogers, 2014) and partnerships involving several players within ecosystems (Adner & Kapoor, 2010; West, 2017).

Moreover, in the past 10 years, digital technologies have progressively increased their role in redesigning and improving how firms run and innovate, established processes to open up a novel opportunity for the ecosystem's management and development. Digital technologies, such as Blockchain, cloud computing, digital platforms, virtual reality (VR) and artificial intelligence (AI), have developed quickly and brought about major changes in the borders, procedures, organisational structures, roles and interactions of businesses (Cennamo et al., 2020). Beyond mere IT installation, digital technologies transform the entire organisation, strategy, business processes, innovation methods and governance structures. Ecosystems in which businesses collaborate and participate in value chains rather than operating alone have emerged because of the spread of digital technology (Cennamo et al., 2020).

There is widespread agreement that an ecosystem involves a collaborative arrangement of hierarchically independent yet interdependent actors that co-evolve over time, despite an ongoing debate about its exact definition and characterisation. The ecosystem in question is often managed by a significant organisation, known as a '*keystone organisation* or *ecosystem leader*' (Adner, 2017; Iansiti & Levien,

2004). Despite ecosystems being viewed as continuously changing, there have been a limited number of research studies that have implemented a qualitative process approach, as recommended by Ritala and Almpanopoulou (2017), to analyse the ecosystem dynamics. Pushpananthan and Elmquist (2022) identified the catalysts that can cause an established company to create a modular platform and ultimately assume the role of a keystone firm in the innovation ecosystem, which advances the knowledge of ecosystem emergence. The study examines how an incumbent company's attempts to innovate, in partnership with a network of individuals and organisations, contribute to the development of an IE. This study offers fresh perspectives on the process of creating modular technology platforms and how they subsequently give rise to an IE (Pushpananthan & Elmquist, 2022).

We took the decision to investigate the creation of an innovation ecosystem in response to Remneland Wikhamn and Styhre's (2023) request to analyse the digital technologies sector. This allowed us to conduct an empirical analysis of how ecosystems are controlled and constructed in real life from the perspective of the leading firm, adding to the body of research on IEs. We also decided to investigate Pushpananthan and Elmquist's (2022) request for information that will help actors make strategic decisions and carefully allocate resources in an ecosystem. Moreover, we try also to fill the gap in the literature through a comprehension of the structure and governance of IEs (Jacobides et al., 2018; Ritala & Almpanopoulou, 2017) as well as understanding the ways through which incumbent firms adopt OI (Chiaroni et al., 2011; Mortara & Minshall, 2011). Based on the above premises, we try to provide an answer to the following research question: How can large organisations develop a stronger innovation ecosystem by leveraging OI?

To provide an answer to the above question, this study adopted an exploratory methodology using the case study approach (Yin, 2009). The case is the multinational, Lutech, that operates in the digital technologies sector, analysing the OI strategies implemented by the corporation as happening in the IE. Our findings provide an understanding of how the OI initiatives and digital technologies involved in the Lutech Campus affect the dynamics of IEs, thereby supporting the processes of collaboration, knowledge exchange and innovation for all the stakeholders and companies participating in Lutech's ecosystem. The operationalisation of the IE dynamics was realised through the analysis of the Lutech Campus Ecosystem project, which seeks to offer a technological and methodological platform to support sustainable entrepreneurship and the incubation of entrepreneurial endeavours and start-ups. This platform, which encompasses several organisations, big businesses, start-ups, small- and medium-sized enterprises (SMEs) and research institutes, is based on the concepts of OI. The establishment of OI enhances an entrepreneurial atmosphere and is intended to foster and augment the expansion and worth of the participating start-ups. Implications for theory and practice close the chapter. The remainder of the chapter is structured as follows. Section 2.2 critically analyses the relationship between OI and IE, as well as the role of the open innovation ecosystem's orchestrators. Then, Sect. 2.3 outlines the research methodology. Subsequently, Sect. 2.4 investigates the Lutech OIE case study. Finally, Sect. 2.5 discusses the case and concludes the chapter.

2.2 Background

The ecosystem notion shows promise for scholarly investigation but remains underexplored in the OI field (Radziwon & Bogers, 2019; Randhawa et al., 2021). Aligning IEs with OI has been theoretically emphasised as a way to enhance value creation. There is, however, insufficient empirical evidence on how to effectively synchronise IE models with various OI strategies (Zhang et al., 2023). Various facets of OI require more investigation, with one emerging area of focus being the IE perspective (Adner, 2017; Adner & Kapoor, 2010) to develop the concept of an open innovation ecosystem (OIEs). This section will critically examine this emerging theoretical construct.

2.2.1 Open Innovation and Innovation Ecosystems for Orchestrating Open Innovation Ecosystems

The OI model has dominated innovation management research in the past two decades. The concept of OI 'refers to a distributed innovation model that involves purposively managed inflows and outflows of knowledge across organisational boundaries, for pecuniary and non-pecuniary reasons, in line with the organisation's business model' (Chesbrough & Bogers, 2014, p. 10). This notion of OI is primarily concerned with the organisational level but soon also started to encompass the ecosystems of organisations and technology at a higher level, as well as inventions and competencies at a lower level. Additionally, OI may facilitate the development of an integrated innovation system in terms of market benefits (Sarkar & Costa, 2008). Companies can eventually develop both incremental and radical innovations and long-term survival by turning to external knowledge from various sources, including suppliers, customers, universities and research labs, innovation intermediaries and businesses operating in other sectors (Baima et al., 2020; Marozzo et al., 2023).

Early studies on OI demonstrated the favourable effects of implementing it in major multinational corporations, including IBM, Lucent and Intel (Chesbrough, 2003), DSM (Kirschbaum, 2005) and Proctor & Gamble (P&G) (Dodgson et al., 2006). Remneland Wikhamn and Styhre (2023) explored the BioVentureHub, an OI initiative by AstraZeneca supporting the life sciences ecosystem. The authors applied the process theory analysis of BioVentureHub to advance the subject of OI by addressing the need for a more thorough understanding of its operations and the ways in which tensions in the enactment process are resolved, as indicated by earlier studies. Further research has investigated the possibility of applying OI approaches in SMEs as well, as demonstrated by Bianchi et al. (2010), Lee et al. (2010) and Van de Vrande et al. (2009). Spithoven et al. (2013) examined the effect of OI methods in SMEs in comparison to large firms due to the increasing interest in OI in both types of organisations. Research indicates that SMEs engage in OI activities more intensely than larger companies. SMEs rely more on OI than large corporations due to the greater effect it has on their earnings (Radziwon & Bogers, 2019).

The extensive literature on OI emphasises the importance of establishing an OIE, which enables interconnected firms to tap into a wider range of external resources, such as knowledge, goods and expertise (Bogers et al., 2019; Chesbrough et al., 2018). Xie and Wang (2020) state that 'firms in OIEs expand organisational resources and allow for collaborations across organisations, which can promote the flow, aggregation and integration of resources' (p. 29). Alam et al. (2022) define an IE as a 'loosely interconnected network of interdependent firms whose functional goal is to co-create capabilities around technologies, knowledge, or skills required to innovate products and services' (p. 438). An OIE is characterised by partner firms whose main objective is OI and where a significant portion of their sponsored activities are designated as OI initiatives (Alam et al., 2022).

IEs aimed at systemic innovation are centred around ecosystem players' collaboration. To foster beneficial collaboration, innovators must be transparent and willing to share with other ecosystem actors the knowledge necessary for systemic innovation (Paasi et al., 2023). In IEs, sharing knowledge is essential to appreciate co-creation. A firm must balance knowledge preservation with opening up and sharing its expertise, however, as knowledge protection is usually necessary to protect value capture in the future (Arora et al., 2016; Foege et al., 2019). Businesses can manage their intellectual property and knowledge in a variety of ways through their partnerships with other organisations through inter-organisational innovation (Luoma et al., 2010; Valkokari et al., 2012). The multilayer viewpoint of ecosystem operations, however, presents obstacles for openness in IEs. Success at the ecosystem level depends on transparency and knowledge exchange, while knowledge protection is required at the business level. Businesses directly manage the exchange and preservation of knowledge at the firm level, but not at the ecosystem level (Paasi et al., 2023).

2.2.2 The Role and Effect of the Open Innovation Ecosystem's Orchestrators

The ecosystem literature primarily consists of conceptual papers that focus on defining, outlining the scope, of setting boundaries for and establishing the theoretical foundations of the ecosystem (Ritala & Gustafsson, 2018). Although discussing what constitutes an ecosystem can enhance our comprehension, it provides limited guidance to how these observed patterns are evolving in reality and over time (Langley, 2007). There is a lack of comprehensive study on how an OIE evolves and changes over time, as noted by Radziwon and Bogers et al. (2019).

Previous studies on IEs have explored various actors from different industries, including creative consumers, product users, communities, universities, government institutions and competitors, all of whom influence each other through their actions (Jacobides et al., 2018; Reynolds & Uygun, 2018). Recent studies emphasise the importance of firms as key strategic actors in IEs, despite the presence of various actors with different characteristics. Jacobides (2019) emphasises that a company's success relies on working together with other companies within a carefully planned ecosystem that covers several sectors. Tang et al. (2020) suggest that interfirm networks offer firms quick and adaptable access to resources from other firms or related industries.

An OIE typically arises when a *strong actor* (such as public institution or large firm) takes the lead and facilitates the spontaneous growth of collaboration amongst players (Heaton et al., 2019). It is difficult to manage the network of creative interfirm interactions due to its complexity, and it frequently needs a central, dependable player to manage its growth (Ritala et al., 2009). Thus, one important skill for putting OI practices into practice is *orchestrating OIE*. Ritala et al. (2009) stated that the ability to orchestrate is particularly required in future-oriented value creation, in the pursuit of both incremental and radical innovations and new business opportunities. Participants must comprehend the significance of having a focal firm orchestrating the networking process for the ecosystem as a whole to function. The ability of the focal firm to link unique experts is necessary for creating value through the pursuit of innovation and knowledge acquisition (Dyer & Nobeoka, 2000).

An OIE orchestrator excels at uniting a collection of actors by streamlining their leadership without exerting formal control or hierarchical influence over the collaborative innovation project. The orchestrator needs to be a prominent player with a central role in the network structure and a well-established reputation. They should provide mentorship and leadership to integrate the network's resources and capabilities (Dhanaraj & Parkhe, 2006). Big multinational corporations can act as orchestrators due to their robust reputations and additional complementary assets, which smaller partners seek to leverage to access their inventive talents. This strategy aims to encourage active participation from all ecosystem partners, particularly start-ups and SMEs, by addressing the obstacles that hinder them from sharing their knowledge and intellectual property to achieve common innovative goals (Marozzo et al., 2023).

The orchestrator's recognised leadership and the agreed-upon rules of engagement play a crucial role in this environment. A large firm should adopt a few methods aimed at effectively orchestrating a burgeoning OIE within an industry unaccustomed to fostering collaborative innovation. Various approaches and activities can be implemented to recruit potential partners and work towards a shared objective. Additional study is required to improve the application of OI and ecosystem principles, as suggested by Randhawa et al. (2021) and Remneland Wikhamn and Styhre (2023). We address the deficiencies by concentrating on the Information and Communication Technologies (ICT) and digital technologies sector, in accordance with the issues raised by Remneland Wikhamn and Styhre (2023) and the call for empirical analysis by Jacobides et al. (2018).

2.3 The Lutech Case Study

We used an exploratory-based strategy to develop our research (Miles et al., 2014). We conducted a single case study on the large corporation Lutech, as described by Yin (2009). Yin (2009) emphasises that using a single case study method is strong and appropriate for the thorough examination of challenging scenarios (Eisenhardt & Graebner, 2007). It is especially suitable for situations that involve novel or not-well-understood processes and behaviours, enabling the examination of theoretical and conceptual frameworks. This method is useful for investigating the 'how' and 'why' questions of current events, as described by Yin (2009), providing a customised methodological strategy. Comprehensive exploratory research is commonly employed to observe and analyse new developments in IEs, characterised by fluid and indistinct borders between firms (Abbassi et al., 2022; Corvello et al., 2023; Hofman et al., 2016).

The research focused exclusively on Lutech, a leading firm in ICT services for digital transformation. Lutech serves as a critical and extreme case, which perfectly matches the goal we wanted to achieve with our study (Eisenhardt, 1989). The selection of the case study was based on Lutech's influence and size in the digital technologies sector. One of its crucial aspects, however, is the company's willingness to adopt OI strategies and spearhead OI projects, which can position it at the centre of an IE. The case was chosen due to its representativeness as a prominent corporation that employs OI strategies and has established itself as a leading firm in fostering an IE. The case was also selected because of its capacity to facilitate the investigation of temporal evolutionary processes. Furthermore, case research is acknowledged as a method to comprehend a developing phenomenon within a real environment (Eisenhardt, 1989; Eisenhardt & Graebner, 2007; Hobday & Rush, 1999; Yin, 2009).

2.3.1 The Lutech Campus Ecosystem

Lutech S.p.A. is an Italian-based multinational company specialising in the installation, expansion, conversion and maintenance of electronic data processing hardware systems and equipment, including applications and basic software. The company also operates in the areas of security, helping in the installation and operation of systems, as well as producing and marketing software and related licences.

In 2023, Lutech launched an industrial project called 'MILE' (Meet the Innovative Lutech Experience) for Research and Development (R&D) and innovation, with a specific focus on artificial intelligence (AI) and OI. This focus on creating data-driven solutions to support start-ups and technology transfer sees the involvement and development of AI technologies and services to guide investments in niche markets, start-ups, technologies and innovations. Complementary services such as acceleration and mentoring for start-ups and smart e-learning will be offered.

The centre plans to create an immersive environment to enable a hybrid concept of real and virtual campus. Moreover, specific hardware and software will be used to run enhanced technology as non-fungible tokens (NFTs) to certify the training and mentoring path: hence, the ranking in line with the development plans of start-ups in line with the Lutech Business.

To develop, orchestrate and create an IE, Lutech launched the project MILE, which enables the development of many initiatives and activities. The Lutech Campus was developed under the MILE project, identified as the group's open innovation hub. One of the objectives of the Lutech Campus is to orchestrate an IE based on a digital platform that promotes sustainable entrepreneurship and facilitates the start-up of new business initiatives. The initiative involves several stakeholders to create a corporate IE based on OI strategies, supporting technology transfer, start-up acceleration and customised online learning. This is coherent with the research stream according to which the intermediaries within an IE could be a powerful instrument for enhancing innovation processes (Corvello et al., 2023).

External intermediaries are responsible for identifying the most promising start-ups on behalf of focal corporations. They are more involved in interacting with the start-up ecosystem (Corvello et al., 2023). This innovative platform acts as a training centre, an incubator for start-ups, a demonstration lab and a venue for the dissemination of cutting-edge technologies, enabling Lutech to collaborate with academic institutions, research centres, technology partners, customers and start-ups to promote collaborative innovation.

One of the objectives of the Lutech Campus is to create a technological and methodological platform that promotes sustainable entrepreneurship and facilitates the start-up of new business initiatives. This platform, based on OI practices, involves various actors, including universities, large companies, start-ups, SMEs and research institutions, with the aim of ensuring economic and environmental sustainability as well as optimising the allocation of resources. The aim of the project is to create an artificial intelligence (AI) framework to provide customised services to promote, support and facilitate training, technology transfer and market access for entrepreneurial initiatives. To promote the growth and value of start-ups, market assessment, forecasting, monitoring and risk assessment processes related to technological innovation and investment will be implemented. The 'Smart Learning Experience Platform', an advanced learning environment, will complement the entrepreneurial ecosystem in question. This platform will provide customised learning paths and interact intelligently with users, adapting learning modes to their needs and characteristics. According to Lutech, the new services developed by the project will address a new market consisting of several public and private institutions, including technology transfer offices, OI hubs, innovation parks, start-ups incubator, start-ups accelerator, academy and co-working, as well as start-ups funded and incubated by these institutions. Using the previously mentioned solutions, these organisations can re-engineer and automate their processes, improving the quality of their services and increasing their production capacity with the same number of staff.

2.3.2 Data Collection and Analysis

The case study analysis used two methodologies to collect and analyse data (e.g. Elia et al., 2020; Marozzo et al., 2023): primary data collection and analysis. These included semi-structured interviews with the head of advanced industry solutions and the head of research and development, along with secondary data analysis, which we used to understand the strategic plans used by Lutech to build and guide the development and management of the OIE, which will feature the 'Lutech Campus Ecosystem', as will be explained in the next section. These data were collected from social media platforms, press releases, industry reports, project documentations and news reports. Secondary data were used as the main source of information, supported by primary data for validation and improvement. The goal was to enhance the theoretical framework and avoid making explanations after the fact. The data analysis process involved an inductive and iterative method as outlined by Strauss and Corbin (1997), where theory was refined using case study data following Eisenhardt's (1989) approach. Following Tellis's methodology (1997), data triangulation included (i) reviewing secondary sources and interview transcripts individually to confirm their validity and clarity; (ii) validating analyses among authors to reach a consensus on interpretation and (iii) collectively triangulating the accepted information from all authors.

Starting in November 2023, we have actively engaged in the field, gathering a wide range of perspectives and ideas (De Massis & Kotlar, 2014), thereby improving our understanding of the situation.

The data-gathering technique entailed active participation in numerous seminars, lectures and conferences organised by the company in collaboration with local institutions. These data offer crucial insights for projects and practices in effectively managing the Lutech ecosystem. Data were collected from November 2023 to April 2024.

During the initial round of interviews with company members, we gathered detailed information on the company's background, resources and organisational framework. Most importantly, we focused on understanding the company's strategic outlook regarding the implementation of OI strategies. Subsequently, further probing questions were asked to further investigate and enhance our comprehension of present technological innovation methods and business requirements. Subsequently, we inquired about the OI strategy and anticipated outcomes to gain a comprehensive perspective. In addition, we examined the company's internal innovation procedures and advancements in terms of collaborative processes with start-ups, considering the overall ecosystem. We conducted a total of four interviews, with each interview lasting between 60 and 150 min. The primary interviews were videotaped and transcribed and were further enhanced by informal discussions during company events and meetings.

Furthermore, alongside the interviews, we carried out brainstorming sessions regarding the adoption and development of digital technologies. We also used secondary interviews available online and email exchanges (Rondi et al., 2024). To enhance the theoretical framework and prevent after-the-fact justifications, secondary data were deliberately employed as the primary source of information, complemented by primary data for the purpose of triangulation (Elia et al., 2020).

The researchers employed an inductive and iterative method to analyse the data and enhance the theory using case study data as a basis (Eisenhardt, 1989; Strauss & Corbin, 1997). Following Tellis's (1997) methodology, data triangulation involved doing individual reviews, collaborating with authors for validation and engaging in group triangulation to confirm the accepted information. As outlined by Eisenhardt (1989), we performed numerous iterations of assessing both secondary and primary data, along with examining the existing literature on IE and OI strategies. The iterative process we employed allowed us to enhance our framework and provided a robust theoretical foundation for our claims.

2.4 An Overview of the Lutech Open Innovation Ecosystem

Lutech initiated the MILE project to develop, orchestrate and create an IE, facilitating the advancement of numerous initiatives and activities. As part of the MILE project, the Lutech Campus was created as the group's open innovation hub. One of the objectives of the Lutech Campus is to organise an IE based on a digital platform that promotes sustainable entrepreneurship and supports the creation of new business ventures. The initiative engages multiple stakeholders to establish an entrepreneurial IE based on open innovation strategies, facilitating technology transfer, business incubation and tailor-made online education. This is in line with research showing that intermediaries within an innovation ecosystem can significantly enhance innovation processes (Corvello et al., 2023).

"External intermediaries are tasked with identifying the most promising start-ups for keystone firms. They show greater commitment to the start-up ecosystem (Corvello et al., 2023). This innovative platform serves as a training centre, a start-up incubator, a laboratory and a venue for the dissemination of advanced technologies, facilitaing Lutech's collaboration with academic institutions, reaearch centres, technology partners, customers and start-ups to foster collaborative innovation."

The Lutech Campus aims to create a technological and methodological platform that promotes sustainable entrepreneurship and supports the creation of new business ventures. This platform, based on OI practices, involves various stakeholders, including universities, large corporations, start-ups, SMEs and research institutions, with the aim of promoting economic and environmental sustainability while optimising resource allocation. The aim of the project is to develop an artificial intelligence (AI) framework that provides tailored services to enhance, support and enable training, technology transfer and market access for entrepreneurial ventures. Market assessment, forecasting, monitoring and risk assessment processes related to technological innovation and investment will be carried out to enhance the growth and value of start-ups. The 'Smart Learning Experience Platform', an advanced educational environment, enhances the relevant entrepreneurial ecosystem. This platform provides customised learning pathways and interacts intelligently with users, adapting learning modalities to their needs and characteristics. Lutech claims that the project's newly developed services will target a market composed of various public and private entities, including technology transfer offices, open innovation hubs, innovation parks, incubators, start-up accelerators, academic institutions, co-working spaces and start-ups funded and supported by these organisations. These companies can improve the quality of their services and increase their production capacity with the same number of employees by re-engineering and automating their operations using the solutions described above.

Lutech's OIE, depicted in Fig. 2.1, focuses on four interconnected areas.

The four areas that make up the Lutech ecosystem include the *identification of OI strategies*, which include a wide range of initiatives to promote entrepreneurial intelligence: Blockchain and NFT certification; technology transfer and education; demonstration labs; accelerators and mentorship programmes for start-ups. In addition, events are planned with the aim of spreading knowledge. The second area is dedicated to *business–institution–research centre cooperation,* which involves collaboration between companies operating in the field of e-learning and ICT and all incubated start-ups. The *actors of the regional innovation system and the regional public policies* for innovation represent the third area of the ecosystem, including the Apulia Region, one of the project's financiers. Firstly, they offer training courses on innovative and cutting-edge topics, developed in collaboration with universities, research centres, industry experts and Lutech's in-house specialists. These courses are aimed at both students and customers of the group. In addition, they select and support innovative start-ups and complement Lutech's offerings by providing strategic and market support. Furthermore, in cooperation with technology partners,

Fig. 2.1 Lutech's open innovation ecosystem. (Source: Authors' elaboration)

they build laboratories where students and customers can experience and see cutting-edge technologies. Finally, they create a platform to organise science outreach events for customers and students, such as Lutech Talks and open days.

2.4.1 The Lutech Open Innovation Ecosystem Technologies

The last area of the Lutech Open Innovation Ecosystem (Fig. 1.1) is dedicated to the ***digital technologies*** that are at the heart of the Lutech Campus Ecosystem's IO strategies. The brokering of digital technologies includes

(i) *Blockchain*, which aims to create a new tangible and lasting value for information and data, enabling the connection between the physical and digital worlds using NFTs and tokens, with the objective of certifying, financing, promoting and engaging.
(ii) C*ybersecurity*, which focuses on risk prediction, visibility maximisation and process management to solve cybersecurity problems.
(iii) *Quantum computing* with power over the financial, pharmaceutical and automotive sectors. It seeks to harness it to perform calculations, simulations and models beyond current limits, creating correlations between data. 5G and the Internet of Things, in particular 5G, will help make digital continuity tangible in industry, accelerating the transfer of business data, improving production information and making production processes more efficient.
(iv) The development of *'digital twins'* of physical assets enables the replication and simulation of objects, processes, systems and infrastructures to optimise production processes and preventive maintenance.
(v) The *metaverse* which aim to ensure the continuity of data related to identity, history, rights, objects, communications and payments, promoting the interoperability and scalability of metaverse usage contexts across the digital world.
(vi) The importance of *artificial intelligence*, which uses the potential of unstructured data, needs to be emphasised. The integration of AI in every process is proposed to improve competitiveness and services. This can be done by using predictive models and automating repetitive tasks.

2.4.2 The Lutech 'AInnovation Centre'

In the Lutech Campus project, AI is a strategically relevant technology. In particular, it will be an essential component of a sub-project called the 'AInnovation Centre', the aim of which is to study, design, implement and test a platform that supports the IE. This platform will focus on the following objectives: the selection of start-ups and entrepreneurial ventures that deserve investment and support during

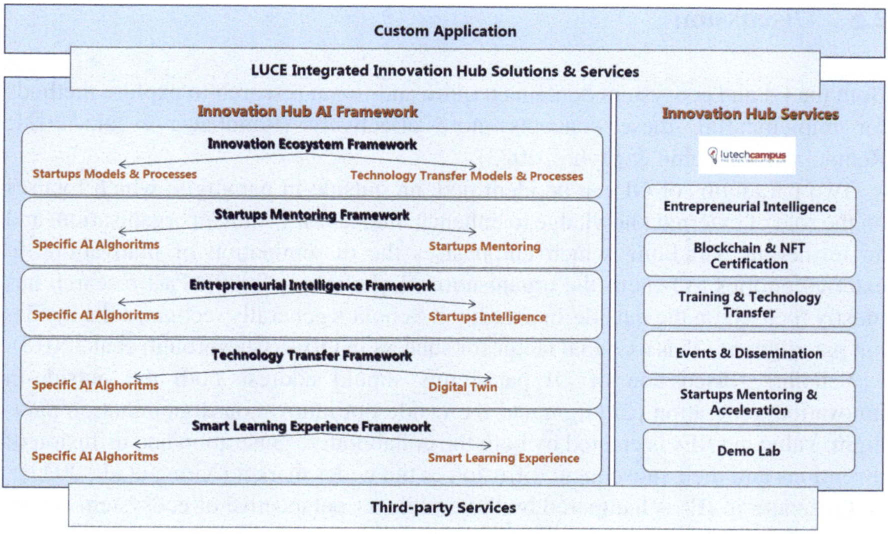

Fig. 2.2 AInnovation Centre architecture. (Source: authors' elaboration from Lutech report)

their development; the transfer of scientific and technological results from research centres and universities to industrial sectors; mentoring to guide start-ups and entrepreneurs through the various stages of their development, providing advice and support on important issues; eLearning, to provide customised online learning using automatic content classification, learning-curve prediction and adaptive content recommendations, with the aim of optimising and accelerating the learning process. The architecture of the AInnovation Centre is depicted in Fig. 2.2, which describes the development of an AInnovation Centre architecture called by Lutech 'LUCE Integrated Innovation Hub Solutions and Services', a system composed of levels and sub-levels aimed at accelerating innovation processes.

The level called 'Innovation Hub AI Framework' aims to use AI technology to support various innovation-oriented sub-processes. In particular, we find among the sub-levels the 'Innovation Ecosystem Framework', consisting of start-up models and processes and the technology transfer models and processes; the 'Startup Mentoring Framework', consisting of AI algorithms to support start-ups and mentoring programmes for start-ups; the 'Entrepreneurial Intelligence Framework', consisting of AI algorithms to support the development of entrepreneurial intelligence and start-up intelligence; the 'Technology Transfer Framework', composed instead of AI algorithms for technology transfer and the use of digital twins for technology transfer; finally, there is a last section that is closely related to the 'Smart Learning Experience Framework', composed of AI algorithms to support a smart learning experience. Finally, at the bottom we find a section solely dedicated to third-party services. On the right-hand side of the framework is a description of the strategies integral to the Innovation Hub Services developed by the Lutech Campus.

2.5 Discussion

Both the OI and ecosystem domains require additional research to explore methods for implementing these concepts more effectively (Randhawa et al., 2021; Remneland Wikhamn & Styhre, 2023).

Two paradigms of OI can be identified: an outside-in paradigm, which focuses on the role of external knowledge to enhance innovation within an organisation, and an inside-out paradigm, which emphasises the dissemination of innovations to external entities to benefit the organisation (Enkel et al., 2009). Past research has mostly focused on the outside-in paradigm. Scholars generally recognise the inside-out paradigm of OI as a crucial factor for success in OIEs (Chesbrough et al., 2018).

Scholarly discussion of OI paradigms should address both the outside-in innovation-generation paradigm and the inside-out innovation-dissemination paradigm. Value in OIEs is created by both the collaborative generation and diffusion of inventions and their subsequent diffusion to the wider market (Xiong et al., 2022).

Openness in IEs is hampered by the multilayer perspective of ecosystem activities, however. Transparency and knowledge-sharing are essential for ecosystem success, while knowledge protection is necessary for economic success. At the company level, businesses oversee knowledge exchange and preservation directly; this is not the case, however, at the ecosystem level (Paasi et al., 2023). There are many OI approaches that could affect enterprises in different ways and that help establish an integrated innovation system (Sarkar & Costa, 2008). By using external knowledge from a variety of sources, such as suppliers, customers, universities and research labs, innovation intermediaries and businesses operating in other sectors, companies can eventually develop both incremental and radical innovations, as well as long-term survival (Baima et al., 2020; Marozzo et al., 2023).

An OIE usually develops when a powerful entity, like a big business or public institution, takes the initiative and encourages participants to collaborate on their own initiative (Heaton et al., 2019). The network of creative inter-firm connections is complicated and difficult to manage; it often requires a core, stable participant to drive its development (Ritala et al., 2009). Therefore, coordinating OIEs is a critical ability for implementing OI practices.

To develop our study, we focused on a single company, 'Lutech', and used the single case study method (Yin, 2009), which we believe is appropriate for examining complex situations in depth. This method is particularly useful for innovative or unfamiliar scenarios as it allows the analysis of theoretical and conceptual frameworks. The investigation examined the entire information and communication technology (ICT) sector, with a special focus on Lutech as an exceptional and significant case. Data were collected and analysed using semi-structured interviews and secondary data analysis from a variety of sources. To confirm the validity of the analysis and interpretation of the results, data triangulation was performed using established methodological methods.

Lutech OIE, manifested through the development of the MILE research project and the development of the Lutech Campus, aims to provide a methodological and technological platform to foster the incubation of entrepreneurial ventures and start-ups and to facilitate sustainable entrepreneurship. This platform is founded on the ideas of OI and includes several organisations, large enterprises, start-ups, SMEs and research institutes.

The Lutech OIE focuses on four related areas: regional public policies for innovation; open innovation strategies; the brokering of digital technologies; collaboration among companies, institutions and research centres; and actors in the regional innovation system. The use of digital technologies, such as Blockchain, cybersecurity, AI, quantum computing, 5G, IoT and metaverse, are examples of open innovation strategies. To promote entrepreneurial intelligence, transfer technologies, provide mentorship for start-ups and organise events to spread knowledge, universities, research centres and technology partners work together to integrate these technologies.

The primary emphasis is on guaranteeing economic and environmental sustainability, maximising resource use and leveraging research outcomes. The project involves creating an AI framework to offer tailored services for identifying and supporting entrepreneurial projects, aiding in their creation, promotion, technology transfer and market entry. Methods for evaluating markets, predicting trends, tracking progress and assessing risks in start-up investments and technical advancements will be determined. An entrepreneurial environment will be established to facilitate and enhance the growth and value of the start-ups involved.

Considering the key role that AI is assuming in numerous industrial and service sectors, the proposal to create a centre (AInnovation Centre) of advanced competence for AI has significant relevance and enormous innovation potential. The strategic importance of AI in today's economy is the main reason for this. Companies that can effectively adopt and integrate AI technologies can gain an important competitive advantage due to the rapid advancement of these technologies. The centre will play a key role in promoting competitiveness and economic growth by providing a supportive ecosystem for AI-based innovation. It also has great potential for innovation. The centre can act as a catalyst for innovation by implementing advanced generative AI methods and creating a supportive environment for experimentation and the implementation of new solutions. The involvement of start-ups and SMEs will also continuously disseminate new approaches and ideas.

2.6 Conclusion and Future Research

The Lutech Campus Ecosystem's OI hub aims to act as a support and technology transfer ecosystem through start-up affiliation initiatives, mentoring, post-diploma and post-graduate training for young technicians and researchers on digital transformation issues and personnel training. This project aims to support this strategy by creating solutions to innovate technology transfer and OI processes. The aim of the project is to support all of Lutech's business lines and provide its customers with new services to introduce and/or strengthen technology transfer and OI initiatives.

The partnership with companies operating in the e-learning and ICT sectors contributed to the design and implementation of the strategy. Active involvement with important research institution, such as the LUM University of Casamassima, will enhance this collaboration.

In conclusion, the project benefits from several recognised principles:

- Artificial intelligence (AI) technology: Artificial intelligence is widely used in the development of data-driven solutions. This enables technology transfer actors and start-ups to find attractive markets and start-ups for investment. AI will act as a catalyst for the choice of technologies, patents and innovations for the project.
- Data-driven approach: The data-driven paradigm will be used to model the technology transfer process and provide packaged solutions for specific use cases.
- 'As a service' services model: The launch of a new 'as a service' offering model is an innovative step in a rapidly growing and fragmented market. This method will make solutions more scalable and less dependent on staff quality and quantity.
- Advanced technologies for training and education: Emerging technologies such as virtual reality (VR) and Blockchain technology (with NFT) will be widely used to manage the learning environment and certify training, mentoring and start-up development.
- An enabling environment for business innovation: Technology transfer, start-up growth and customised online learning will be facilitated through the creation of a platform to support a dedicated business IE.
- Partnership and collaboration with several SMEs: This makes it more innovative. Each SME will help with a particular aspect of the project, bringing a variety of knowledge and experience that will contribute to the overall success.

This study adds to the existing body of knowledge on IEs. We have built upon the research conducted by Marozzo et al. (2023), Baima et al. (2020), Bogers et al. (2019), Chesbrough et al. (2018), Alam et al. (2022) and Paasi et al. (2023) in our major contribution to this field.

Upon receiving the request from Remneland Wikhamn and Styhre (2023) to assess the digital technology sector, we conducted an examination of the evolution of an innovation ecosystem. Our objective was to perform an empirical examination that expanded the current corpus of research on IEs. Specifically, we examined how ecosystems are controlled and established in the real world, with a special focus on the perspective of the leading enterprise.

Pushpananthan and Elmquist (2022) emphasised the necessity of providing knowledge to assist individuals in making strategic decisions and distributing resources effectively within an ecosystem. To resolve this issue, we provided a concrete illustration of an IE initiative spearheaded by a large corporation. This organisation undertook both an industrial and a research initiative, with the goal of enhancing collaborative processes with a diverse range of stakeholders, such as institutions, SMEs, start-ups, research centres, accelerators, incubators and universities.

The case study we examined enhances the existing body of literature by integrating the conception of an IE led by a large corporation, using OI methodologies and incorporating the effect of digital technology. The Lutech case study serves as a prime example of a theoretical and practical approach. Using digital technology is crucial for facilitating collaborative endeavours with stakeholders, such as start-ups, inside the ecosystem. Furthermore, they are the primary catalysts for ongoing expansion and advancement. There are also numerous management implications, considering the approach used to build the IE model that will help design new IEs and orchestrate existing ones so that they can be more successful.

The study has limitations that could serve as the basis for future research. We should analyse the case study offered using a longitudinal technique, which was not used here. Exploring process view theory could enhance our analysis by providing a comprehensive understanding of all stages, from idea development to pilot project implementation. Future research could also investigate OIEs in many sectors and industries outside our current study.

Acknowledgments This chapter provides a contribution to the research related to the ongoing research project 'PRIN INSPIRE Digital Innovation EcoSystem Development for the Circular Economy: the startups' perspective' (CUP E53D23016450001) fuelled by PNRR grants.

References

Abbassi, W., Harmel, A., Belkahla, W., & Ben Rejeb, H. (2022). Maker movement contribution to fighting COVID-19 pandemic: Insights from Tunisian FabLabs. *R&D Management, 52*(2), 343–355.

Adner, R. (2006). Match your innovation strategy to your innovation ecosystem. *Harvard Business Review, 84*(4), 98.

Adner, R. (2017). Ecosystem as structure: An actionable construct for strategy. *Journal of Management, 43*(1), 39–58.

Adner, R., & Kapoor, R. (2010). Value creation in innovation ecosystems: How the structure of technological interdependence affects firm performance in new technology generations. *Strategic Management Journal, 31*(3), 306–333.

Alam, M. A., Rooney, D., & Taylor, M. (2022). Measuring inter-firm openness in innovation ecosystems. *Journal of Business Research, 138*, 436–456.

Arora, A., Athreye, S., & Huang, C. (2016). The paradox of openness revisited: Collaborative innovation and patenting by UK innovators. *Research Policy, 45*(7), 1352–1361.

Baima, G., Santoro, G., Busso, D., & Quaglia, R. (2020). Exploring the outcomes of the external revealing of knowledge: A case study in the craft beer industry. *Business Process Management Journal, 26*(5), 1183–1201.

Bianchi, M., Campodall'Orto, S., Frattini, F., & Vercesi, P. (2010). Enabling open innovation in small-and medium-sized enterprises: How to find alternative applications for your technologies. *R&D Management, 40*(4), 414–431.

Bogers, M., Sims, J., & West, J. (2019). What is an ecosystem? Incorporating 25 years of ecosystem research. *Academy of Management Proceedings, 2019*(1), 11080.

Cennamo, C., Dagnino, G. B., Di Minin, A., & Lanzolla, G. (2020). Managing digital transformation: Scope of transformation and modalities of value co-generation and delivery. *California Management Review, 62*(4), 5–16.

Chen, J., Yin, X., & Mei, L. (2018). Holistic innovation: An emerging innovation paradigm. *International Journal of Innovation Studies, 2*(1), 1–13.

Chesbrough, H. W. (2003). *Open innovation: The new imperative for creating and profiting from technology*. Harvard Business Press.

Chesbrough, H., & Bogers, M. (2014). Explicating open innovation: Clarifying an emerging paradigm for understanding innovation. In *New frontiers in open innovation* (pp. 3–28). Oxford University Press.

Chesbrough, H., Lettl, C., & Ritter, T. (2018). Value creation and value capture in open innovation. *Journal of Product Innovation Management, 35*(6), 930–938.

Chiaroni, D., Chiesa, V., & Frattini, F. (2011). The open innovation journey: How firms dynamically implement the emerging innovation management paradigm. *Technovation, 31*(1), 34–43.

Corvello, V., Felicetti, A. M., Steiber, A., & Alänge, S. (2023). Start-up collaboration units as knowledge brokers in corporate innovation ecosystems: A study in the automotive industry. *Journal of Innovation & Knowledge, 8*(1), 100303.

De Massis, A., & Kotlar, J. (2014). The case study method in family business research: Guidelines for qualitative scholarship. *Journal of Family Business Strategy, 5*(1), 15–29.

de Vasconcelos Gomes, L. A., Facin, A. L. F., Salerno, M. S., & Ikenami, R. K. (2018). Unpacking the innovation ecosystem construct: Evolution, gaps and trends. *Technological Forecasting and Social Change, 136*, 30–48.

Dhanaraj, C., & Parkhe, A. (2006). Orchestrating innovation networks. *Academy of Management Review, 31*(3), 659–669.

Dodgson, M., Gann, D., & Salter, A. (2006). The role of technology in the shift towards open innovation: The case of Procter & Gamble. *R&D Management, 36*(3), 333–346.

Dyer, J. H., & Nobeoka, K. (2000). Creating and managing a high-performance knowledge-sharing network: The Toyota case. *Strategic Management Journal, 21*(3), 345–367.

Eisenhardt, K. M. (1989). Building theories from case study research. *Academy of Management Review, 14*(4), 532–550.

Eisenhardt, K. M., & Graebner, M. E. (2007). Theory building from cases: Opportunities and challenges. *Academy of Management Journal, 50*(1), 25–32.

Elia, G., Petruzzelli, A. M., & Urbinati, A. (2020). Implementing open innovation through virtual brand communities: A case study analysis in the semiconductor industry. *Technological Forecasting and Social Change, 155*, 119994.

Enkel, E., Gassmann, O., & Chesbrough, H. (2009). Open R&D and open innovation: Exploring the phenomenon. *R&D Management, 39*(4), 311–316.

Foege, J. N., Lauritzen, G. D., Tietze, F., & Salge, T. O. (2019). Reconceptualizing the paradox of openness: How solvers navigate sharing-protecting tensions in crowdsourcing. *Research Policy, 48*(6), 1323–1339.

Gawer, A., & Henderson, R. (2007). Platform owner entry and innovation in complementary markets: Evidence from Intel. *Journal of Economics & Management Strategy, 16*(1), 1–34.

Heaton, S., Siegel, D. S., & Teece, D. J. (2019). Universities and innovation ecosystems: A dynamic capabilities perspective. *Industrial and Corporate Change, 28*(4), 921–939.

Hobday, M., & Rush, H. (1999). Technology management in complex product systems (CoPS)-ten questions answered. *International Journal of Technology Management, 17*(6), 618–638.

Hofman, E., Halman, J. I., & Van Looy, B. (2016). Do design rules facilitate or complicate architectural innovation in innovation alliance networks? *Research Policy, 45*(7), 1436–1448.

Iansiti, M., & Levien, R. (2004). Strategy as ecology. *Harvard Business Review, 82*(3), 68–78.

Jacobides, M. G. (2019). In the ecosystem economy, what's your strategy? *Harvard Business Review, 97*(5), 128–137.

Jacobides, M. G., Cennamo, C., & Gawer, A. (2018). Towards a theory of ecosystems. *Strategic Management Journal, 39*(8), 2255–2276.

Kirschbaum, R. (2005). Open innovation in practice. *Research-Technology Management, 48*(4), 24–28.

Langley, A. (2007). Process thinking in strategic organization. *Strategic Organization, 5*(3), 271–282.

Lee, S., Park, G., Yoon, B., & Park, J. (2010). Open innovation in SMEs—An intermediated network model. *Research Policy, 39*(2), 290–300.

Luoma, T., Paasi, J., & Valkokari, K. (2010). Intellectual property in inter-organisational relationships—Findings from an interview study. *International Journal of Innovation Management, 14*(03), 399–414.

Marozzo, V., Abbate, T., Cesaroni, F., Crupi, A., & Di Minin, A. (2023). Orchestrating an Open Innovation Ecosystem in low-tech industries: the case of Barilla's Blu1877. *Technology Analysis & Strategic Management*, 1–16.

Miles, M. B., Huberman, A. M., & Saldana, J. (2014). *Qualitative data analysis: A methods sourcebooks*. Sage.

Moore, J. F. (1993). Predators and prey: A new ecology of competition. *Harvard Business Review, 71*(3), 75–86.

Mortara, L., & Minshall, T. (2011). How do large multinational companies implement open innovation? *Technovation, 31*(10–11), 586–597.

Nambisan, S., & Baron, R. A. (2013). Entrepreneurship in innovation ecosystems: Entrepreneurs' self–regulatory processes and their implications for new venture success. *Entrepreneurship Theory and Practice, 37*(5), 1071–1097.

Paasi, J., Wiman, H., Apilo, T., & Valkokari, K. (2023). Modeling the dynamics of innovation ecosystems. *International Journal of Innovation Studies, 7*(2), 142–158.

Pushpananthan, G., & Elmquist, M. (2022). Joining forces to create value: The emergence of an innovation ecosystem. *Technovation, 115*, 102453.

Radziwon, A., & Bogers, M. (2019). Open innovation in SMEs: Exploring inter-organizational relationships in an ecosystem. *Technological Forecasting and Social Change, 146*, 573–587.

Randhawa, K., West, J., Skellern, K., & Josserand, E. (2021). Evolving a value chain to an open innovation ecosystem: Cognitive engagement of stakeholders in customizing medical implants. *California Management Review, 63*(2), 101–134.

Remneland Wikhamn, B., & Styhre, A. (2023). Open innovation ecosystem organizing from a process view: A longitudinal study in the making of an innovation hub. *R&D Management, 53*(1), 24–42.

Reynolds, E. B., & Uygun, Y. (2018). Strengthening advanced manufacturing innovation ecosystems: The case of Massachusetts. *Technological Forecasting and Social Change, 136*, 178–191.

Ritala, P., & Almpanopoulou, A. (2017). In defense of 'eco'in innovation ecosystem. *Technovation, 60*, 39–42.

Ritala, P., & Gustafsson, R. (2018). Q&A. Innovation and entrepreneurial ecosystem research: Where are we now and how do we move forward? *Technology Innovation Management Review, 8*(7), 52–57.

Ritala, P., Armila, L., & Blomqvist, K. (2009). Innovation orchestration capability—Defining the organizational and individual level determinants. *International Journal of Innovation Management, 13*(04), 569–591.

Ritala, P., Agouridas, V., Assimakopoulos, D., & Gies, O. (2013). Value creation and capture mechanisms in innovation ecosystems: A comparative case study. *International Journal of Technology Management, 63*(3–4), 244–267.

Rondi, E., Magrelli, V., Debellis, F., & De Massis, A. (2024). The evolution of craft work in the strategic development of a family enterprise. *Strategic Entrepreneurship Journal*. https://doi.org/10.1002/sej.1503

Sarkar, S., & Costa, A. I. (2008). Dynamics of open innovation in the food industry. *Trends in Food Science & Technology, 19*(11), 574–580.

Scaringella, L., & Radziwon, A. (2018). Innovation, entrepreneurial, knowledge, and business ecosystems: Old wine in new bottles? *Technological Forecasting and Social Change, 136*, 59–87.

Spithoven, A., Vanhaverbeke, W., & Roijakkers, N. (2013). Open innovation practices in SMEs and large enterprises. *Small Business Economics, 41*, 537–562.

Strauss, A., & Corbin, J. M. (1997). *Grounded theory in practice*. Sage.
Tang, H., Ma, Z., Xiao, J., & Xiao, L. (2020). Toward a more efficient knowledge network in innovation ecosystems: A simulated study on knowledge management. *Sustainability, 12*(16), 6328.
Tellis, W. (1997). Application of a case study methodology. *The Qualitative Report, 3*(3), 1–19.
Valkokari, K., Paasi, J., & Rantala, T. (2012). Managing knowledge within networked innovation. *Knowledge Management Research & Practice, 10*, 27–40.
Van de Vrande, V., De Jong, J. P., Vanhaverbeke, W., & De Rochemont, M. (2009). Open innovation in SMEs: Trends, motives and management challenges. *Technovation, 29*(6–7), 423–437.
West, J. (2017). Open source platforms beyond software: From ICT to biotechnology. In *Entrepreneurship, innovation, and platforms* (Vol. 37, pp. 337–370). Emerald Publishing Limited.
West, J., & Bogers, M. (2014). Leveraging external sources of innovation: A review of research on open innovation. *Journal of Product Innovation Management, 31*(4), 814–831.
Xie, X., & Wang, H. (2020). How can open innovation ecosystem modes push product innovation forward? An fsQCA analysis. *Journal of Business Research, 108*, 29–41.
Xiong, B., Kuan Lim, E. T., Tan, C. W., Zhao, Z., & Yu, Y. (2022). Towards an evolutionary view of innovation diffusion in open innovation ecosystems. *Industrial Management & Data Systems, 122*(8), 1757–1786.
Yin, R. K. (2009). *Case study research: Design and methods* (Vol. 5). Sage.
Zahra, S. A., & Nambisan, S. (2012). Entrepreneurship and strategic thinking in business ecosystems. *Business Horizons, 55*(3), 219–229.
Zhang, J., Yu, B., & Lu, C. (2023). Exploring the effects of innovation ecosystem models on innovative performances of start-ups: The contingent role of open innovation. *Entrepreneurship Research Journal, 13*(4), 1139–1168.

Chapter 3
Competencies and Skills for Public Administration: A Digital Journey

Valentina Ndou and Giusi Miccoli

Abstract Managing digital transformation goes beyond the realm of technology, requiring significant disruption to organisational structure, culture and leadership. This chapter emphasises that digital transformation of public administration is fundamentally about people and the development of digital capabilities and competencies that align all activities, processes and culture to organisational objectives. The Fourth Industrial Revolution has underscored the critical need for reskilling human resources and building dynamic organisational capabilities to manage advanced technologies. However, research on the competencies required for digital transformation remains limited and fragmented. This chapter aims to address this gap by analysing the competencies needed to manage digital transformation in public administration. It provides a framework for developing the necessary skills for civil servants and administrators, crucial for leading the digital transformation of the public sector.

Keywords Digital transformation · Organisational change · Digital capabilities · Public administration · Competencies · Fourth industrial revolution · Reskilling · Dynamic capabilities

3.1 Introduction

Managing digital transformation is not just a matter of technology. It also entails a disruption of organisational structure, culture and leadership, and thus poses considerable challenges in terms of skills and competencies (Bharadwaj et al., 2013; Jackson & Dunn-Jensen, 2021). The digital transformation is firstly about people

V. Ndou (✉)
Department of Engineering for Innovation, University of Salento, Lecce, Italy
e-mail: valentina.ndou@unisalento.it

G. Miccoli
Strategic Advisor for Personnel Development Policies, Rome, Italy

G. Passiante (ed.), *Digital Innovation Management*, Applied Innovation and Technology Management, https://doi.org/10.1007/978-3-031-80426-7_3

and the development of digital capabilities and competencies (Secundo et al., 2021) that coordinate all activities, processes, people and culture and align them to specific organisational objectives (Kiron et al., 2016; Nambisan et al., 2020).

It has been argued that just 30% of digital transformation initiatives are successful; this is because firms do not blend digital and human capabilities to apply them to the different targets (Gartner, 2022).

The recent debate on the effects of the Fourth Industrial Revolution has highlighted the profound change in the set of skills that is essential for managing advanced technologies and the related disruptive changes in business activities and models (WEF, 2023). Accordingly, studies have stressed the necessity for human resource reskilling (Doherty & Stephens, 2021; Goldmann, 2021) and the importance of building organisational dynamic capabilities (Vial, 2021).

Nevertheless, research addressing the need for new competencies to manage digital transformation has been limited and fragmented so far (Matarazzo et al., 2021). In the last years, studies have begun to investigate the required set of skills and capabilities for supporting digital change in the manufacturing and service sectors (Chirumalla, 2021; Ostmeier & Strobel, 2022; Schlegel & Kraus, 2023). Indeed, more research is needed to advance the current knowledge on the new generation of capabilities, mindsets, skills and competencies at the organisational level for digital transformation. This is especially relevant today for public administrative staff who are required to join, follow and manage the digital transformation of the public sector.

The Next Generation EU (20209) agenda has been highlighted as priorities in revitalising the economic system of its members' digital growth, the modernisation of public administration and the strengthening of the administrative capacity of the public sector.

Achieving such goals, however, requires a new set of skills and competencies. Indeed, the digital transformation of public administration underlies the relevance of new digital competencies (knowledge and skills), required to deal with innovation and change in the new digital environment.

In this chapter we aim to analyse the gap in the skills and competencies required to manage the digital transformation of public administration. We also provide a framework of new competencies needed to be developed to equip civil servants and administrators with the necessary skills that could lead the way towards digital transformation of the PA sector.

3.2 Digital Transformation and the Need for New Skills

The rapid advancement of digitisation, catalysed by the global Covid-19 pandemic, has underscored the urgent necessity of acquiring new skills to meet the evolving demands of the future workforce. In their recent OECD report (Manca & Oses Arranz, 2022), researchers delved into current trends concerning the interplay between the job market and the requisite skills amidst the digital transition. They contend that the adoption of emerging technologies, including AI, robotics, automation systems and IoT, is fundamentally altering how individuals learn and work, consequently necessitating adaptations within educational and occupational frameworks. Thus, it is imperative to closely monitor these evolving learning and employment dynamics to formulate policies aimed at facilitating the effective acquisition of the digital skills essential for meaningful participation in rapidly transforming labour markets and societies.

Digital skills emerge as the linchpin of technological advancement, giving rise to novel, highly skilled professional roles within the technological domain. The digital revolution fosters the emergence of fresh job opportunities and organisational paradigms while challenging existing ones. Consequently, there has arisen a demand for new skilled professionals equipped with a comprehensive array of both foundational and specialised technological competencies.

Moreover, findings from the World Economic Forum's *Future of Jobs* report (2023) posit that, while technology presents both challenges and opportunities for labour markets, most employers anticipate a positive effect on job creation. The report forecasts significant shifts in job roles over the next 5 years, with approximately 23% undergoing transformation, characterised by a growth rate of 10.2% juxtaposed with a decline of 12.3%. Survey data from 803 companies suggest a net decrease of 14 million jobs, representing 2% of current employment, with 69 million new roles projected to be created and 83 million eliminated.

Foremost among the technologies driving job creation is big data, with 65% of respondents anticipating job growth in related domains. Roles like data analysts, big data specialists, AI and machine learning specialists and cybersecurity professionals are projected to witness substantial growth, with an average increase of 30% by 2027. Training in AI and big data use is slated to be a primary focus for 42% of surveyed companies over the next half-decade, alongside analytical and creative thinking skills. Notably, digital commerce is poised to witness the most significant surge in job opportunities, with an estimated 2 million new roles expected to emerge, encompassing positions like e-commerce specialists, digital transformation experts and digital marketing strategists.

Conversely, even roles experiencing the swiftest decline are affected by technology and digitalisation, with clerical or secretarial positions, including bank tellers, cashiers and data entry clerks, anticipated to dwindle rapidly.

Furthermore, AI emerges as a pivotal driver of potential algorithmic displacement, with nearly 75% of surveyed companies poised to adopt AI technology. While 50% of organisations foresee job growth stemming from AI adoption, 25% anticipate job losses (Fig. 3.1).

It is expected that employment for data analysts and scientists, big data specialists, AI and machine learning specialists and cybersecurity professionals will grow by an average of 30% by 2027 (Fig. 3.2).

Moreover, investments aimed at facilitating the green transition and mitigating climate change are fuelling substantial job growth across the green, education and agriculture sectors. As consumer awareness regarding sustainability issues continues to rise, there is a notable shift towards industry transformation, ushering in new

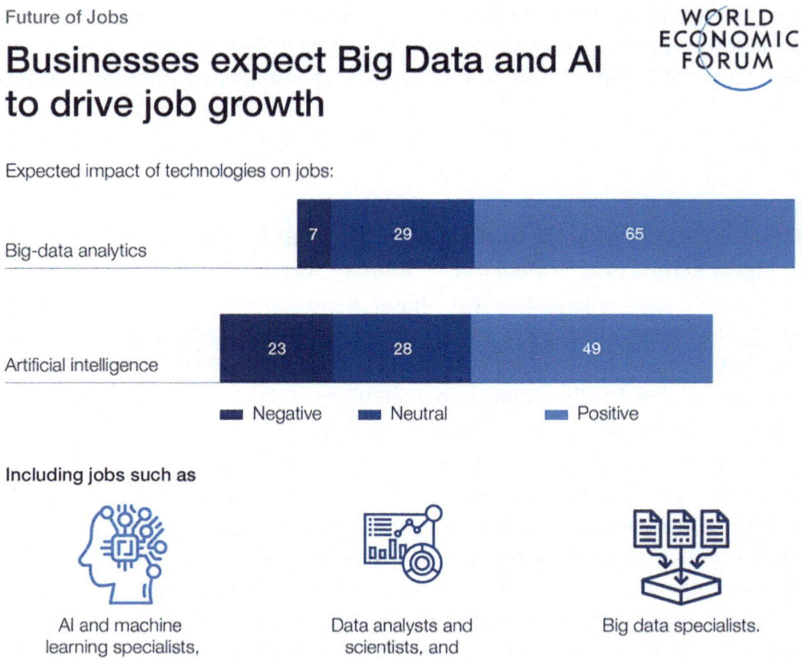

Fig. 3.1 Expected effects of technologies on jobs. (Source: WEF, 2023; Future of jobs, World Economic Forum, April 2023)

Fastest growing vs. fastest declining jobs

Top 10 fastest growing jobs		Top 10 fastest declining jobs	
1.	AI and Machine Learning Specialists	1.	Bank Tellers and Related Clerks
2.	Sustainability Specialists	2.	Postal Service Clerks
3.	Business Intelligence Analysts	3.	Cashiers and ticket Clerks
4.	Information Security Analysts	4.	Data Entry Clerks
5.	Fintech Engineers	5.	Administrative and Executive Secretaries
6.	Data Analysts and Scientists	6.	Material-Recording and Stock-Keeping Clerks
7.	Robotics Engineers	7.	Accounting, Bookkeeping and Payroll Clerks
8.	Big Data Specialists	8.	Legislators and Officials
9.	Agricultural Equipment Operators	9.	Statistical, Finance and Insurance Clerks
10.	Digital Transformation Specialists	10.	Door-To-Door Sales Workers, News and Street Vendors, and Related Workers

Fig. 3.2 Jobs lost and jobs created. (Source: WEF, 2023; World Economic Forum, Future of jobs report 2023)Note: The jobs which survey respondents expect to grow most quickly from 2023 to 2027 as a fraction of present employment figures

opportunities within the labour market. Most respondents anticipate that investments geared towards facilitating the green transition of companies will yield the most significant net job creation effects. As nations strive to expand their use of renewable energy sources, roles like renewable energy engineers and solar energy system installation engineers are expected to experience heightened demand. Additionally, these investments will stimulate the proliferation of generalist roles in sustainability, including sustainability specialists and environmental protection professionals, with an estimated growth of approximately 1 million jobs.

The most substantial absolute increases in job opportunities, however, are projected to occur in the education and agriculture sectors. While certain repetitive tasks may be automated, it is crucial to acknowledge that digital tools necessitate programming and monitoring by qualified personnel. The use of advanced technologies for intellectually demanding tasks underscores the significance of 'human' skills, such as empathy, intuition and creativity in anticipating the evolution of emerging labour markets.

Analytical thinking and creative thinking are deemed the most crucial skills for workers in 2023, a trend expected to persist over the next 5 years. Furthermore, technological literacy, particularly in areas like AI and big data, is projected to become increasingly indispensable, with business strategies placing a heightened emphasis on these skills over the next 5 years (Fig. 3.3).

The urgency of retraining is increasingly apparent as companies face challenges related to skills gaps and talent acquisition, hindering their transformation efforts. This underscores a clear necessity for comprehensive training and retraining initiatives across all sectors. Surveys indicate that six out of every ten workers will require training before 2027, yet it is believed that only half of employees currently have access to adequate training opportunities. Additionally, the report estimates that, on average, 44% of an individual worker's skills will need updating to align with future business needs.

Addressing the disparity between workers' existing skills and the evolving requirements of businesses necessitates a reskilling and upskilling revolution to

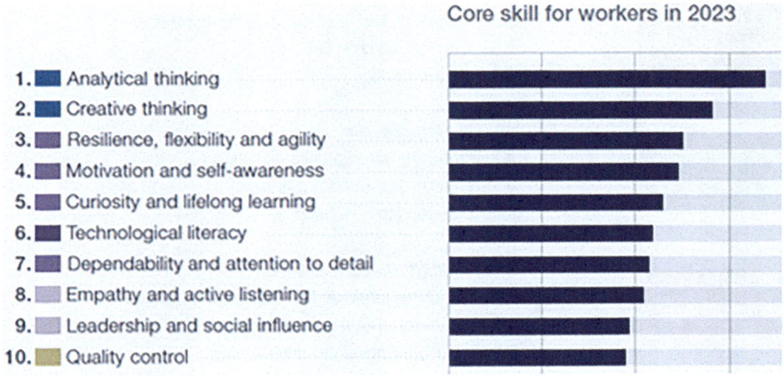

Fig. 3.3 Core skills for the future. (Source: WEF, 2023)

foster learning and retraining opportunities, particularly in digital competencies. A significant portion of surveyed companies (45%) express that government funding for skills training would facilitate the connection of talent to employment.

Thus, it becomes imperative to cultivate digital competencies and enhance the skill sets of current workforces, with a focus on key areas such as cloud computing, cybersecurity, data analysis and software development for future success.

Digital competencies are defined as the 'confident, critical and responsible use of and engagement with, digital technologies for learning, at work and for participation in society. It is defined as a combination of knowledge, skills and attitudes' (Council recommendation on key competencies for lifelong learning 2018 in European Commission (2018a)). This definition encompasses both technical and soft skills, emphasising not only proficiency with digital tools but also the ability to comprehend the complexities of the work environment, adeptly navigate ever-changing contexts and leverage digital tools to support business objectives. Moreover, skills such as innovation and creative thinking are essential for leading the transformative changes driven by digitalisation.

The DigComp (Vuorikari et al., 2022) framework outlines five core dimensions of digital competence, each encompassing key areas essential for navigating the digital landscape effectively. These dimensions provide a comprehensive framework for individuals to develop and enhance their digital skills (Fig. 3.4).

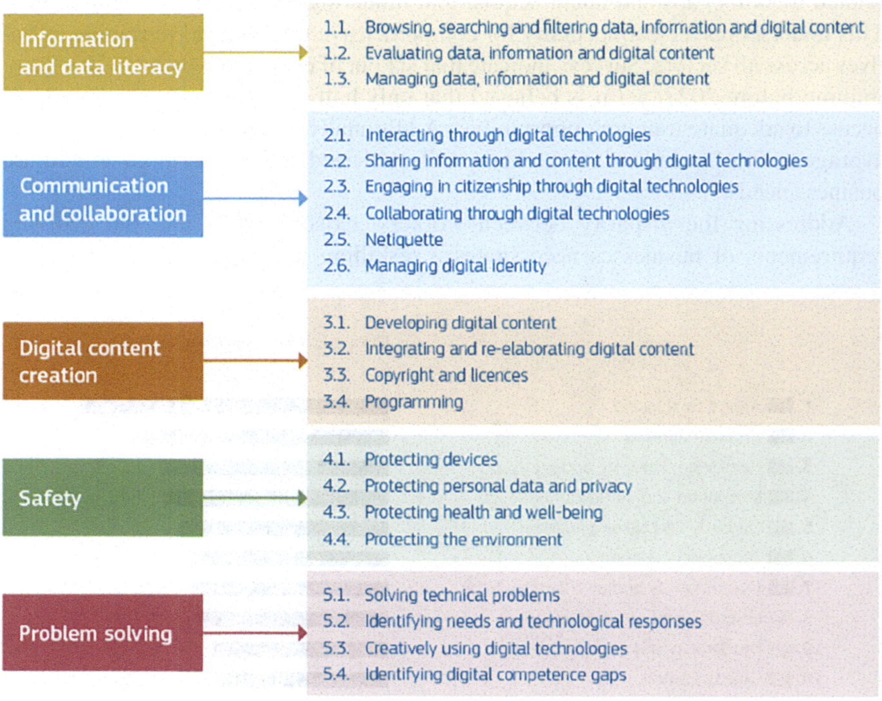

Fig. 3.4 DigComp reference model, (Source: Vuorikari et al., 2022)

More specifically, the dimensions deal with

- *Information and data literacy*: This dimension involves the ability to articulate information needs and effectively locate and retrieve digital data and content. It also includes the capacity to assess the relevance and credibility of sources, as well as the skills to manage and organise digital information. Furthermore, individuals should be proficient in storing, managing and organising digital data to facilitate its efficient access and retrieval.
- *Communication and collaboration*: In today's interconnected world, effective communication and collaboration through digital technologies are essential. This dimension emphasises the ability to interact and collaborate with others using digital tools while being mindful of cultural and generational diversity. Individuals should also be capable of engaging with digital services for both public and private purposes, demonstrating participatory citizenship. Additionally, managing one's digital presence, identity and reputation is vital in maintaining a positive online image.
- *Digital content creation*: This dimension focuses on the creation and editing of digital content, encompassing various forms, such as text, multimedia and graphics. Individuals should possess the skills to produce high-quality digital content and integrate it into existing knowledge domains. Understanding copyright laws and licensing agreements is crucial for ethical content creation, along with the ability to provide clear instructions for computer systems.
- *Safety*: Ensuring safety in digital environments is paramount, encompassing the protection of devices, personal data and privacy. Individuals should be equipped to safeguard themselves against cyberthreats and understand the importance of maintaining physical and psychological well-being in digital spaces. Awareness of the environmental effects of digital technologies and responsible use practices are also integral aspects of this dimension.
- *Problem-solving*: Digital competence includes the ability to identify and address needs and problems within digital environments. This dimension emphasises problem-solving skills, both conceptual and practical, to navigate challenges effectively. Individuals should leverage digital tools to innovate processes and products, staying abreast of technological advancements to adapt and thrive in a rapidly evolving digital landscape.

In summary, the DigComp framework provides a holistic approach to digital competence, encompassing essential skills and competencies across various dimensions. It serves as a valuable guide for individuals seeking to enhance their digital proficiency and adaptability in an increasingly digitalised world.

3.3 Digital Skills and Competencies for PA

The importance of implementing digital transformation in the public sector has been widely emphasised due to the multitude of benefits it offers for government, citizens and businesses. As public administrations undergo the digitalisation of processes and adopt new tasks, it becomes imperative for civil servants to possess digital competencies to serve the public more efficiently and effectively (Lember, 2017). Despite changes in policy and governance, many digitalisation initiatives fail to achieve the desired outcomes, possibly due to a lack of digital literacy and competencies among both internal and external stakeholders, as suggested by Rupp (2017). Therefore, the digital transformation of public administration necessitates the development of various competencies, crucial for public administration education and the preparation of future civil servants for the modernisation of administration (Kausch-Zongo & Schenk, 2022).

Indeed, the Digital Economy and Society Index (DESI) monitors all EU countries' progress in digitisation across multiple metrics, encompassing connectivity, human capital, Internet service usage, integration of digital technology and provision of digital public services, underscoring the critical nature of human capital and digital skills and emphasising their importance in shaping interactions and modern work practices. With an increasing demand for digital competencies in the workplace, it becomes vital for employees, regardless of sector, to possess these skills. As reliance on the Internet and digital tools grows, adapting to evolving skill requirements becomes imperative. Without a strong grasp of digital skills, the ability to drive innovation and maintain competitiveness is compromised.

A digitally literate workforce and population are essential for facilitating the digital transition. The Path to the Digital Decade proposal, defined by EU in 'The Digital Decade policy programme', underscores this importance, along with initiatives aimed at infrastructure development and the digital transformation of businesses and public services. Specific targets have been outlined to guide and incentivise actions by the EU and its member states by 2030, including ensuring that at least 80% of the population possesses basic digital skills and increasing the number of ICT specialists to 20 million, constituting approximately 10% of total employment, while also ensuring gender equality in this field by 2030.

According to the DESI report, in 2021, despite 87% of individuals aged 16–74 regularly accessing the Internet, only 54% had basic digital skills (Fig. 3.5).

DESI also evaluates the accessibility of online public services by examining whether crucial services can be completed entirely online within member states. It is widely recognised that fully harnessing the potential of digital technologies presents a significant challenge for governmental entities. The availability of public services online has shown a steady increase over the past decade, particularly accelerated by the Covid-19 pandemic, during which digital interactions became commonplace. The digitisation of public administration brings about various advantages, including heightened efficiency and cost savings for both governments and businesses, alongside increased transparency and openness.

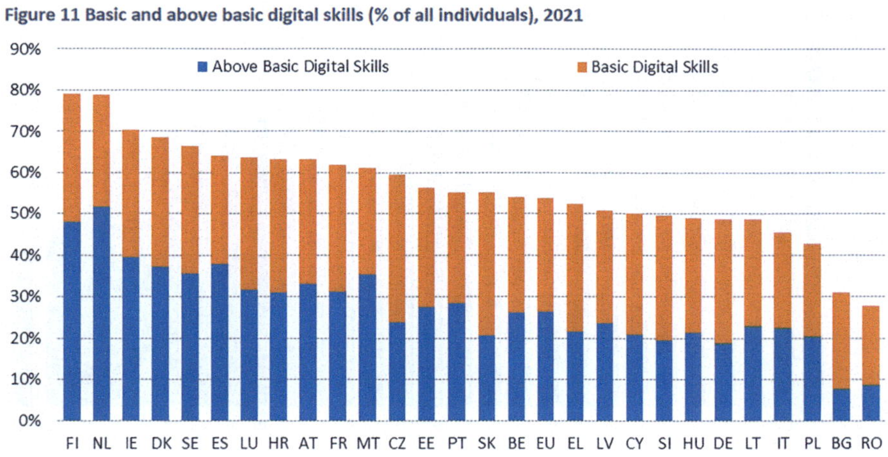

Fig. 3.5 EU countries' digital skills performance

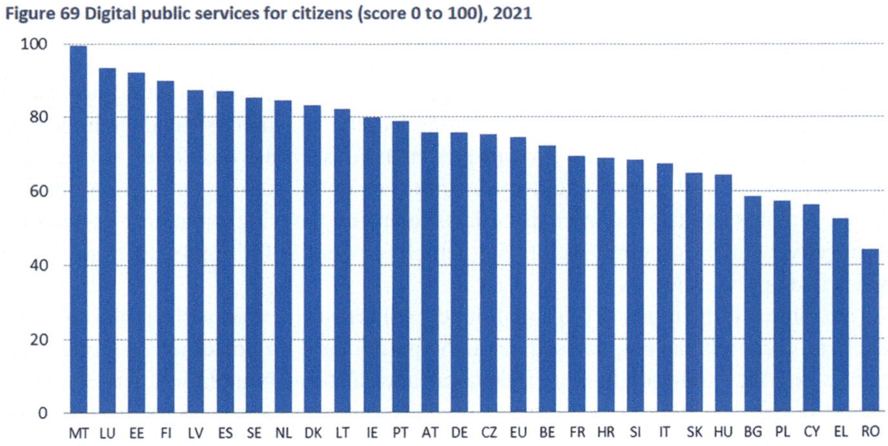

Fig. 3.6 Digital public services for citizens. (Source: e-Government Benchmark, Capgemini)

Per the latest DESI report, the quality scores for digital public services reached 75 out of 100 for citizens and 82 out of 100 for businesses in 2021 (Figs. 3.6 and 3.7). Estonia, Finland, Malta and the Netherlands received the highest scores for digital public services in DESI, while Romania and Greece scored the lowest. The Path to the Digital Decade proposal aims to ensure that all essential public services for citizens and businesses are fully accessible online by 2030. Nonetheless, progress varies both among and within member states.

While the implementation of fundamental digital public services, such as online form access and appointment scheduling, is progressing steadily, providing more advanced services leverageing state-of-the-art digital technologies, such as AI, big data and robotics, requires significant investment. The European Interoperability

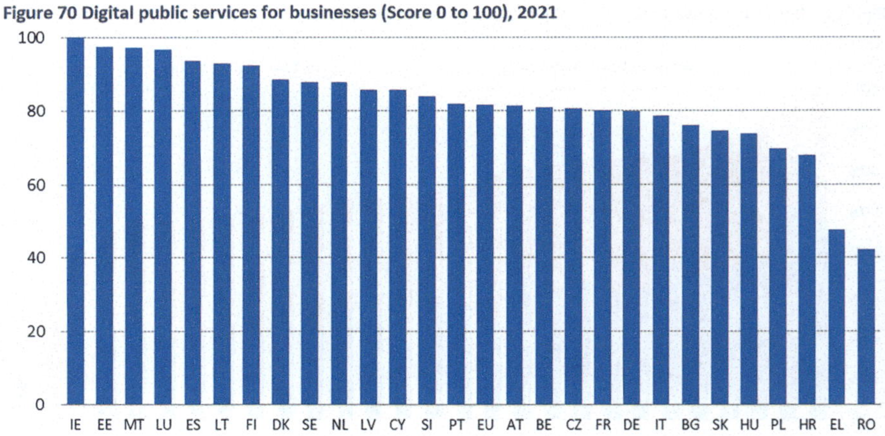

Fig. 3.7 Digital public services for businesses. (Source: e-Government Benchmark, Capgemini)

Framework provides comprehensive guidelines for establishing interoperable digital public services.

The DESI 2022 findings indicate that, while many member states are progressing in their digital evolution, businesses' adoption of critical digital technologies, such as AI and big data, remains low, even among leading EU nations. Inadequate levels of digital skills impede future growth prospects, exacerbate the digital divide and heighten the risk of digital exclusion as more essential services transition online. There is a pressing need to intensify efforts to ensure the widespread deployment of connectivity infrastructure, notably 5G, which is essential for highly innovative services and applications.

In summary, the urgency of propelling digital transformation and streamlining its execution cannot be emphasised enough, particularly in fostering interoperable public services transcending geographical and sectoral boundaries. An essential aspect of this endeavour is equipping civil servants with the necessary digital skills and competencies to effectively lead this transformative process. Beyond merely improving public service delivery, cultivating a digitally proficient workforce acts as a catalyst for innovation and efficiency across various industries and regions.

Moreover, investing in the ongoing development of digital skills among civil servants is not just beneficial but imperative. Such investments enable governments to unleash the full potential of digital transformation, leading to enhancements in service delivery, responsiveness and citizen engagement. Ultimately, the successful integration of digital technologies into public service delivery hinges on empowering and upskilling civil servants, paving the way for a more connected, efficient and responsive public sector capable of meeting the evolving needs of citizens in the digital era.

3.4 Public Administration and Industry 4.0 and 5.0: Gaps in Skills and Competencies for Public Administration

3.4.1 Public Administration Readiness for Digital Transformation

The National Recovery and Resilience Plan (PNRR), framed into the NextGenerationEU programme (https://commission.europa.eu/strategy-and-policy/recovery-plan-europe_en), represents a fundamental opportunity to address the structural challenges of the Italian Public Administration (PA) and to build a better future for generations. The European Union's country-specific recommendations (CSRs) have emphasised the need to improve the functioning and effectiveness of the PA, with a particular focus on investing in the skills of public employees (European Commission, 2022).

Over the past 20 years, spending review policies have led to a gradual impoverishment of the population employed in the PA, both quantitatively and qualitatively. In the public sector, two long-standing critical issues persist: a shortage of personnel and an ageing workforce, coupled with a lack of skills adequate to the rapid changes in society and the economy. For example, in the case of Italy, despite significant signs of change, the number of public workers remains low compared to other European countries, with an average age exceeding 50 years (excluding the police and armed forces), the limited presence of young people under 30 and a shortage of training and specialised skills to address the challenges of the PNRR. Of the 3.7 million public workers, a staggering 1.35 million are over 55 years old, representing 36% of the total. It is projected that, within the next 10 years, over a third of these employees will retire, posing a significant challenge for human resource management and maintaining operational continuity in public services (ForumPA, 2024).

In addition to challenges related to the quantitative and qualitative characteristics of public sector personnel, it is now a priority to provide efficient and accessible services to citizens and businesses by investing in the modernisation and digital transformation of the PA. The digitisation of infrastructure and public services is essential for reducing bureaucracy and bridging the gap between entities and individuals, especially after the digital acceleration caused by the pandemic.

According to the RRF Regulation, each member state is required to allocate a minimum of 20% of its total allocation under the Recovery and Resilience Plan (RRP) to initiatives that support the digital transition or address challenges arising from it. Within this allocation, 37% is designated for the digitalisation of public services and government processes. The EU's Next Generation Recovery and Resilience Plan aims to significantly enhance the competitiveness and productivity of the country's system through various components, one being the digitalisation of public administration.

The broad-spectrum interventions of this component include

- *Transition to digital infrastructures, with a 'cloud-first' approach*: Investment in migrating the data and IT applications of central and local PA entities to the cloud environment, supporting administrations in their transformation journey.
- *Action on full interoperability between administrative data*: Investment in technologies focusing on interconnecting administrative databases to enable cross-cutting and universal access to services based on the 'once only' principle.
- *Enhancement of digital services* offered to citizens, accompanying the transformation of the PA's digital architecture. This entails affecting internal processes deemed most critical and improving the user experience and accessibility of digital services through common quality standards.
- *Consistent strengthening of cybersecurity* to address the growing cyber threats due to digitalisation.

The NextGeneration EU plan could thus play a fundamental role in promoting digital transformation, the development of Industry 4.0 and the evolution towards Industry 5.0, creating favourable conditions for sustainable, inclusive and resilient economic growth, but technological innovation is advancing so rapidly that it is leading to the rapid evolution of challenges related to technology obsolescence, with many PA infrastructures and IT systems outdated and inadequate for modern needs. Addressing obsolescence requires significant investments in technological upgrades, personnel training and targeted digitalisation strategies. Only the integration of investments in technology, training and process focus can induce real transformation of the PA and support a country's competitive system (Miccoli, 2023).

3.4.2 What Are the Levers?

- *Digitisation and automation of processes*: The NextGeneration EU plan encourages the digitisation and automation of processes, urging administrations to adopt innovative technological solutions to enhance efficiency, productivity and service quality.
- *Training and digital skills*: The plan includes initiatives for basic and specialised digital skills training and development to enable personnel to use tools and technologies in work management and service delivery and develop specialised skills useful for e-leadership and supporting continuous organisational and technological innovation. The Department of Civil Service has developed the digital skills framework, which defines the set of minimum skills required of each public employee to enable them to actively participate in the digital transformation of PA. The framework, which also refers to DigComp, is a model considered an interesting best practice at the European level.
- *Process change*: The introduction of innovative technologies necessitates a rethink of work processes and administrative work management, transitioning administrations from vertical structures organised by silos to leaner and less hierarchical structures founded on office integration.

3.4.3 Changing Perspective: Towards a Goal-Oriented and Results-Driven Public Administration

To tackle the challenges of technological innovation and effectively manage the Recovery and Resilience Plan, it is necessary to simultaneously invest in process transformation, technological innovation and training and development, adopting a dynamic and strategic approach to change management. For PA to be future-oriented and strategic for the country's competitive system, the determined embrace of change management is essential to promote the efficiency and innovation of services and the satisfaction of citizens and businesses.

This entails embarking on an administrative transition path from an approach based on the directiveness of laws to one focused on objectives and results (Miccoli, 2023). Although regulations provide an important framework, focusing solely on them could limit the effectiveness and efficiency of administrative action. Working towards objectives enables PA to focus on the concrete effects on citizens and society rather than just compliance with procedures. Furthermore, goal orientation promotes greater flexibility and responsiveness to changing social, technological and economic needs. Lastly, promoting such an approach encourages responsibility and transparency within the administration, innovation and creativity, paving the way for new and innovative solutions. By balancing regulatory compliance with a focus on objectives and results, PA can become more effect-oriented, flexible, responsible and innovative, with the ultimate goal of promoting the well-being of society and citizens.

3.5 The Framework of New Competencies

To accompany the transition of the PA from an approach based on the directiveness of laws to one centred on objectives and results, it is necessary to consider a framework of new competencies for public sector personnel articulated in soft skills, project management competencies, process work competencies and digital skills (Fig. 3.8).

The following section details the specific competencies required within the PA.

3.5.1 Soft Skills

Soft skills are strategically crucial in PA as they contribute to the effective management of change, the promotion of a results-oriented organisational culture and the improvement of the quality of public services. In a constantly evolving context, soft skills allow the PA to face increasingly complex challenges and quickly adapt to the changing needs of citizens, encourageing innovation and professional growth.

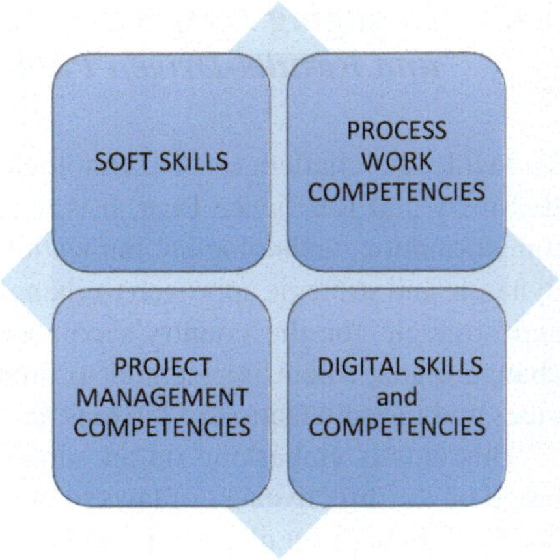

Fig. 3.8 Framework of new competencies

The crucial soft skills for effectively managing change and promoting a collaborative and efficiency-oriented work environment include (Goleman, 2020):

- *Effective communication*: Conveying information and instructions, communicating with colleagues, stakeholders and citizens, motivating personnel, managing conflicts and maintaining a steady flow of information during change.
- *Leadership and decision-making ability*: Being able to lead and make strategic decisions involving and inspiring others to follow a common vision.
- *Change management*: Being able to manage and adapt to changes, anticipating challenges, mitigate risks and develop strategies to address the new context.
- *Empathy and emotional intelligence*: Understanding the emotions and perspectives of others to maintain an atmosphere of trust and collaboration during change.
- *Problem-solving*: Being able to address complex problems, think creatively and find innovative solutions to overcome obstacles.
- *Teamwork and collaboration*: Effectively working in groups, encouraging the diversity of perspective and valuing the abilities, skills and talents of each individual to achieve common goals.
- *Flexibility and adaptability*: Being ready to change approaches and strategies when necessary to address new challenges, review and modify viewpoints; being open to change.
- *Negotiation and conflict management skills*: Being able to understand the positions involved in a conflict, negotiate between parties, manage conflict situations and reach compromises for the common good.
- *Critical and analytical thinking*: Critically evaluating information, making informed decisions and analysing the consequences of actions.
- *Resilience and stress management*: Managing personal and organisational stress, guiding others in difficult times and being resilient in times of uncertainty and instability.

Developing and cultivating these soft skills can make the administrative transition more effective, improve change management and foster a healthier and more productive organisational climate.

3.5.2 *Project Management Competencies*

These skills are vital for planning, coordinating and efficiently overseeing administrative transformation projects, ensuring adherence to timelines and budgets and attaining the desired results. They are indispensable for effectively managing complexity, facilitating change implementation and supporting administrative transition systematically. It is widely recognised that the failure of many digital transformation initiatives stems from the lack of a conducive mindset towards change, both within businesses and among individuals and the absence of a culture that fosters digital transformation.

It is crucial to acknowledge that digital transformation transcends mere technological advancements; it also entails a comprehensive process involving the radical reimagining of work environments, processes, organisational structures, customer requirements, product offerings and, most importantly, the development of skills and capabilities necessary to foster a proactive approach in managing change.

In this context, innovative project management is fundamental. Although within the framework of the NextGeneration EU plan there have been funds allocated for project designers, such as engineers, architects and freelancers, aimed at assisting municipalities and businesses in drafting and presenting projects, what seems to be missing in many cases is the figure of 'Innovation Project Manager' (Ndou & Ingrosso, 2022), a professional figure who goes beyond merely managing the project, controlling timelines, activities and costs. Instead, in line with the ongoing technological revolution, they play a key role in serving businesses and organisations in defining and managing innovation projects through

- Identification and development of new technology-based ideas to create economic and social value compatible with challenges.
- Creativity and innovative strategies to enable a profound paradigm shift, making necessary changes to structures and organisational roles to create value.
- Support and creation of an innovation ecosystem crucial for connecting businesses, public administration and individuals, enabling innovation processes through cross-collaboration and proactive sharing of knowledge and experiences.
- Identification of the skills necessary to develop through differentiated training paths, reskilling and upskilling interventions for personnel to support businesses and public administration towards an open, innovative and flexible digital transition.
- Support for businesses and public administration in defining improvement initiatives with a new cultural and managerial model based on cross-disciplinary collaboration.

The current scenario requires not only learning new methods, techniques and tools for project management but, above all, training talented individuals with the awareness that change is constant. The strategy governing change aims at creating Learning Organisations: organisations capable of facilitating people's learning and continuously transforming themselves.

3.5.3 Working with Process Competencies

In addition to soft skills and project management competencies, administrative transition requires the ability to work with processes (Hammer & Champy, 2009). Focusing on processes helps analyse administrative activities, identifying strengths and areas for improvement and then simplifying and optimising them. To support administrative transition, there are several process-related competencies:

- *Analysis of existing processes*: Conducting in-depth analysis of existing administrative processes, identifying strengths, inefficiencies and areas for improvement.
- *Process redesign*: Redesigning processes using methodologies like continuous improvement or reengineering to make them more efficient, results-oriented and aligned with change objectives.
- *Standardisation and documentation*: Standardising processes and documenting them clearly and accessibly to facilitate the management of various phases and activities.
- *Continuous improvement*: Implementing continuous improvement cycles, regularly assessing process effectiveness and making changes to adapt to changing needs or situations.
- *Technological integration*: Integrating new tools and digital solutions harmoniously within administrative processes to enhance overall efficiency.
- *Resource optimisation*: Identifying and optimising the use of resources, such as time, money and personnel, within processes to maximise efficiency.

In summary, process-related competencies are essential for identifying, optimising and managing administrative processes to adapt them to changes, maximise efficiency and ensure that the entire organisation aligns with transition and change objectives.

3.5.4 Digital Skills and Competencies

Finally, a significant investment in digital skills (Syllabus, 2023) is necessary for administrative and digital transition. Living in the digital age means navigating through data, information and online services. But what differentiates data from information? And how can we best use the digital tools at our disposal?

The articulation presented here refers to the digital skills framework proposed by the Department of Public Function. This framework defines the minimum set of digital competencies required for each civil servant.

- *Data* vs. *information*: Being able to collect useful data from the internet and organise it effectively is a necessary skill in the public sector. Data are the raw building blocks, while information is the wall we construct with them, so it is important to be able to collect, process and use data, information and documents. Skills in managing big data are in fact considered among the main core skills for the future (WEF, 2023).
- *Digital identity and online services*: Accessing institutional online services requires a digital identity. Knowing authentication tools is crucial for safely navigating the digital world.
- *Communication and sharing*: Using different tools, from emails to social media, allows public sector employees to communicate and share information. Choosing the most suitable method based on content and context is important for daily interactions within the administration and with other administrative structures, as well as for sharing information and work documents.
- *Digital transformation*: Understanding the strategies and actors involved in digital transformation is essential to keep up with changes. Transitioning to digital offers multiple opportunities to intervene in PA processes by simplifying them, speeding them up and making them more transparent.

3.5.5 Cybersecurity

Being aware of and preventing cyberattacks is crucial for protecting computer systems and the data they contain. Cybersecurity is an important individual skill that preserves personal and institutional data, documents and usage systems.

Among the digital competencies, the development of e-leadership skills is also envisaged. These skills involve understanding the changes brought about by digitalisation and the ability to guide such changes. They are not possessed exclusively by IT personnel but also by managers and officials who can accompany the PA in the technological change of processes and public services (Iacono, 2021).

Navigating the digital world may seem complex, but, with adequate preparation, the Italian PA can operate safely and effectively.

3.6 Conclusions: Competencies in Evolution

Investing in the development of skills within PA personnel has far-reaching benefits that extend beyond the immediate operational improvements. Firstly, a well-trained and skilled workforce can lead to greater public trust and confidence in government institutions. When citizens perceive that civil servants possess the necessary expertise and competencies to address their needs effectively, it fosters a positive relationship between the government and the public, enhancing overall governance.

Secondly, by nurturing a culture of continuous learning and skill development, the PA can better adapt to evolving societal needs and expectations. As societies become increasingly complex and interconnected, the ability to quickly adapt to new challenges and emerging trends becomes paramount. Skilled personnel are better equipped to navigate these complexities and respond proactively to changing circumstances, ensuring that government services remain relevant and effective.

Moreover, investing in skills development can have significant economic implications. A highly skilled public sector workforce is better equipped to drive economic growth and development by implementing policies and initiatives that promote innovation, entrepreneurship and sustainable development. Skilled personnel can identify opportunities for economic advancement, effectively allocate resources and collaborate with other stakeholders to achieve common goals, ultimately contributing to broader socioeconomic progress.

Additionally, a focus on skills development can help mitigate the various risks and challenges faced by the PA, ranging from cybersecurity threats to demographic shifts. By equipping personnel with the necessary skills to address these challenges, governments can enhance their resilience and capacity to withstand unexpected disruptions, safeguarding the continuity of essential services and protecting the interests of citizens.

In essence, investing in skills development within the PA is not just about improving operational efficiency; it is about building a more capable, responsive and resilient government that can effectively meet the needs of society, drive economic prosperity and navigate the complexities of the modern world.

References

Bharadwaj, A., El Sawy, O. A., Pavlou, P. A., & Venkatraman, N. V. (2013). Digital business strategy: Toward a next generation of insights. *MIS Quarterly*, 471–482.

Chirumalla, K. (2021). Building digitally-enabled process innovation in the process industries: A dynamic capabilities approach. *Technovation, 105*, 102256.

Doherty, O., & Stephens, S. (2021). The skill needs of the manufacturing industry: Can higher education keep up? *Education+ Training, 63*(4), 632–646.

ForumPA. (2024). *Annual report*. ForumPA.

Goldmann, S. (2021). Illuminating digital transformations: A literature review to conceptualize the impact of technologies on human capital. In *Proceedings of the 2nd world conference on management and economics* (pp. 2–17).

Goleman, D. (2020). *Emotional intelligence: Why it can matter more than IQ*. Bloomsbury Publishing.

Hammer, M., & Champy, J. (2009). *Reengineering the corporation: Manifesto for business revolution, a*. Zondervan.

Iacono, G. (2021). *E-leadership: Come guidare la trasformazione (digitale) della PA*. FrancoAngeli.

Jackson, N. C., & Dunn-Jensen, L. M. (2021). Leadership succession planning for today's digital transformation economy: Key factors to build for competency and innovation. *Business Horizons, 64*(2), 273–284.
Kausch-Zongo, J., & Schenk, B. (2022). General technological competency and usage in public administration education: An evaluation study considering on-the-job trainings and home studies. *Smart Cities and Regional Development (SCRD) Journal, 6*(1), 55–65.
Kiron, D., Kane, G. C., Palmer, D., Phillips, A. N., & Buckley, N. (2016). Aligning the organization for its digital future. *MIT Sloan Management Review, 58*(1).
Lember, V. (2017). The increasing role of digital technologies in co-production. In T. Brandsen, T. Steen, & B. Verschuere (Eds.), *Co-production and co-creation engaging citizens in public services*. Routledge.
Manca, F., & Oses Arranz, A. (2022). *Skills for the digital transition: assessing recent trends using big data*. OECD.
Matarazzo, M., Penco, L., Profumo, G., & Quaglia, R. (2021). Digital transformation and customer value creation in made in Italy SMEs: A dynamic capabilities perspective. *Journal of Business Research, 123*, 642–656.
Miccoli G. (2023). *La PA sarà efficiente solo se orientata ai risultati: il cambio che serve*, in Agenda Digitale, 18 dicembre 2023. https://www.agendadigitale.eu/cittadinanza-digitale/la-pa-sara-efficiente-solo-se-orientata-ai-risultati-il-cambio-che-serve/
Nambisan, S., Lyytinen, K., & Yoo, Y. (2020). Digital innovation: Towards a transdisciplinary perspective. In *Handbook of digital innovation* (pp. 2–12). Edward Elgar Publishing.
Ndou, V., & Ingrosso, A. (2022). *Per fare la PA digitale servono i "progettisti dell'innovazione": chi sono e perché sono cruciali*. Agenda digitale, 17 giugno 2022. https://www.agendadigitale.eu/cittadinanza-digitale/per-fare-la-pa-digitale-servono-i-progettisti-dellinnovazione-chi-sono-e-perche-sono-cruciali/
Ostmeier, E., & Strobel, M. (2022). Building skills in the context of digital transformation: How industry digital maturity drives proactive skill development. *Journal of Business Research, 139*, 718–730.
Rupp, C. (2017). *E-Government in Europa—Warum es in Österreich gut funktioniert. Public Governance Herbst/Winter*. Institut für den öffentlichen Sektor.
Schlegel, D., & Kraus, P. (2023). Skills and competencies for digital transformation–a critical analysis in the context of robotic process automation. *International Journal of Organizational Analysis, 31*(3), 804–822.
Secundo, G., Mele, G., Del Vecchio, P., Gianluca, E., Margherita, A., & Ndou, V. (2021). Threat or opportunity? A case study of the digital-enabled redesign of entrepreneurship education in the COVID-19 emergency. *Technological Forecasting and Social Change, 166*, 120565.
Vial, G. (2021). Understanding digital transformation: A review and a research agenda. *Managing Digital Transformation*, 13–66.

Websites

European Commission. (2018a). Proposal for a COUNCIL RECOMMENDATION on Key Competences for Lifelong Learning. Brussels. [Online]. Available: https://ec.europa.eu/education/sites/education/files/recommendation-key-competences-lifelonglearning.pdf
European Commission, Country Specific Recommendations. (2022). Retrieved at https://commission.europa.eu/publications/2022-european-semester-country-specific-recommendations-commission-recommendations_en
Gartner. (2022). *Digital transformation success: Best practices in strategy and execution*. Retrieved at https://www.gartner.com/en/information-technology/topics/digital-transformation.
Syllabus. (2023). Retrieved at: https://www.syllabus.gov.it/portale/web/syllabus/

Vuorikari, R., Kluzer, S., & Punie, Y. (2022). DigComp 2.2, The Digital Competence framework for citizens: With new examples of knowledge, skills and attitudes. Publications Office of the European Union. https://data.europa.eu/doi/10.2760/115376

WEF. (2023). *Annual report 2022–2023*. Retrieved at: https://www3.weforum.org/docs/WEF_Annual_Report_2022-23.pdf

Chapter 4
Digital Human Resource Management: Innovative Methods to Build a People-Centred Organisation in the Healthcare Industry

Alessandro Margherita, Hila Chalutz-Ben Gal, and Guy Topaz

Abstract The management of human resources is increasingly leveraging digital innovation to enhance strategic decisions related to the governance of people within organisations. In particular, digital human resource management is a trend of major interest for scholars and practitioners in the current scenario, characterised by growing volatility, uncertainty and complexity. Such conditions in fact require organisations to increasingly put human resources at the centre of their resilience-building and transformation processes. Advanced decision support capabilities are crucial to build people-centred organisations. New theory contributions and practitioner advancements are thus needed to provide robust conceptual frameworks and real-life applications. Given such a scenario, this chapter analyses digital innovation in the HR function in the healthcare sector as a challenging and complex domain. The chapter also reports the experience of the Meir Medical Centre, part of the Clalit Health Services Group, the largest provider of health services in Israel. Lessons and managerial guidelines are extracted and presented to HR managers aiming to undertake successful initiatives of digital-enhanced HR.

Keywords Business analytics · Digital innovation · Healthcare · Human resource management · Human resource analytics · Organisational transformation · People-centred organisation

A. Margherita (✉)
Department of Engineering for Innovation, University of Salento, Lecce, Italy
e-mail: alessandro.margherita@unisalento.it

H. Chalutz-Ben Gal
The Alexander Kofkin Faculty of Engineering, Bar-Ilan University, Ramat Gan, Israel
e-mail: hila.chalutz-ben-gal@biu.ac.il

G. Topaz
Meir Medical Center, Clalit Health Services, Kfar Saba, Israel
e-mail: guyto@clalit.org.il

G. Passiante (ed.), *Digital Innovation Management*, Applied Innovation and Technology Management, https://doi.org/10.1007/978-3-031-80426-7_4

4.1 The New Scenario and the Centrality of Human Resource Management (HRM)

The business world is being transformed by several intertwined forces, such as global geopolitical crises and emergencies and pressing sustainability challenges, which have highlighted the importance of organisational resilience and workforce optimisation. Human resources (HR) managers are particularly challenged to readapt to transforming employee needs, re-allocate human resources and prepare the workforce to ensure business continuity against unprecedented disruptions (Margherita & Heikkilä, 2021). From this perspective, the innovative strategies, practices and methods of human resource management (HRM) are crucial to improve the abilities of organisations to face challenging scenarios and optimise workforce capabilities to effectively face extant or emerging challenges.

In such a puzzling scenario, exponential digital technologies, such as AI and advanced analytics, are deeply transforming industries and providing new tools to generate business intelligence as a core organisational capability. In particular, the management of human resources is increasingly adopting advanced design, analysis and visualisation technologies to enhance strategic decisions related to the management of people within organisations, especially in relation to individual-specific job design, leadership, rewards, selection and training.

In 1997, Ghoshal and Bartlett introduced the idea of the *individualised corporation* as a fundamentally different management philosophy that leverages the power of the individual as the driver of value creation and the generation of a post-bureaucratic entrepreneurial environment (Mullins et al., 2001). People-centred cultures assume that all the people inside the organisation are important and that people working together perform at higher levels. These cultures share key features, such as people-first core values, leadership, open communication, trust, change responsiveness and organisational resiliency (Black & La Venture, 2017).

Through the years, interest in more people-centred management models and organisations has increased in the practitioner context. The international standard ISO 27500:2016 'Human-centred organisation' (ISO, 2016) describes the values that make an organisation human-centred and the significant business benefits that can be achieved, as well as the risks for the organisation of not being human-centred. The standard draws on an extensive body of ergonomics and human factors knowledge and presents the rationale and general principles of human-centredness based on principles like capitalising on individual differences, ensuring well-being, valuing employees and creating a meaningful work environment.

Digital innovation in HR management can provide a broad spectrum of approaches, methods and applications to analyse people-related data and build more people-centric HR governance as a strategic capability in the current scenario. Organisations can use digital HRM to achieve valuable outcomes by integrating agile HR and company operations, prioritising issues, integrating different approaches and methods, preparing and validating data and transforming insights into actions to improve business outcomes.

New academic contributions and practitioner advancements are envisioning what managerial, technological and process innovations can contribute to boosting organisational performance by leveraging technology-enhanced HR management. Recent studies have analysed human resources analytics and the effect of machine learning on turnover, company performance and employee role and skill fit (e.g. Avrahami et al., 2022; Ben-Gal, 2019; Chalutz Ben-Gal, 2023; Fitz-enz, 2010; Pessach et al., 2020).

Among the sectors mostly affected by socio-technical transformations and extensive requirements in terms of preparing a competent and resilient workforce, the healthcare industry deserves particular attention. In line with such a fast-growing trend, in this chapter we review the extant literature on digital innovation of the HR function, with a specific focus on healthcare as an extremely challenging and complex domain. We also report the experience of the Meir Medical Centre, part of the Clalit Health Services group. Based on the interaction with company managers and the direct involvement of one of the authors, we report some initiatives conducted to build a people-centred organisation by leveraging the potential of technology innovation and advanced analytics.

The rest of the chapter is structured as follows. First, we describe the theory and practitioner background on digital HRM as a strategic organisational capability. Next, we describe the trends of digital HRM in the healthcare sector. We then present the case of Clalit Health Services, and in the final section we discuss guidelines for HR managers aiming to undertake successful initiatives of digital-enhanced HR.

4.2 Digital Human Resource Management

In the last 10 years, scholars have discussed the transformation of HR in the digital era and how digital innovation and advanced analytics can move people managers to the centre of organisational decision-making, thus improving strategy (Lal, 2015; Levenson, 2018). With the rise of big data, digital technologies and data science techniques in human resources scenarios (e.g. Angrave et al., 2016; Edwards, 2019), the need for and potential of building specific human resources analytics capabilities have received increased attention (Kryscynski et al., 2017). Big data can be applied to every stage of the hiring process and the entire workforce planning and management cycle (Isson & Harriott, 2016), including attraction, acquisition, development and retention.

The management of human resources has thus gradually increased the adoption of advanced data analysis and visualisation models and techniques, since the extensive use of quantitative analysis to build explanatory and predictive models can drive decisions and actions involving personnel and build an evidence-based approach to managing people processes. Human resource (HR) analytics (or people analytics) includes a large family of methods and applications aimed at analysing people-related data and building robust and effective HR-centred organisational processes (Margherita, 2021). Various examples of how digital transformation can support HRM processes include, of course, advanced analytics and more performing algorithms and AI features (HR analytics), but also robotic process automation (RPA) to support the automation of specific HR tasks, IoT tools to enable better monitoring of employee health or behaviour, Blockchain to allow smart contracts and more efficient management of employee documentation and so forth.

HR analytics is a fact-based approach to driving people-related decision-making and actions (Bassi et al., 2010; Davenport et al., 2007). The use of objective facts can provide company managers with insightful information needed to govern the employees for organisational success. HR analytics adopts logical and systematic analysis and visualisation of HR-related data (van den Heuvel & Bondarouk, 2017). Further examples of HR analytics are represented by applications for employee turnover prediction, performance prediction, succession planning, recruitment and retention, diversity and inclusion, career planning and internal mobility support.

HR analytics requires a strategic approach to integrating science and agility (McIver et al., 2018), with the goal of enhancing organisational competitive advantage and driving business success (Minbaeva, 2018; Schiemann et al., 2017), increasing managerial efficiency and organisational effectiveness (Singh & Nath, 2020; Zeidan & Itani, 2020) and enhancing employee performance (Sharma et al., 2022).

Analytics can be related to different stages or maturity levels. First, descriptive analytics is related to using organisational internal and external data and HR information to generate ratios, metrics, dashboards and reports, focusing mostly on the past. Second, predictive analytics is about data-derived insights and decisions and includes statistical techniques, data mining and advanced algorithms able to analyse process or workflow data, predictions and create scenarios. Predictive analytics has then led to a generation of prescriptive analytics based on the availability of large and diversified HR data, where HR gets decision options to optimise performance and reshape the HRM decision-making process (Fitz-enz & Mattox II, 2014; Krumeich et al., 2016; Lepenioti et al., 2020).

Digital innovation of the HR function and processes can provide managers with the insightful information needed to manage employees for organisational success, with a proven effect on strategic decision-making. An area of potentially disruptive innovation is AI. The potential of AI can be explored across several different scenarios, including turnover prediction, candidate search, staff rostering, HR sentiment analysis and résumé data acquisition with information extraction and employee self-service. The effect of digital technologies is also particularly relevant in web-based applications for competence showcasing and visualisation, skills-matching, chatbot-based HR interaction and hiring and talent experience management.

Digital HR can support advanced people management through innovative data acquisition, processing and visualisation capabilities and provide features, such as the real-time analysis of competence gaps, the normalisation of job descriptions and rankings, optimised talent management, customised onboarding and predictive modelling of engagement. All these functionalities can support organisational transformation journeys. Advanced HR management can valorise multiple sources of user-generated and user-related data, with the goal of creating dashboards for HR managers and project managers, who increasingly require synthetic data and infographics about human resources to build effective HR-centred organisational processes.

4.3 Digital HRM in Healthcare

Digital innovation can reshape the employee experience and behaviour if organisations can establish complementarities between technology and HR practices. Since organisations need to identify ways to assess the business effect of HR and the process needed to maximise productivity (e.g. Muscalu & Şerban, 2014; Phillips & Phillips, 2014), a shift towards actionable, high-impact HRM is needed to drive organisational agility and performance.

These new requirements, along with changes in society's demographics and dynamics, particularly affect the healthcare system and the management of HR in the industry. Digital technologies are increasingly relevant in healthcare, and HR digitisation is a fundamental development that has grown exponentially in popularity over the years, along with the strategic relevance of the healthcare ecosystem given the ageing population and the arising societal challenges and forces. As healthcare professionals strive to construct resilient and future-proof healthcare systems, digitising the sector is now a primary focus.

The term *digital transformation* in healthcare refers to the way an organisation leverages technology and digital solutions to improve the patient experience, streamline operations and make on-demand medical care more accessible. The transformative process includes electronic health records, online appointments, telemedicine, Software as a Medical Device (SaMD) and AI-powered medical applications, technologies and devices (Chalutz-Ben Gal, 2023; Kadosh & Chalutz Ben-Gal, 2021). These technologies completely transform how patients interact with healthcare providers, how their information is shared among healthcare key stakeholders and how treatment options are chosen.

Healthcare organisations that combine good HR management practices with effective HR technology are more productive. In a scenario where patients' expectations have shifted dramatically as they tend to demand more personalised and convenient care, digitalisation has the potential to reduce the workload of healthcare providers, including medical doctors and assistants, resulting in faster and more effective healthcare services. Digitalisation in healthcare may thus boost overall employee and patient satisfaction and enable better diagnoses based on modern technology solutions.

Healthcare providers in many regions of the world are experiencing workforce shortages. According to the WHO, there will be a global shortage of 12.9 million competent healthcare professionals by 2035. As a result, it is more critical than ever to safeguard the emotional and physical well-being of healthcare personnel. Digitisation can provide cost-cutting opportunities and increase citizens' access to healthcare services. Specific ways this may be accomplished are the adoption of electronic health records, consolidated citizens' data and databases, faster access to health services and reduced time to service.

Technology can automate data collection and communication while validating the events that claim to lower healthcare expenses and improve patient satisfaction. Digital transformation is thus critical to the future of healthcare systems. The benefits of using digitisation for healthcare HRM are evident in terms of improved doctor–patient relationships, automated administrative tasks, easy communication among multiple healthcare providers, improved process mapping, real-time health data, data protection and security, transparency and the enrichment of employees' training development (Bhattacharyya et al., 2021; Mohamed et al., 2023).

Digitalisation can lead to better HRM, which ultimately leads to good patient outcomes. It is reasonable to believe that the enormous array of digital breakthroughs that will emerge soon will be beneficial to both healthcare providers and patients. This advancement will prioritise the patient's well-being, benefiting several stakeholders in the healthcare industry. HR departments can now employ digital technologies and make digital tools available so that employee satisfaction can be increased, with the added benefit of great workplace branding.

4.4 Building a People-Centred Organisation at Meir Medical Centre (Clalit Group)

4.4.1 Company Introduction

Innovation in the HRM is particularly relevant to an extremely challenging and complex domain, such as healthcare. Given this, we brought to our discussion the presentation of a relevant case represented by Clalit Health Services. Clalit is the largest health management organisation (HMO) in Israel. Widely known as 'Kupat Holim Clalit', it was established in 1911 as a mutual-aid society. When the state of Israel was founded in 1948, Clalit was instrumental in providing medical care for the massive influx of new immigrants. Today, it is the largest provider of public and semi-private health services in Israel. Under Israeli law, it is run as a not-for-profit entity.

As of 2024, Clalit serves over 4.7 million insured members, representing slightly over half of the Israeli population. Clalit runs its own network of hospitals in Israel (although it provides services, especially emergency care, for members of the other national health funds as well). It operates 14 hospitals, including psychiatric hospitals and a rehabilitation hospital, all university-affiliated. Clalit employs about 48,000 doctors and other employees. In 2010, Clalit established the Clalit Research Institute, whose mission is to turn data into decision-making insights that can be translated into policies for transforming healthcare delivery and clinical practice. Figure 4.1 shows the Clalit headquarters in Tel Aviv. Figure 4.2 shows the website of the Clalit Research Institute.

Fig. 4.1 Clalit headquarters in Tel Aviv

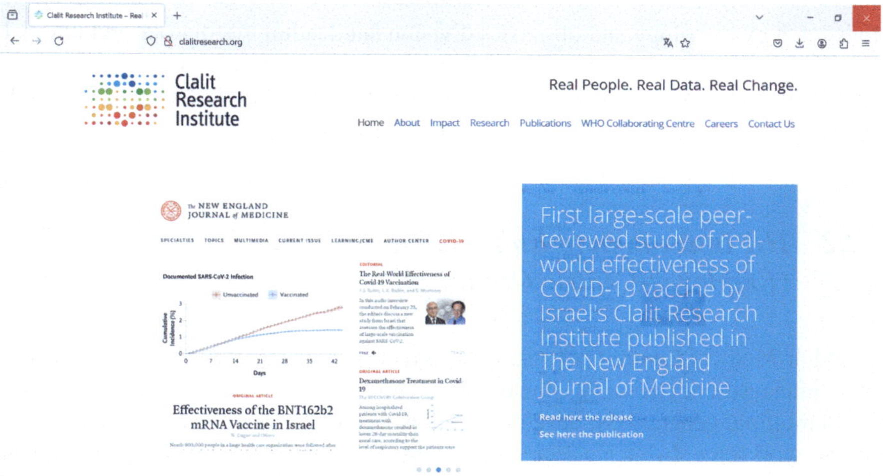

Fig. 4.2 The Clalit Research Institute (CRI) webpage

The Clalit Research Institute (CRI) and the Meir Medical Centre collaborate on medical research and healthcare projects. The CRI focuses on conducting research using real-world data from Clalit Health Services' extensive patient database to improve healthcare outcomes, treatments and policies.

We focused our study on the Meir Medical Centre, which is part of the Clalit group. The Meir Medical Centre was established in 1956. Initially serving as a hospital for tuberculosis patients, within a few years it was converted into a general hospital. Located in the city of Kfar Saba in the Sharon region, Meir Medical Centre serves approximately 800,000 residents of the area. The hospital has around 800 inpatient beds and numerous centres of medical excellence, including a surgical

Fig. 4.3 The Meir Medical Centre in Kfar-Saba

division, a gynaecology and obstetrics division and leading paediatrics and internal medicine wards. The emergency medicine department treats, as of 2023, over 200,000 patients annually—a number that ranks it fourth in patient volume in Israel. Figure 4.3 shows the Meir Medical Centre in Kfar-Saba.

4.4.2 *HR Innovation to Enhance Onboarding (Employee-Centric Organisation)*

The Meir Medical Centre operates in a healthcare environment that is facing many talent management challenges, including recruiting and retaining top talent, appealing to multiple generations, developing talent to meet future needs and engaging a diverse workforce. In such a scenario, the organisation knows that using digital HR can enhance its organisational performance and generate positive returns in terms of employee retention, leadership development and service quality and effectiveness, which ultimately drives business outcomes and growth. Engaged employees create a better patient experience, stay with their employer longer, help recruit other top talent and create a positive work culture.

As a forward-thinking healthcare system leader, Meir Medical Centre aims to capitalise on employee-related opportunities resulting from shifting workforce patterns, as well as by using people analytics. People analytics helps refocus the workforce planning lens from a qualitative one to a quantitative one, enabling the organisation to scientifically unlock and measure the value of people to the organisation. Analytics can help view employees as critical assets in the value chain that can be analysed and optimised to benefit individuals and the company as a whole. HR analytics can also allow the uncovering of opportunities to transform HR practices, optimise talent-focused programmes and increase employee satisfaction. In the healthcare industry, there is a growing maturity gap among many organisations in how to best leverage data for greater organisational value. Today's healthcare leaders must broaden their analytics focus to include internal HR applications.

In the past 5 years, the Meir Medical Centre has invested in building new forms of people-related 'intelligence'—data-driven and more robust HR-centred management plans aimed at generating a better talent management process. The HR function maintains huge amounts of human capital data, which are being analysed and implemented in critical medical and business operations. Meir Medical Centre uses predictive analysis to increase its overall ability to predict attrition risks, select high-performing job applicants, analyse engagement, understand employee productivity and performance, determine leadership training needs and potential and manage staffing needs based on leave-of-absence trends. The medical internship in Israel is a yearlong period following the completion of one's medical studies and before the beginning of the residency. In this important first year of their actual professional journey, the interns—a unique yet heterogeneous population—face major challenges and various dilemmas in different respects—professional, ethical and personal. During the year, an emphasis on practical work, learning and growth is placed, and the interns need to adapt to a challenging lifestyle and a new organisational system, as well as the heavy responsibility and psychological burden that come with the nature of their job responsibilities. Throughout the internship, the young doctors are required to choose their future field of specialisation—a decision that at this time must be taken even though professional and personal implications are sometimes unclear.

In recent years, healthcare ecosystems have undergone profound alterations: the population is getting older, and public medical demands and needs are on the increase. Medical providing techniques are advancing and becoming increasingly technological and AI-based (Chalutz-Ben Gal, 2023; Kadosh & Chalutz Ben-Gal, 2021). There is growth in the amount of knowledge and specificities of skill-fit (Chalutz-Ben Gal, 2023) required from a doctor, who faces a continuous process of caregiver–patient relationship change. Moreover, the physician population is changing as the generation is changing and the 'Y' generation enters the game. Additionally, at the national level in Israel, there is an increase in the number of interns, which complicates the medical intern's ecosystem country-wide.

In 2019, the Meir Medical Centre recognised the need for a deep change in the way interns are trained and developed. Thus, it initiated a profound managerial and organisational interventional process to build a high-quality, robust and state-of-the-art internship programme aimed at increasing the proportion of interns who choose to remain as medical residents at the institute and to support them professionally.

As a first step, an internal examination and characterisation analyses were conducted within Meir's higher management to identify the human capital characteristics and skills of the future physician. This included five broad characteristics: (a) compassionate and empathetic; (b) professional and knowledgeable; (c) technologically adept; (d) investigative and innovative; and (e) in possession of leadership skills.

As the second step, Meir examined key factors that are central to the interns themselves when selecting medical specialisation and a future profession. Additionally, the interns' expectations, concerns and satisfaction levels with the internship programme at the hospital were also assessed. A digital hospital-wide survey was administered among a population of 70 interns. Figure 4.4 illustrates the specific expectations of the intern population from the internship. The survey results indicate that the important parameters for interns in choosing a department for specialisation include (a) a collegial atmosphere; (b) the quality of the theoretical instruction; (c) practical bedside clinical learning and (d) work–life balance.

Awareness of employees' and interns' expectations and capabilities is crucial for Clalit since the organisation knows that the future of healthcare depends on real-life innovative solutions, and these are strongly based on the availability of motivated and competent human capital. In this regard, it is relevant to mention the Clalit Entrepreneurship and Innovation Programme (ETGAR), which is an initiative dedicated to the development of innovations and disruptive technologies addressing the current challenges of Clalit's healthcare providers and patients (https://www.clalit-innovation.org/).

Some digital innovation examples in which employees and interns are involved include (a) predictive medicine; (b) precision and personalised medicine; (c) patient-centred healthcare services, based on the use of behavioural science and applied computational modelling; (d) an employee self-service portal to improve and enhance efficiency at Meir Medical Centre; and (e) online performance management systems to digitise the evaluation process using a platform where managers and employees can set, track and review performance goals.

Clalit is also interested in understanding the concerns of current and future employees. Figure 4.5 shows some of those concerns, which can be associated with the (physical and mental) workload and the high professional requirements that can

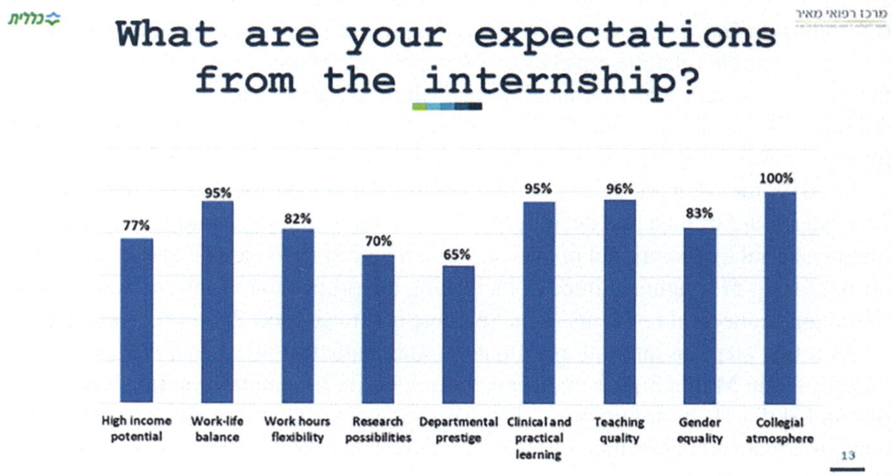

Fig. 4.4 Intern expectations from the internship

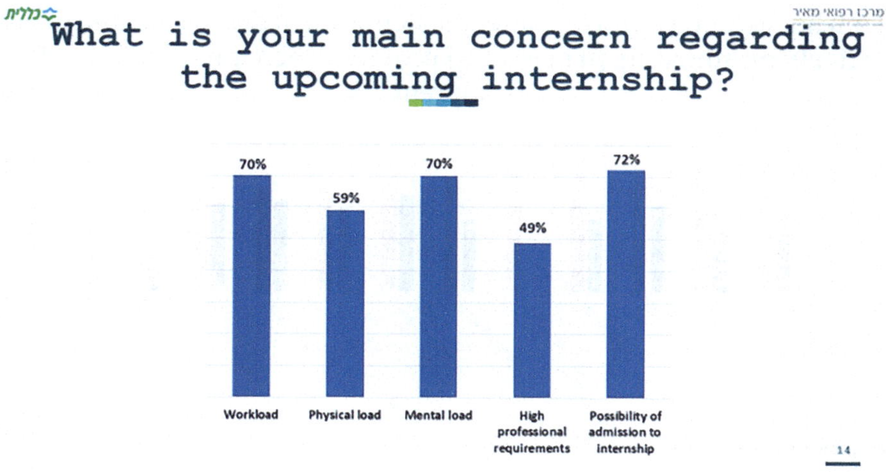

Fig. 4.5 Internship main concerns

potentially originate (for example) from the transformation of the workplace deriving from the adoption of disruptive technology.

Satisfaction with the internship year at the hospital was also examined by the feedback given by interns to departments, and the scores were unsatisfactory. To further focus on human capital development and training initiatives, a new training programme was introduced, focusing on four main axes based on the organisation's expectations and the interns' needs:

1. Establishment of the elite programme 'Marom'.
2. Improvement of bedside teaching through staff integration into the process.
3. Construction of 'mini-internship programmes'.
4. A monthly digital 'intern feedback' process that focuses on how the departments evaluate interns and how interns evaluate the quality of teaching.

During the 5-year programme, there has been a noticeable improvement in the achievement of various goals and KPIs. As a result, Meir Medical Centre has become more sought after for medical internship selection, and the proportion of interns at Meir who are graduates of the Meir internship programme has increased from 26% in 2019 to 39% in 2023.

Survey results indicate that the improvement in the interns' desire to stay at the hospital, as well as the positive connections among hospital departments and their connection to the process, has improved significantly. According to a survey conducted in 2023, compared to the feedback survey of departments conducted in 2018, a noticeable improvement in intern satisfaction with departments of the hospital is evident. In terms of satisfaction and regarding the question of whether they would recommend an elective rotation in departments, there has been a major transactional improvement throughout nearly all departments (Fig. 4.6).

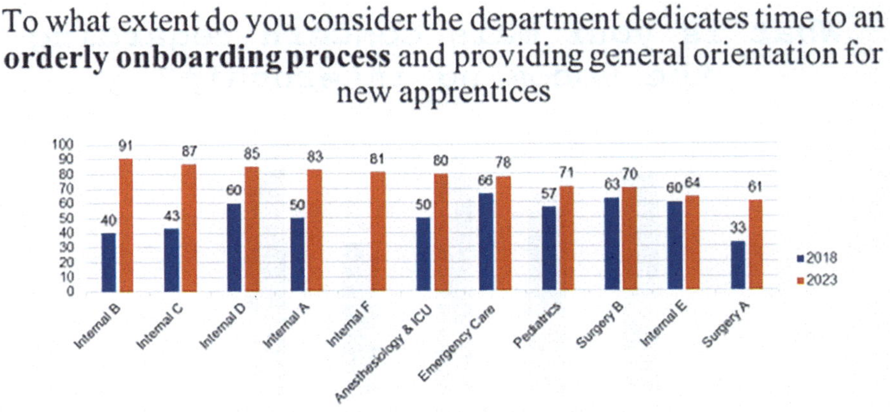

Fig. 4.6 Annual comparison survey 2018–2023

Table 4.1 HR analytics domains in the Meir Medical Centre

Human resource task	Sample challenges	Tool[a]	Expected ROI
Workforce planning	High-demand jobs and attrition	Predictive	High
Job analysis	Robustness of job components	Descriptive	Low
Recruitment and selection	Centralised vs. decentralised	Predictive	High
Training and development	Training ROI	Descriptive and predictive	Medium
Compensation	Total/shift compensation scenarios	Descriptive and predictive	Medium
Performance management	Performance management cycle scenarios	Descriptive	Low
Retention	Whether retention can be predicted	Descriptive and predictive	Medium

[a]**Descriptive analytics** tools may include descriptive statistics, graphs and plots, benchmarking tools, KPI-based methods (scorecards), business intelligence (BI) dashboards and advanced survey analytics. **Predictive analytics** tools may include regression and parametric modelling (including logistic regression), time-series analysis, classification methods (e.g. decision trees, SVM, discriminant analysis, neural networks, deep learning), clustering (K nearest neighbours, K-means) anomaly detection, profiling, association rules, link analysis, causality modelling (Bayesian networks), text analysis and NLP and attrition modelling
Adapted from Chalutz-Ben Gal (2019)

Table 4.1 presents the HR analytics' domains in the Meir Medical Centre and the expected return on investment (ROI) associated with each domain. Some of the methods presented are already being executed in the hospital, while others are in their formative phase. For example, in the domain of workforce planning, key challenges at Meir are, for example, high-demand physicians and specific wards with high attrition. Predictive analytics tools are employed in those cases to anticipate specific needs and reduce risks. Moreover, the table presents the breadth of analytics tools to be adopted across different HR tasks. While some tasks predominantly rely on descriptive analytics, such as job analysis and performance management, others leverage predictive analytics for more forward-looking insights, as seen in recruitment, selection and retention. The expected ROI varies across these domains, reflecting the differing effects of analytics implementation. The plan for Meir is to adopt and implement these analytics tools gradually to address HR challenges and optimise clinical and organisational performance.

As demonstrated in Table 4.1, using advanced predictive models and KPI-based tools—for example, regression analyses, time-series forecasting and machine learning techniques—may increase Meir Medical Centre's ROI, based on forecasting in the various people-centred domains (e.g. staffing, recruitment, retention). For example, workforce planning, recruitment and selection and retention are especially critical for the intern population as the next generation of physicians; thus, the use of predictive tools is important. Applying these HRA methods and technologies allows the centre to adjust its HR strategies based on the predicted trends in job demand. For recruitment, predictive analytics helps determine which recruitment channels and strategies yield the best candidates, reducing the time and cost per hire.

4.4.3 HR Innovation to Enhance Patient Satisfaction (Patient-Centric Organisation)

HRM innovation in a patient-centric organisation may affect and digitally innovate HRM processes and performance by maintaining high levels of ROI (Chalutz-Ben Gal, 2019). The integration of patient monitoring into HRM processes assists healthcare activities in improving the quality of care and innovating HR practices, resulting in a more responsive, efficient and patient-focused workforce (Bhattacharyya et al., 2021). This approach enhances patient satisfaction and contributes to a more motivated and skilled healthcare team.

A crucial indicator of service quality and patient satisfaction is *hospital readmission*, which is defined as an additional admission within 30 days after discharge, whether it is to the same hospital or to a different institution. The 30-day readmissions rate is an indicator of hospital treatment quality.

Over the years, extensive research has been conducted on the subject, and several risk factors for readmission have been identified, such as age, length of stay, certain underlying diseases and the number of medications taken by the patient. The readmission rate varies among medical centres and countries. According to the Israeli Ministry of Health, the readmission rate to internal medicine departments in Israel averages about 19%. Many healthcare systems have tried to deal with this phenomenon, but, to date, there is no single strategy to reduce the readmission rate, and it seems that a combination of medical and managerial activities is required to reduce the readmission rate.

During the first quarter of 2023, there was an average increase of nearly 5% compared to previous years in the readmission rate to the internal medicine departments at Meir Medical Centre. Upon systematic review of the medical records, no significant difference was observed in readmission rates between the various internal medicine departments, and no clinical explanation was found for the phenomenon. Compared to prior years, there was no significant difference in patients' illness characteristics. Finally, no change was observed in the administration treatment protocols of the departments.

These days, a complex model to predict patient readmissions is being constructed to move from the descriptive HR analytics stage to a more predictive stage. The model is based on an advanced statistical algorithm. Understanding that sociotechnical factors may influence the decision for readmission and therefore a significant component of the predictive model includes data related to the physician's skills and expertise (e.g. whether an intern is an emergency-medicine physician), their stage of training (e.g. resident or specialist) and the workload in the specific shift the physician worked.

The Israeli Ministry of Health monitors healthcare quality metrics at the national level. These metrics are continuously measured and tracked among all hospitals in Israel. The hospital's medical quality unit oversees the matter and monitors the compliance of hospital departments with various metrics. Based on the performance in 2022, several key metrics were identified as focal points at the Centre in 2023.

The KTV index is a measure that evaluates the quality of dialysis performed and is influenced by several parameters. Dialysis patients typically undergo three sessions per week, and the Israeli Ministry of Health measures the KTV value for the second dialysis session of the week. A value of 75% is considered acceptable. The institute's management, medical staff and hospital computer systems have characterised an automatic report that extracts all the necessary data from information systems (such as the duration of dialysis and laboratory test results). Quality dialysis data for all institute patients are received mid-month. Each physician receives his or her patient scores, and, if necessary, an immediate re-evaluation of KTV measurement is performed. Automatic and continuous digital accessibility of data to the treating physicians, emphasising discrepancies, led to a significant improvement in clinical performance within a short period, as can be seen in Fig. 4.7.

Another important quality measure is performing brain imaging within 25 min of arrival at the hospital in cases of suspected acute stroke. In such a medical emergency, rapid diagnosis and swift medical intervention are crucial to save the patient's life and preserve their functions. A median score of 50% constitutes compliance with the metric.

In early 2023, a decline in performance in this area was identified. Urgent action was taken in collaboration with the relevant departments (the emergency room, neurology department and imaging institute). A daily report was implemented that automatically retrieves data from the electronic health records pertinent to investigating the event: triage admission time, the attending nurse, the treating physician, the physical examination time, CT scan ordering time, CT scan performance time and the necessity of medical intervention. The report is distributed in the morning to

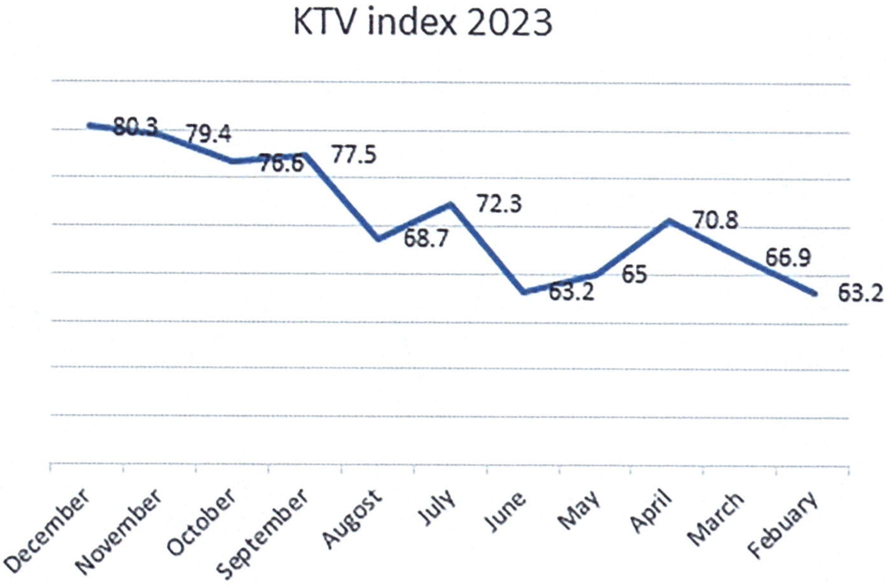

Fig. 4.7 KTV index continuous monitoring and improvement

the relevant persons and reflects all cases of stroke from the previous day. Through the daily report distribution, which began in April 2023, Meir successfully identified critical process failures, such as nursing–medical communication issues and more complex cases requiring diagnosis, provided feedback and appropriate training for relevant staff members and succeeded in meeting the metric (Fig. 4.8).

4.5 Discussion and Conclusions

Organisations are required to support business continuity while leveraging exponential technologies to support sustainable digital transformation. The complex socio-technical scenario will increasingly require an enhancement of individual and group resilience and the ability to cope with disruptive transformation processes. New contributions and practitioner advancements are thus required to envision what managerial, technological and process innovations can contribute to boosting employee well-being and building people-centred organisations.

A human-centred organisation can have a deep effect on its customers, employees and the wider community. The organisational ability to capitalise on individual differences and create a meaningful work environment requires a more sophisticated approach to knowing and analysing processes and human resources. Advanced intelligence and decision support are crucial to building people-centred organisations. In particular, the adoption of innovative methods in HRM is today crucial to

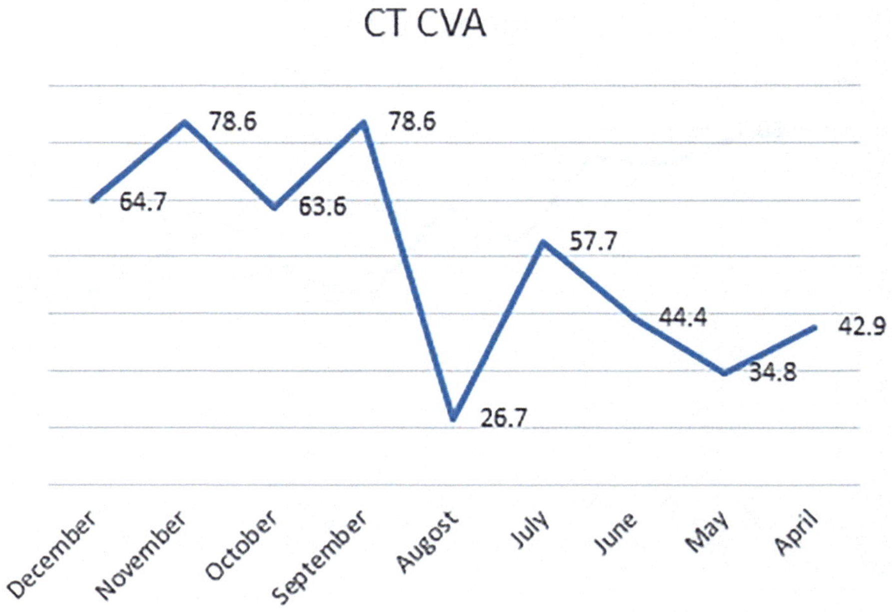

Fig. 4.8 CT CVA 2023 measures

developing a new form of intelligence on a multidimensional set of human resources features, capabilities, needs and expectations.

Digital innovation in HR can provide a broad spectrum of approaches, methods and applications to analyse people-related data and build effective HR management processes. Organisations can successfully use digital HR to achieve valuable outcomes by integrating HR and company operations, integrating different approaches and methods, preparing and validating data and transforming insights into actions to improve business outcomes. Understanding digital HR in driving organisational performance is essential today, and HR professionals need to develop an integrated management view to provide the best actions regarding the management of human capital. The digital transformation of the HR function also affects individual roles and perceptions and employee outcomes, including burnout, stress and job satisfaction (Christensen et al., 2020).

In the healthcare ecosystem, the digital innovation of HR can support people management decisions and the cost-effectiveness evaluation of healthcare organisations. There are a range of issues that affect healthcare, including the growing use of health services during the pandemic, emergency situations, complex forms of technology, worker expectations, work intensification and government reporting requirements. Underdeveloped HR processes and outdated management perceptions cannot make decisions about the well-being of healthcare staff. Some answers can be found in the use of HR analytics and AI (Cavanagh et al., 2023).

Advanced analytics can support healthcare leaders' decisions and strategies to enhance efficiency along the healthcare value chain. Big data analytics can add to the efficiency of the decision-making process, assisting in the collection, management and integration of data in healthcare organisations (Sousa et al., 2019). The strategic imperative of a people-centred organisation (Rao & Choudhury, 2017) is of increasing interest in the post-pandemic scenario, characterised by growing volatility, uncertainty and complexity. Changing environmental conditions require organisations to integrate many variables associated with employees' personal and professional characteristics (e.g. knowledge, skills, attitude and cumulated expertise) and the organisation. Innovative HR analytics and advanced reporting and visualisation features and dashboards can support the transformation of healthcare. This is particularly relevant in healthcare, and future HR managers will need to adopt an outside/inside approach, where the external environment and stakeholders influence what HR does inside the organisation (Ulrich & Dulebohn, 2015).

Digital innovation of HR in healthcare aims at providing fact-based recommendations to conduct HR-centred transformation plans (e.g. organisational redesign, capability development, workflows digitalisation, logistic and operations redesign). Advanced intelligence and decision support are crucial to building people-centred organisations, and new studies are thus needed to provide robust conceptual frameworks and conduct real-life applications with the vision to support organisations willing to put HR at the centre of their transformation and value creation processes.

This chapter provided food for thought in discussing how innovative HR management can support organisational renewal and transformation in challenging times. The chapter provides guidelines to undertake data analytics initiatives aimed at building more employee-centric and patient-centric organisations in the healthcare industry.

We defined five dimensions along which to discuss how Clalit Health Services, and particularly the Meir Medical Centre, has created organisational value by adopting an innovative approach in HR management. First, concerning *People*, the case of Meir Medical Centre has shown the relevance of investing in talent and human resources (e.g. interns) to enhance the service and quality level of the organisation, and the use of digital technology is primarily positioned in this endeavour to ensure effectiveness and efficiency. The efforts invested in expanding physicians' skills, both clinical and technological, are growing. The Meir culture of continuous learning and feedback adds to this dimension. By investing in this dimension, Clalit is improving employee satisfaction and retention and increasing its professionals' ability to deliver high-quality patient care.

As for the *Process* dimension, the case shows the relevance of defining the proper procedures and tasks with related owners to define the smooth conditions to generating new customer and patient data and employee data useful in improving core activities. Some of the hospital's resources are already digitised, reducing administrative tasks, improving patient data accuracy and assisting in accurate decision-making. Since Covid-19, some clinical specialisations (e.g. radiology and OBGYN) have expanded remotely by adding the digital monitoring of patients. Concerning *Platforms*, the case of Meir Medical Centre shows the relevance of a company's information systems and applications, which can integrate data and allow for the reporting and visualisations for decision-makers. In those cases, for some processes

Clalit uses advanced HR information systems (HRIS) to gather insights into workforce dynamics, identify trends and make data-driven decisions. These platforms enable better communication, collaboration and transparency within the organisation, enabling Clalit to align its HR processes with its management goals.

In relation to the *Policy* dimension, the case of Meir Medical Centre shows the critical importance of the top management's commitment to ensuring a strategy definition and application and innovative HR management. Finally, concerning the *Planet*, the trends of green HR and the sustainable management of resources have required organisations to readapt or innovate HR practices to reduce waste and enhance process efficiency and external influence. Clalit promotes eco-friendly workplace practices and support community engagement projects focused on environmental conservation.

HR managers should be able today to embrace digital innovation in their organisations and to integrate their HR strategy with their overall business goals, including by addressing three key challenges: first, to come up with a systemic design of what human resources means and implies for the healthcare organisation, thus including a clear effort to identify medical resources and patients as human agents of the organisations; second, to identify the foundational aspects of HR-related algorithms and decision-support systems, which have a clear effect on individual emotions and well-being; and third, to describe how the digital innovation of HRM can support the ability of organisations to face disruptive changes.

References

Angrave, D., Charlwood, A., Kirkpatrick, I., Lawrence, M., & Stuart, M. (2016). HR and analytics: Why HR is set to fail the big data challenge. *Human Resource Management Journal, 26*(1), 1–11.

Avrahami, D., Pessach, D., Singer, G., & Ben-Gal, H. C. (2022). A human resources analytics and machine-learning examination of turnover: Implications for theory and practice. *International Journal of Manpower, 43*(6), 1405–1424.

Bassi, L., Carpenter, R., & McMurrer, D. (2010). *HR analytics handbook*. Reed Business.

Ben-Gal, H. C. (2019). An ROI-based review of HR analytics: Practical implementation tools. *Personnel Review, 48*(6), 1429–1448.

Bhattacharyya, D. S., Dutta, G. K., Nowrin, I., Shafique, S., Islam, M. Z., Riazul Islam, B. M., & Anwar, I. (2021). Implementing a digital human resources management tool in the government health sector in Bangladesh: A policy content analysis. *BMC Health Services Research, 21*(1), 1346.

Black, J., & La Venture, K. (2017). The human factor to profitability: People-centered cultures as meaningful organizations. *Journal of Organizational Psychology, 17*(2), 24–34.

Cavanagh, J., Pariona-Cabrera, P., & Halvorsen, B. (2023). In what ways are HR analytics and artificial intelligence transforming the healthcare sector? *Asia Pacific Journal of Human Resources, 61*(4), 785–793.

Chalutz Ben-Gal, H. (2023). Person–skill fit: Why a new form of employee fit is required. *Academy of Management Perspectives, 37*(2), 117–137.

Chalutz-Ben Gal, H. (2019). An ROI-based review of HR analytics: Practical implementation tools. *Personnel Review, 48*(6), 1429–1448.

Chalutz-Ben Gal, H. (2023). Artificial intelligence (AI) acceptance in primary care during the coronavirus pandemic: What is the role of patients' gender, age and health awareness? A two-phase pilot study. *Frontiers in Public Health, 10*, 931225.

Christensen, J. O., Finne, L. B., Garde, A. H., Nielsen, M. B., Sørensen, K., & Vleeshouwes, J. (2020). *The influence of digitalization and new technologies on psychosocial work environment and employee health: A literature review*. STAMI-rapport.

Davenport, T. H., Harris, J. G., Jones, G. L., Lemon, K. N., Norton, D., & McCallister, M. B. (2007). The dark side of customer analytics. *Harvard Business Review, 85*(5), 37.

Edwards, M. R. (2019). HR metrics and analytics. In M. Thite (Ed.), *E-HRM: Digital approaches, directions and applications*. Routledge.

Fitz-enz, J. (2010). *The new HR analytics. Predicting the economic value of your company's human capital investments*. American Management Association.

Fitz-enz, J., & Mattox, J. R., II. (2014). *Predictive analytics for human resources*. Wiley.

Ghoshal, S., & Bartlett, C. A. (1997). *The individualized corporation*. Harper Audio.

ISO—International Standard Organization. (2016). *ISO 27500:2016: The human-centred organization — Rationale and general principles*. International Organization for Standardization.

Isson, J. P., & Harriott, J. S. (2016). *People analytics in the era of big data: Changing the way you attract, acquire, develop, and retain talent*. Wiley.

Kadosh, E., & Chalutz Ben-Gal, H. (2021). AI acceptance in primary care during COVID-19: A two-phase study of patients' perspective. In *Academy of management proceedings* (Vol. 2021 (1), p. 13461). Academy of Management.

Krumeich, J., Werth, D., & Loos, P. (2016). Prescriptive control of business processes. *Business and Information Systems Engineering, 58*(4), 261–280.

Kryscynski, D., Reeves, C., Stice-Lusvardi, R., Ulrich, M., & Russell, G. (2017). Analytical abilities and the performance of HR professionals. *Human Resource Management, 57*(3), 715–738.

Lal, P. (2015). Transforming HR in the digital era: Workforce analytics can move people specialists to the center of decision-making. *Human Resource Management International Digest, 23*(3), 1–4.

Lepenioti, K., Bousdekis, A., Apostolou, D., & Mentzas, G. (2020). Prescriptive analytics: Literature review and research challenges. *International Journal of Information Management, 50*, 57–70.

Levenson, A. (2018). Using workforce analytics to improve strategy execution. *Human Resource Management, 57*(3), 685–700.

Margherita, A. (2021). Human resources analytics: A systematization of research topics and directions for future research. *Human Resource Management Review*, 100795.

Margherita, A., & Heikkilä, M. (2021). Business continuity in the COVID-19 emergency: A framework of actions undertaken by world-leading companies. *Business Horizons, 64*(5), 683–695.

McIver, D., Lengnick-Hall, M. L., & Lengnick-Hall, C. A. (2018). A strategic approach to workforce analytics: Integrating science and agility. *Business Horizons, 61*(3), 397–407.

Minbaeva, D. B. (2018). Building credible human capital analytics for organizational competitive advantage. *Human Resource Management, 57*(3), 701–713.

Mohamed, N., Al-Jaroodi, J., Jawhar, I., & Kesserwan, N. (2023). *Leveraging digital twins for healthcare systems engineering*. IEEE Access.

Mullins, J., Linehan, M., & Walsh, J. S. (2001). People-centred management policies: A new approach for the 21st century. *Irish Journal of Management, 22*(1), 127.

Muscalu, E., & Şerban, A. (2014). HR analytics for strategic human resource management. In *Proceedings of the 8th international management conference management challenges for sustainable development*. Bucharest, Romania.

Pessach, D., Singer, G., Avrahami, D., Ben-Gal, H. C., Shmueli, E., & Ben-Gal, I. (2020). Employees recruitment: A prescriptive analytics approach via machine learning and mathematical programming. *Decision Support Systems, 134*, 113290.

Phillips, P. P., & Phillips, J. (2014). *Making human capital analytics work: Measuring the ROI of human capital processes and outcomes*. O'Reilly.

Rao, V. P., & Choudhury, R. R. (2017). A strategic imperative for better business: Designing the people-centered organization. *Asian Journal of Management, 8*(4), 1247–1256.

Schiemann, W. A., Seibert, J. H., & Blankenship, M. H. (2017). Putting human capital analytics to work: Predicting and driving business success. *Human Resource Management, 57*(3), 795–807.

Sharma, S., Sharma, A. K., Agarwal, M., & Kumar, P. (2022). Enhancing employee productivity through high performance work practices: Evidence from IT sector. *World Journal of Management and Economics*.

Singh, S., & Nath, D. V. (2020). An assessment in the green HRM practices with job satisfaction and its impact on organisational commitment. *International Journal of Management, 11*(9).

Sousa, M. J., Pesqueira, A. M., Lemos, C., Sousa, M., & Rocha, Á. (2019). Decision-making based on big data analytics for people management in healthcare organizations. *Journal of Medical Systems, 43*, 1–10.

Ulrich, D., & Dulebohn, J. H. (2015). Are we there yet? What's next for HR? *Human Resource Management Review, 25*(2), 188–204.

van den Heuvel, S., & Bondarouk, T. (2017). The rise (and fall?) of HR analytics: A study into the future application, value, structure, and system support. *Journal of Organizational Effectiveness: People and Performance, 4*(2), 157–178.

Zeidan, S., & Itani, N. (2020). HR analytics and organizational effectiveness. *International Journal on Emerging Technologies, 11*(2), 683–688.

Chapter 5
Digital Factory 5.0: Experimenting Digital Innovation in the Reverse Logistics Process

Gianluca Elia, Gianpaolo Ghiani, Emanuele Manni, Francesco Nucci, Stefano Giuri, and Alberto Paglialunga

Abstract The increasing attention to human-related factors, sustainable development issues and organisational resiliency is contributing to the rise of the Industry 5.0 paradigm. Looking at such principles, companies aiming to enlarge their businesses are called to experiment with digital innovation. In the last decade, and especially due to the Covid-19 pandemic, online commerce has registered significant growth, with a consequent increase in the number of products returned. From this perspective, the reverse logistics process plays a crucial role in the competitiveness of companies operating in the online commerce industry because it affects the level of customer satisfaction, retention and engagement. This chapter focuses on reverse logistics of LGH srl, an Italian company operating in the logistics sector to deliver furniture for houses, bathrooms and gardens. After an introduction to the reverse logistics process, the chapter presents the innovative solution designed by LGH in collaboration with a multidisciplinary research team. The solution leverages the use of a cobot and a decision support system to support the analysis, inspection and decisions related to the management of returned products. Through the description of the digital solution that innovates the reverse logistics process of LGH, the case highlights not only the economic and business effects but also the effects on the workers' role and the environmental dimension.

Keywords Digital innovation · Digital transformation · Industry 5.0 · Reverse logistics · Sustainable development

G. Elia (✉) · G. Ghiani · E. Manni · F. Nucci
Department of Engineering for Innovation, University of Salento, Lecce, Italy
e-mail: gianluca.elia@unisalento.it; gianpaolo.ghiani@unisalento.it; emanuele.manni@unisalento.it; francesco.nucci@unisalento.it

S. Giuri · A. Paglialunga
LGH srl – gruppo DEGHI, Lecce, Italy
e-mail: sgiuri@deghi.it; direzione@deghi.it

G. Passiante (ed.), *Digital Innovation Management*, Applied Innovation and Technology Management, https://doi.org/10.1007/978-3-031-80426-7_5

5.1 The Emergence of the Industry 5.0 Paradigm

Industry 5.0, unlike the paradigm of Industry 4.0 coined in Germany in 2011 and mostly focused on the adoption of new digital technologies (e.g. big data, cloud computing, artificial intelligence, 3D printing, simulations, cybersecurity) to improve organisational efficiency, production systems and economic performances, complements such an approach by including positive effects on environmental sustainability, human centricity and social inclusion and resiliency (Breque et al., 2021).

More specifically, production systems based on the Industry 5.0 paradigm pursue environmental sustainability by promoting circular processes for reusing, repurposing and recycling natural resources to reduce waste and increase resource efficiency and effectiveness (Xu et al., 2021). Such systems must also guarantee human centricity in terms of a safe and inclusive work environment that takes care of the physical and mental health of workers by ensuring the achievement of individual well-being, the safeguarding of fundamental rights, such as human dignity or privacy, and the upskilling and re-skilling process for better career opportunities and work–life balance (Xu et al., 2021). Finally, an Industry 5.0-based system must develop resiliency capabilities in individuals and organisations that make them more robust and flexible in responding to any typologies of crises (e.g. business, geopolitical, natural, health) and adapting to unexpected changes, thus reaching a new equilibrium, which is possibly more respectful than the previous one (Breque et al., 2021; EESC, 2021).

In other words, whereas Industry 4.0 is focused on technology, Industry 5.0 is driven by an extended concept of value (Xu et al., 2021) that encompasses not only the economy (e.g. profitability, growth) and society dimensions (e.g. employment and other social problems, human-centricity and workers' well-being) but also an ecological dimension and respect for the planet (e.g. CO_2 reduction, circular economy practices).

In this view, Industry 5.0 aims to design new scenarios in which organisations can experiment with the twin transition process (Husain et al., 2022; Montresor & Vezzani, 2023; Rehman et al., 2023), which leverages digital technologies for creating value by mitigating the environmental effect of business activities and providing the opportunity to participate to the entire society, by preserving the central role of human beings and developing new capabilities for ensuring resiliency and anti-fragility. In such a way, Industry 5.0 shapes a future that links the economic and financial performances of organisations with social stability, workers' well-being, environmental respect and resource preservation. Unlike Industry 4.0, which is focused on individual technologies, Industry 5.0 adopts a systemic approach that integrates technological, environmental, social and governance issues (Xu et al., 2021).

The Industry 5.0 paradigm represents a source of digital innovation grounded in the potential of new digital technologies (e.g. pervasiveness, interoperability, adaptability) and combines four complementary dimensions: the centrality of people and their competencies, the merging of physical spaces with virtual places, the strategic role of knowledge-based assets as the most valuable resources and data-driven decision-making processes (Leng et al., 2022).

Moreover, to undertake a digital transformation process based on the Industry 5.0 paradigm effectively, two further elements are strongly recommended: an entrepreneurial mindset and an open innovation approach. The former is required to stress the creative capabilities and solution-oriented dimension of the process (Bennyson et al., 2023), whereas the latter accelerates value development and favours stakeholders' involvement and collaborative learning (Madhavan et al., 2022).

The result of such an approach is an intelligent, flexible and adaptable system in which there is a strict collaboration between humans and machines so that humans can augment their creativity and intelligence and machines can ensure the processes' efficiency and the resources' productivity.

5.2 The Relevance of Reverse Logistics in the E-Commerce Sector

Logistics plays an important role in the e-commerce sector because it determines the shipping of physical products to the end customers. Its performance in terms of costs and on-time delivery affects customers' satisfaction and consumers' purchasing behaviour, generating a positive effect on consumers' trust and brand loyalty (Cano et al., 2022).

Logistics is a bi-directional process comprising forward and reverse logistics. The former is responsible for moving the goods from the manufacturer to the customers (Govindan et al., 2015), whereas the latter extends forward logistics by including the opposite flow of products from the point of consumption back to the company (Rogers & Tibben-Lembke, 2001). Both forward and reverse logistics contribute to closing the loop and merging the physical, informational, financial and reputational flows that connect companies with end customers, thus acting as enablers for the circular economy (Ding et al., 2023).

Table 5.1 provides a synthesis of the main differences between forward and reverse logistics.

In the wider domain of the circular economy, more than forward logistics, reverse logistics is becoming a crucial area of investigation because it focuses on the management of goods that travel back in the supply chain from the end customers to the vendors (Ding et al., 2023; Mallick et al., 2023). Furthermore, the growth of e-commerce transactions, especially since the pandemic, makes reverse logistics a key driver of the competitive advantage of online businesses.

The recent pandemic has changed the purchasing behaviour of consumers, who significantly increased their online purchases (Guthrie et al., 2021). At the same time, beyond criteria simply based on the price, wide choice availability and delivery time, services and policies for reverse logistics also play a central role in

Table 5.1 The main differences between forward and reverse logistics

Dimension	Forward logistics	Reverse logistics
Planning of activities	Activities (especially production and distribution) are scheduled to minimise inventory stocks	It is difficult to schedule the activities because it is very difficult to foresee the requests for returns
Typology of flows	Direct flows, one-to-many	Inverse flows, many-to-one
Target of the flows	End customer	Manufacturing company or distributor/ reseller
Value of the product	The value increases every time the product goes to the next step	The value decreases every time the product performs a step (the costs increase and the product can be damaged)
Packaging	Standard and intact	Often absent or damaged

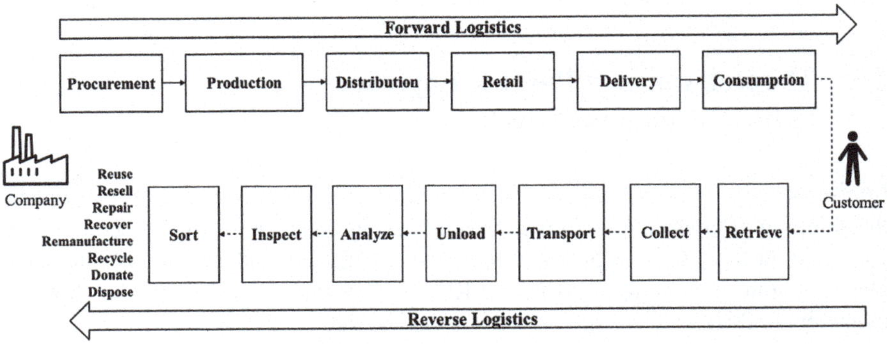

Fig. 5.1 A systemic view of forward (continuous line) and reverse (dashed line) logistics

maintaining customer loyalty (Röllecke et al., 2018) and enhancing customer satisfaction (Mahindroo et al., 2018).

The relevance of reverse logistics is also confirmed from both economic and environmental perspectives. Morgan et al. (2018) estimated that the economic effect of reverse logistics in online businesses is between $800 million and $1 billion and an accurate organisation of reverse logistics activities may contribute to optimising the cost function (e.g. the procurement of materials, transportation of goods, management of waste) and reducing the negative effect of the economic activity on the environment (Dutta et al., 2020; Islam et al., 2021).

By focusing on reverse logistics, the American Reverse Logistics Executive Council defines reverse logistics as.

> the process of planning, implementing and controlling the efficient, cost-effective flow of raw materials, in-process inventory, finished goods and related information from the point of consumption to the point of origin to recapture value or proper disposal. (Rogers & Tibben-Lembke, 1999)

Figure 5.1 provides a systemic view of forward and reverse logistics.

Forward logistics includes the procurement of raw materials from suppliers, the design and production of goods, the distribution through different partners at different levels and finally the delivery to the customers and the consumption.

In reverse logistics, it is possible to identify seven key steps. *Retrieve* represents the initial step in which the end customer gives the good back to the company through its delivery to a third-party partner, the carrier or the company itself. After that, there is the *Collect* step, which focuses on grouping the returned goods using different criteria (e.g. typology of product, geographical provenience, customer segment). Then, the *Transport* step ensures that the collected products arrive at the company by using its own transportation means or logistics service providers and carriers. Once the returned products reach the company, the *Unload* step is executed to place and organise them within a reserved area located in the company's warehouses. Here, dedicated personnel execute the *Analyse* step with the aim of verifying the messages from the customer and check the details of the returned good. At this point, personnel perform the *Inspect* step by opening the packaged product and validating its status and any further information needed to take a decision and identify possible causes of the return. Finally, the returned goods enter into the *Sort* step, which consists of organising the returns in specific sub-groups depending on the different decisions which could be *reuse* (e.g. continuing to exploit in other contexts the residual value of the returned goods); *resell* (e.g. selling again the returned goods because they are still marketable with the same characteristics); *repair* (e.g. resetting the initial functionalities by substituting worn or damaged components thus obtaining a product that is similar to the original one); *recover* (e.g. realising a new product, often one that performs better than the original one, simply by substituting some components with more updated modules and technologies); *remanufacture* (e.g. recreating from scratch the product by substituting obsolete modules and components with more updated and used ones); *recycle* (e.g. disassembling the product to extract functioning components and valuable materials that can be used to reinsert the product into the market or repair other products); *donate* (e.g. donating the returned goods to charities, thus consolidating the corporate brand and image) and *dispose* (e.g. throwing away the goods according to current laws).

Reverse logistics can be considered a transversal process, crossing the entire company's operations and thus playing a relevant role in the entire company's competitiveness (Davidavičienė & Al Majzoub, 2021). It affects the inbound logistics for the management of inventory and suppliers. It also influences the manufacturing and assembling activities for issues related to the production methods and quality standards adopted, as well as the recovery and reuse of materials. It has also effects on the outbound logistics for the choice of carriers. Finally, it has a strong marketing effect for the themes of customer satisfaction, customer loyalty and brand reputation.

Most of the existing studies focus on the efficient execution—in terms of reduced time and costs—of reverse logistics activities by proposing initiatives at the strategic level (e.g. secondary market forecasting), tactical level (e.g. modular design for recycling) and operational level (e.g. identification of third-party collection centres; Wilson & Goffnett, 2022).

For this purpose, organisations can leverage multiple drivers of their reverse logistics process, such as, according to Agrawal et al. (2015) and Ahlén and Johansson (2023): making middle and top managers more aware of and committed to the importance of reverse logistics for the company's success; exploiting the technology's interoperability to integrate different systems; influencing political decisions; reserving a financial budget for investments in the area of reverse logistics; enhancing coordination among activities and resources; and promoting a culture oriented to continuous improvement.

Instead, the study and analysis of data and information flows to forecast product returns and reduce the number of returned goods through a more robust decision-making, the reorganisation of the supply chain and the identification of key performance indicators represent a field of research and application that may generate promising and valuable results (Agrawal et al., 2015; Dutta et al., 2020), thus combining economic advantages with operational efficiency and environmental protection.

5.3 Experimenting with Digital Innovation in LGH's Reverse Logistics Process

The company LGH carries out logistics activities involving the handling of goods on behalf of third parties. These activities include warehousing, storage and all related handling operations, such as packaging, labelling and reconditioning. Moreover, the company is involved in the design, organisation and management of goods flows from suppliers' origins to customer delivery points, including post-sales services. This encompasses the supply of necessary human and material resources. Furthermore, LGH manages warehouses and storage facilities, including customs warehouses, for goods of all types. They also rent out related spaces to third parties along with associated ancillary services. The company plans, coordinates, monitors and manages shipping and transportation services both domestically and internationally. Their headquarters are in the hinterland of Lecce, in the south-eastern part of Italy.

Specifically, LGH manages logistics for goods processed on the e-commerce site www.deghi.it, one of the largest in the Italian market. They prepare spaces, vehicles, equipment and the necessary resources to ensure the proper execution of entrusted services, adhering to the highest quality standards in the industry.

The objective of the company was to speed up the analysis phase of returns from orders originating from the e-commerce website. In recent years, the volume of online sales has significantly increased, and, consequently, the number of returned products that need analysis has also grown proportionally.

Previously, the returns-analysis phase was carried out manually, both in terms of evaluating the returned items and updating data in the order management information system. The company deals with a wide variety of objects (such as sinks, furniture, faucets and assembly kits), which require different procedures, depending on the product category.

This manual approach caused process slowdowns and a non-negligible error rate as repetitive manual tasks were prone to mistakes. The company has consequently requested to optimise this process to improve efficiency and decrease errors.

5.3.1 Reengineering the Reverse Logistics Process in LGH

To speed up the returns analysis process, a study of the operations was carried out to evaluate timing and identify bottlenecks.

The returns department has been facing a significant increase in volume for several years. Each package returned by a customer is sent directly to the returns department. This department, which has authorised the return, already has the relevant data in its information system. Each package must be checked for two reasons: firstly, to verify the customer's reason for returning the parcel and, secondly, to determine whether the returned product can be put back on the market or whether it needs to be repaired or disposed of.

Before the innovation, the activities carried out by the return's office staff were as follows:

- Visually inspect the external condition of the package and note the barcode to check whether the return is present in the information system.
- Shake the package and listen to detect any broken pieces inside.
- Open the package and observe the condition of the products inside.
- Inspect each individual product.
- Verify whether all the products that should be in the package are indeed present.
- Take photos using a smartphone to document any issues.
- Download the photos to a computer and send them to the customer support department along with the evaluator's assessment of the return.

The last two activities, although less critical than the others, contribute significantly to increased processing time and errors. For example, the photos must be taken by the worker, who has only one hand free to manipulate the items. Finally, the employee must transfer the photos from the smartphone to the computer and ensure that they are correctly associated with each return case.

5.3.2 *Digital Innovation Initiatives for Reverse Logistics in LGH*

The Industry 5.0 paradigm has several implications for reverse logistics in the e-commerce sector. It allows for the adoption of a customer-centric approach, leveraging data-driven decision-making, fostering collaborative supply chain networks and embracing circular economy initiatives. Therefore, by optimising reverse logistics operations, e-commerce companies can improve customer satisfaction, reduce costs and contribute to sustainability goals.

In this view, the company LGH has re-engineered the entire reverse logistics process by introducing automation for capturing the returned products' photos and storing them in the company's information system. In addition, the manual data update phase in the information system was significantly reduced by implementing management software to track the status of returns. Finally, all the data stored in the company's information system and properly linked through an intelligent middleware have the potential to be further processed to support decision-making processes in managing and forecasting product returns.

For this purpose, LGH has launched three main initiatives to experiment with digital innovation in reverse logistics (Elia et al., 2024). They are

- A cobot-based cell to support the inspection and analysis of returned goods.
- An Anomaly Detection System for early warning and recommendations.

5.3.3 *A Forecasting System for Predicting Future Returns*

5.3.3.1 A Cobot-Based Cell to Support Inspection and Analysis of Returned Goods

The basic idea behind the proposed innovation is to use a cobot (a collaborative robot) to assist the returns office staff in taking photos (Gualtieri et al., 2021). The cobot is suitable for use in an environment where both an operator and fragile items are present (Hjorth & Chrysostomou, 2022). In addition, the cobot cell management software can be configured to automatically send the photos to the information system. The advantages of this proposal are as follows:

- Enhanced safety: By not handling the smartphone for taking photos, the staff members have both hands free to focus on their primary tasks. Mentally, they can concentrate more on handling the objects rather than taking photographs.
- Reduced processing time: With free hands, the staff can manipulate objects more quickly. Moreover, they do not need to manually transfer photos from the smartphone to the computer since the captured photos are automatically sent to the information system;

- Decreased errors: Staff members no longer need to worry about correctly associating the photos with specific returns as the photos are automatically sent to the correct party.

The design of a robotic cell heavily depends on the specific application context and the corresponding case study. Analysing the current situation to identify weaknesses is crucial for determining where collaborative automation can be introduced. In this case, the cell employs a cobot that operates closely with operators under safe conditions.

The cobot does not perform typical manipulation tasks but instead assists the operator in capturing photographs to document the condition of the returned product for analysis. The chosen cobot model is the 'Omron TM12', equipped with a 'uEye XC iDS' camera. In addition to the cobot, the cell includes the following components:

- A PLC (programmable logic controller) to execute specific tasks for the cobot.
- A set of physical buttons to activate and deactivate the cobot's operation.
- A touchscreen monitor that allows the operator to issue various commands.
- A computer connected to both the cobot and the company's information system for interaction with the returns management software.
- A workbench on which the packages containing the products to be analysed are placed.

The communication flow within the cell allows for information exchange between the operator and Cobot Omron TM12. Data flow occurs through the cell's management software and the PLC, as depicted in Fig. 5.2.

The management software streamlines the operator's work by controlling the cobot's movements and providing return data (such as item descriptions). It manages access to the company's information system. It is not necessary for the operator to have detailed knowledge of the cobot's specific movements.

To optimise the cobot's movements, the management software does not directly command the manipulator. Instead, it communicates with a PLC (programmable logic controller) by sending high-level logical movement commands (Kostenko,

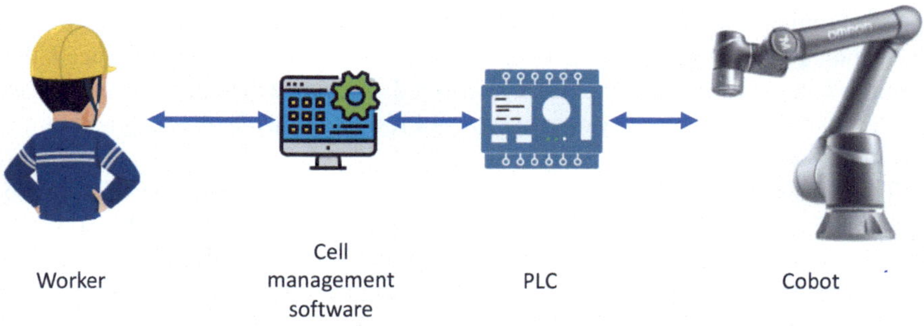

Fig. 5.2 The architecture of the cobot-based cell

2019). The PLC accurately translates these commands into cobot movements. Communication between the PLC and the cobot is facilitated by an application developed by Omron.

In the data reading phase, the use case involves the following steps:

- The operator receives the package to inspect and performs one of the following actions:

  Scans the NAR barcode on the package.
  Enters customer data (SSN, email, phone number, name).

- By querying authorised returns using this data, the system should provide.

  A list of items contained in the package (including composition).
  A list of any object photos (if available).

- Return information, including details of the issue reported by the customer (e.g. 'Item X broken', 'Item Y missing' or 'right of withdrawal').

In the data updating phase, the operator uploads photos to a folder with a unique return identifier. If the return is not suitable for traditional resale, the operator, after consulting the warehouse stock, can decide whether to recondition it (for high stock levels) or use it as a replacement (for low stock levels).

In summary, the operator can set the outcome of the return by configuring the status to one of the following values:

- Product suitable for resale.
- Product to be reconditioned.
- Product to be used as spare parts.
- Product to be sold in an outlet.
- Product to be disposed of.

The management software primarily supports the operator in three fundamental respects:

- Interaction with the company's order database.
- Interaction with the cobot.
- Interaction with auxiliary systems for the in-depth inspection of objects.

A preliminary step was to analyse the company's information system to define the technical requirements for the integration. Before the innovation introduced, the operator had to move to a computer away from the workbench to perform queries in the company's information system and record results in the database, generating a significant time loss.

The software interface, however, has been custom-tailored to the operator to maximise daily work support. The screen on the cell, connected to a Windows 10 PC, allows the operator to search for a return and verify all relevant information (including status) by extracting real-time data from the company's database.

A straightforward interface enables the operator to search for a return based on the barcode on the package (scanned using a simple barcode reader integrated with

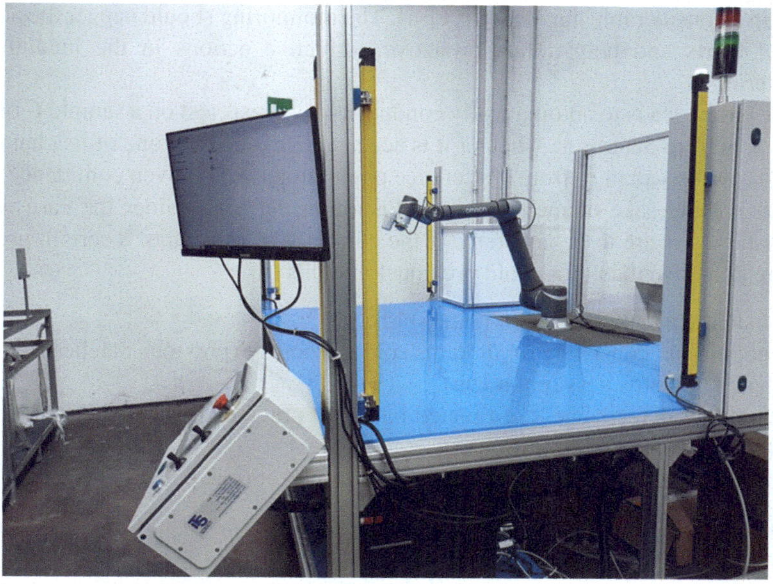

Fig. 5.3 The cobot-based cell

the computer). If the return code is unavailable or unreadable, the operator can search for the return using other package data, such as the customer's SSN, phone number, email or name.

Figure 5.3 shows the robot cell that has been installed and is fully functional in the LGH returns department.

5.3.4 An Anomaly Detection System for Early Warning and Recommendations

In the context of Industry 5.0, which emphasises the integration of advanced technologies with human-centric approaches, Anomaly Detection Systems play a critical role in enabling human–machine collaboration and intelligent decision-making. By providing early warnings and actionable recommendations, these systems empower human operators and decision-makers to respond effectively to anomalies, optimise processes and enhance overall productivity, efficiency and safety within industrial settings.

The system designed for LGH returns management had the ambitious goal of generating, in a semi-automatic manner, recommendations aimed at anticipating the onset of returns, thereby reducing company costs and customer service disruptions. In other words, the objective of the system is to identify anomalous situations (anomaly detection) that if not addressed promptly and proactively would likely result in a considerable number of returns. The monitoring should trigger the activation of alerts and help define proactive corrective actions in the medium- to short term.

The basic idea is to automatically conduct a hypothesis test on a sample C of size n (e.g., daily) to determine whether it is acceptable to consider one of its characteristics, p, 'worse' than p_0 from a reference population, with a given confidence level of 1-α. For the sake of methodology illustration, let us consider the case where automatic alerts are to be generated if the currently sold batch of a certain product is more defective than those sold previously. In this case:

- C: batch currently on sale (n items sold).
- P: population consisting of all items sold previously (previous batches sold).
- p: batch defectiveness (unknown),
- p_0: product defectiveness, estimated based on previous batches (here, historical data are assumed to be sufficient),
- 1-α: the confidence level set by the decision-maker (e.g. 0.9)

The null hypothesis to be tested is

$$H_0 : p \le p_0$$

To perform the test, the number X of returned (non-conforming) items in sample C is used, as detected from the company database (e.g. daily).

X is distributed binomially with parameter (unknown) p, and therefore, the probability that X is greater than a certain k (survival function) is equal to

$$P(X > k) = \sum_{i=k+1}^{+\infty} \binom{n}{i} p^i (1-p)^{n-i}$$

This probability increases with p. Therefore,

$$P(X > k) = \sum_{i=k+1}^{+\infty} \binom{n}{i} p^i (1-p)^{n-i} \le$$

$$P_{H_0}(X > k) = \sum_{i=k+1}^{+\infty} \binom{n}{i} p_0^i (1-p_0)^{n-i}$$

This implies that an alert will be triggered if $X > k^*$, where k^* is defined by

$$k^* = \underset{k}{\operatorname{argmin}} \sum_{i=k+1}^{+\infty} \binom{n}{i} p_0{}^i (1-p_0)^{n-i} < \alpha$$

The model is embedded in a batch procedure of Early Warning and Recommendation, which, executed with appropriate frequency (see Table 5.2), allows for the generation of a wide range of recommendations aimed at reducing returns and their effect on costs and the level of service provided to the customer. Table 5.2 shows the variables and parameters of the model (C, P, p, p_0, n, X) for the different cases identified during the study. Hereafter, by product, we refer to all the references corresponding to variants differing in terms of, for example, format, size, colour or dimension.

For each case described in Table 5.2, the batch procedure

- Estimates the model parameters.
- Checks whether the corresponding alert should be triggered.
- Suggests the most appropriate recommendation.

5.3.5 A Forecasting System for Predicting Returns

Another way to improve the management of returns is trying to determine in advance the approximate number of items that will be returned each day. In the following, we illustrate the methodology employed to predict the number of returns that could be received and examined in a day, as well as the number of expected shipments. To this end, a time-series analysis of returns and shipments was conducted by means of the following steps.

1. *Data collection*: First, a dataset was created by extracting from the company database the historical data related to returns and shipments, starting from January 1, 2021. After cleaning the data of any anomalies or input errors, the historical data were then divided into a training set (used to train the forecasting models) and a test set (used to assess the models). For instance, Fig. 5.4 shows the obtained time series of the returns.
2. *Time-series decomposition*: The time-series dataset was then decomposed into its components: trend, seasonality and residual (or noise). This decomposition helps in understanding the underlying patterns and variations in the data.
3. *Model selection*: To identify the most appropriate forecasting model, both the additive and multiplicative models were considered.
4. *Model training*: Both models were trained using the historical data making up the training set so that they were able to learn to capture the underlying patterns and relationships in the data.
5. *Model evaluation*: Once trained, the models' performances were evaluated using the test set and computing two indicators: the *sum of squared errors* (SSE) and the *mean absolute percentage deviation* (MAPD). Such indicators showed that the most appropriate model was the multiplicative one.
6. *Forecasting*: After training and validating the model, forecasts about returns and shipments can be made for future time periods. In addition to the predicted values, we also provided a 90% confidence interval to give a range of values for the

Table 5.2 The variables and parameters of the model for anomaly detection

Problem	C, X	P, p_0	Corrective action *(if the alert is activated)*	Frequency
Poor quality of a batch (currently for sale) of a given product?	C = the n units of the batch X = the number of units of the batch returned due to inadequate quality	P = the units previously sold of the reference (previous batches) p_0 = fraction of customers who returned the product due to inadequate quality	Conduct a sample check on the batch and then, if necessary, remove the batch from sale. Eventually, initiate a recourse action against the supplier.	Daily
Non-compliance of a batch (currently for sale) of a given product?	C = the n units of the batch X = the number of units of the batch returned due to non-compliance	P = the units previously sold of the reference (previous batches) p_0 = fraction of customers who returned the product due to non-compliance	Conduct additional potential sample checks; remove the batch from sale. Eventually, initiate a recourse action against the supplier.	Daily
Poor quality of a product?	C = the n units sold of the product X = the number of units from the batch returned due to poor quality	P = the previously sold units of products from the same category p_0 = fraction of customers who returned products of the same category due to poor quality	Carry out further possible sample checks. Assess the cost–benefit of removing the product from sale. Eventually initiate a recourse action against the supplier. Consider halting purchases of the product.	Weekly
Product damaged more frequently than products in the same category?	C = the n units sold of the product X = the number of units of the product returned due to damage	P = the units previously sold of products from the same category p_0 = the fraction of customers who returned products from the same category due to damage	Consider requesting from the supplier better packaging, potentially providing feedback and suggestions. Also evaluate whether to add additional packaging during shipping.	Weekly

(continued)

Table 5.2 (continued)

Problem	C, X	P, p_0	Corrective action (*if the alert is activated*)	Frequency
Non-compliance of a product?	C = the n units sold of the product X = the number of units of the product returned due non-compliance	P = the units previously sold of products from the same category p_0 = the fraction of customers who returned products from the same category due to non-compliance	Update the technical datasheet or highlight key aspects in the documentation/website that customers should check before making a purchase.	Weekly
Product category damaged most frequently compared to others?	C = the n units sold of the product category X = the number of units of the product category returned due to damage	P = the units previously sold of products from other categories p_0 = the fraction of customers who returned products from other categories due to damage	Evaluate whether to add additional packaging to all products in the category.	Monthly
The products from supplier F have a lower standard compared to other suppliers in the same product category CP?	C = the n units sold of products (in the CP category) from supplier F X = the number of units from the CP product category from supplier F returned for some reason	P = the units previously sold of CP category products by suppliers $F' \neq F$ p_0 = fraction of customers who returned CP category products from other suppliers $F' \neq F$	Evaluate whether to stop sourcing from that supplier. Identify alternative suppliers.	Weekly
Is customer CC a *serial returner*? In other words, does the incidence of returns significantly exceed that of customers ordering the same categories of products?	C = the n units purchased by customer CC X = the number of units purchased by customer CC and returned	P = the units purchased by other customers with the same profile p_0 = fraction of purchased units returned by customers with the same profile as CC	The customer might be a serial returner. Evaluate whether to prevent the customer from making future purchases. Alternatively, provide guidelines to avoid compliance issues, etc.	Weekly

(continued)

Table 5.2 (continued)

Problem	C, X	P, p_0	Corrective action *(if the alert is activated)*	Frequency
Does carrier T have a higher incidence of breakages compared to other carriers?	C = the n units transported by carrier T X = the number of units transported by T and damaged	P = The units transported by carriers T' ≠ T p_0 = fraction of units transported by carriers T' ≠ T and damaged	Handle the issue with the carrier or replace it.	Weekly

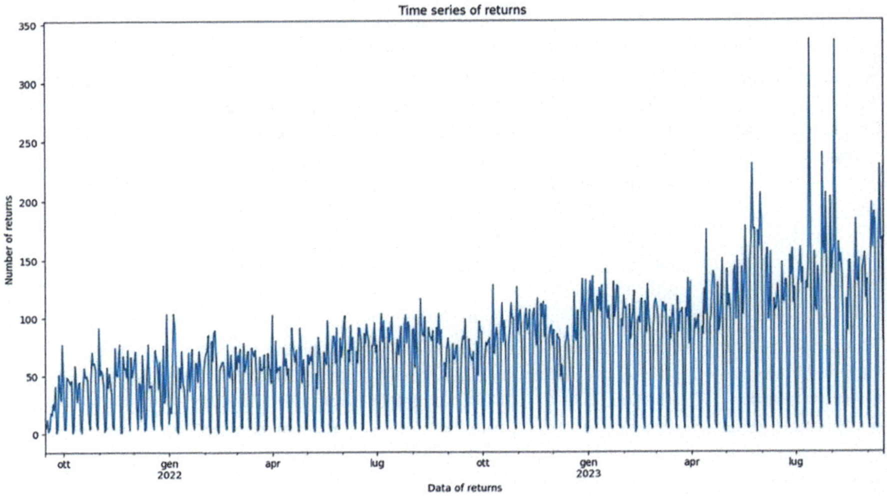

Fig. 5.4 Time series of returned goods

forecasts and provide an estimate of the uncertainty associated with the forecasts themselves.

7. *Dashboard creation*: The forecasted values, along with additional relevant information about the predictive model, are presented in a dashboard to visualise and interpret the forecasted figures easily. Figure 5.5 shows this aspect of the dashboard.

5.4 The Effect of Digital Innovation Initiatives on LGH

The three initiatives launched by LGH and described above to experiment with digital innovation in reverse logistics generate a synergistic effect combining efficiency gains, revenue growth and enhanced decision-making. It is also interesting to note that the final joint effect of such initiatives contributes to diminishing the

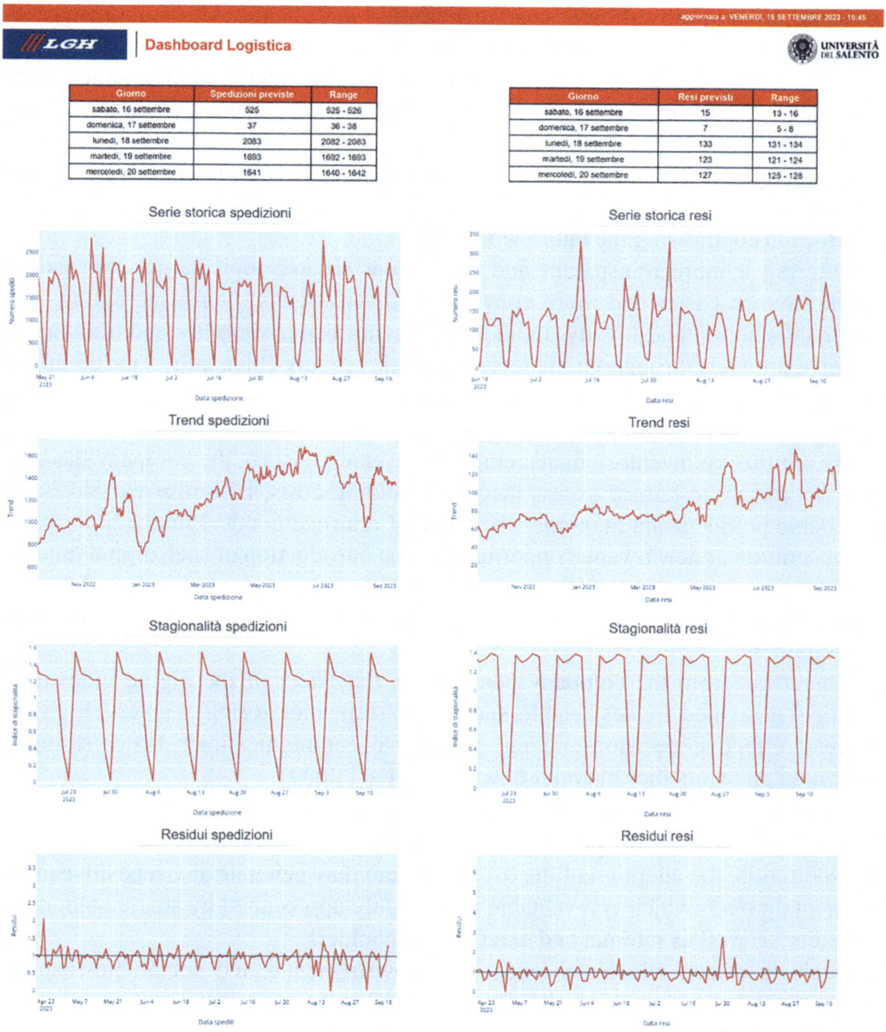

Fig. 5.5 Dashboard for monitoring shipments and returns

environmental effect of the LGH business activities, thus contributing to increasing the company's sustainability rating.

More specifically, the cobot-based cell for the inspection and analysis of returned goods enhances workers' safety and efficiency due to the reduction in time for performing an inspection, taking a decision, sharing information and providing customers' feedback.

The system for anomaly detection, instead, generates early warnings and recommendations that may support managers in evaluating suppliers and their offers, identifying defective products to withdraw from the market and allocating the right time and attention to different customer profiles and identities to maximise revenues. Such anomalies, if not addressed promptly and proactively, would likely result in a considerable increase in returns. Hence, the overall system aims at anticipating the onset of returns, thereby reducing company costs and customer service disruptions.

Finally, the system can predict future returns and provide managers with valuable inputs to schedule correctly the required workforce and resources for managing returns, thus optimising the entire workload.

Offering a more transparent and convenient reverse logistics process makes product return easier and more convenient for customers, hence increasing customer satisfaction and loyalty. In addition, having better visibility and tracking of returned products throughout the reverse logistics supply chain allows the company to make informed decisions about the disposition of returned products, such as whether to restock, refurbish, resell or recycle them.

By optimising inventory management in reverse logistics, the company has also the opportunity to reduce excess inventory holding costs, minimise write-offs for unsellable products and maximise the value of returned goods. Finally, in terms of the generation of new revenue opportunities, the introduction of such digital innovation practices in reverse logistics makes it possible to leverage returned products for resale through secondary markets, liquidation channels or refurbished goods programmes.

Therefore, from the company perspective, the effect of the digital innovation practices described creates benefits such as real-time monitoring of reverse logistics process, effective decision-making, responsive communications, better resource allocation and smoother material flows (Sun et al., 2022).

By combining the waste reduction achieved through the multiple destinations of returned products and the pollution decrease due to the elimination of unnecessary transportation, the adoption of the overall system may generate also a positive environmental effect, which is a valuable issue highly appreciated by shareholders and investors, as well as internal and external stakeholders.

Such an effect, which has economic, environmental and social dimensions, makes customers aware not only of the economic relevance of the value embedded into used products but of the human-centricity and social responsibility towards the environment (Pokharel & Mutha, 2009), thus envisioning a trade-off among such the three dimensions (Ramos et al., 2014) that is grounded in the reverse logistics 5.0 framework (Sun et al., 2022).

5.5 Conclusions

Digital technologies today represent a booster towards business innovation and environmental sustainability. They may also operate as powerful enablers to improve working conditions in terms of increasing security, reducing physical fatigue, enhancing the quality of decision-making process and better organising activities.

All these issues have been observed in a digital innovation project carried out in collaboration with LGH srl, an Italian company that has experimented with the innovation of its reverse logistics process. Indeed, this chapter has described the results of such project that are grounded in

- Modelling decision-making problems to support the management process of returns.
- Implementing a cobot-based cell to support the inspection and analysis of returned goods.
- Designing modules to support the decision-making process by extracting and presenting information useful to decision-makers and providing automatic suggestions.
- Designing a performance analysis module.

Designing an automatic early warning module generating (semi-)automatic recommendations aimed at anticipating the occurrence of returns, thus reducing company costs and customer dissatisfaction.

Such innovation implemented within the company allows for experimenting with both Industry 4.0 and Industry 5.0 paradigms. Coherently with Industry 4.0, the project and system realised relies on connectivity and data integration by emphasising seamless communication between machines and data-driven processes. Besides, along the automation and robotics dimension, the cobot-based cell implemented ensures efficient production and process optimisation.

The Industry 5.0 perspective highlights human-centricity and collaboration. Such issues have been considered in several aspects of the project, mainly including the human-centric design of man–machine interfaces that empowers workers' productivity and enhances security and ergonomics and the up-skilling process of workers aimed at enhancing human capabilities and promoting continuous learning.

The overall adoption of the results of the digital innovation project has allowed the company to experiment with the flexibility and adaptability of the entire process of returned product management, thanks to the modular design of the solution and the dynamic integration between the software layer and the legacy systems. The final solution has thus contributed to realising the circular economy scenarios, where products are designed for longevity, repairability and recycling.

Future work should focus on making returns easier and more convenient for customers and e-commerce companies by providing multiple return options (e.g. drop-off locations and pickup services) to increase customer satisfaction and loyalty. Moreover, further effort should be made in integrating AI modules into the reverse logistics processes to proactively address challenges and optimise operations.

Acknowledgement This chapter was developed with the financial support of Apulia region (Italy) in the framework of the project 'A.LO.SOL.'—Advanced Logistics SOLutions.

References

Agrawal, S., Singh, R. K., & Murtaza, Q. (2015). A literature review and perspectives in reverse logistics. *Resources, Conservation and Recycling, 97*, 76–92.

Ahlén, A., & Johansson, E. (2023). Overcoming barriers for functional reverse logistics in e-commerce—A systematic literature review. *Report, E2023*, 007.

Bennyson, R., Christiansen, L., & Laursen, E. S. (2023). Cooperative development of a technical, entrepreneurial mindset in manufacturing. In *International conference on cooperative design, visualization and engineering* (pp. 123–134). Springer.

Breque, M., De Nul, L., & Petridis, A. (2021). *Industry 5.0: Towards a sustainable, human-centric and resilient European industry*. European Commission, Directorate-General for Research and Innovation.

Cano, J. A., Londoño-Pineda, A., & Rodas, C. (2022). Sustainable logistics for e-commerce: A literature review and bibliometric analysis. *Sustainability, 14*(19), 12247.

Davidavičienė, V., & Al Majzoub, M. (2021). Performance of reverse logistics in electronic commerce: A case study from Lebanon and Syria. *Transport, 36*(3), 260–282.

Ding, L., Wang, T., & Chan, P. W. (2023). Forward and reverse logistics for circular economy in construction: A systematic literature review. *Journal of Cleaner Production, 388*, 135981.

Dutta, P., Mishra, A., Khandelwal, S., & Katthawala, I. (2020). A multiobjective optimization model for sustainable reverse logistics in Indian E-commerce market. *Journal of Cleaner Production, 249*, 119348.

EESC—European Economic and Social Committee. (2021). *Industry 5.0*. Available online https://ec.europa.eu/info/research-and-innovation/research-area/industrial-research-and-innovation/industry-50_en

Elia, G., Ghiani, G., Manni, E., & Margherita, A. (2024). A system for anomaly detection in reverse logistics: An application into an e-commerce company. *Measuring Business Excellence*. https://doi.org/10.1108/MBE-01-2024-0002

Govindan, K., Soleimani, H., & Kannan, D. (2015). Reverse logistics and closed-loop supply chain: A comprehensive review to explore the future. *European Journal of Operational Research, 240*(3), 603–626.

Gualtieri, L., Rauch, E., & Vidoni, R. (2021). Emerging research fields in safety and ergonomics in industrial collaborative robotics: A systematic literature review. *Robotics and Computer-Integrated Manufacturing, 67*, 101998.

Guthrie, C., Fosso-Wamba, S., & Arnaud, J. B. (2021). Online consumer resilience during a pandemic: An exploratory study of e-commerce behavior before, during and after a COVID-19 lockdown. *Journal of Retailing and Consumer Services, 61*, 102570.

Hjorth, S., & Chrysostomou, D. (2022). Human–robot collaboration in industrial environments: A literature review on non-destructive disassembly. *Robotics and Computer-Integrated Manufacturing, 73*, 102208.

Husain, S., Sohag, K., & Wu, Y. (2022). The response of green energy and technology investment to climate policy uncertainty: An application of twin transitions strategy. *Technology in Society, 71*, 102132.

Islam, M. S., Moeinzadeh, S., Tseng, M. L., & Tan, K. (2021). A literature review on environmental concerns in logistics: Trends and future challenges. *International Journal of Logistics Research and Applications, 24*(2), 126–151.

Kostenko, K. V. (2019). Real-time communication between robot PLC and PC over Ethernet-based protocols. *arXiv preprint, arXiv*, 1902.01924.

Leng, J., Sha, W., Wang, B., Zheng, P., Zhuang, C., Liu, Q., Wuest, T., Mourtzis, D., & Wang, L. (2022). Industry 5.0: Prospect and retrospect. *Journal of Manufacturing Systems, 65*, 279–295.

Madhavan, M., Wangtueai, S., Sharafuddin, M. A., & Chaichana, T. (2022). The precipitative effects of pandemic on open innovation of SMEs: A scientometrics and systematic review of industry 4.0 and industry 5.0. *Journal of Open Innovation: Technology, Market, and Complexity, 8*(3), 152.

Mahindroo, A., Samalia, H. V., & Verma, P. (2018). Moderated influence of return frequency and resource commitment on information systems and reverse logistics strategic performance. *International Journal of Productivity and Performance Management, 67*(3), 550–570.

Mallick, P. K., Salling, K. B., Pigosso, D. C., & McAloone, T. C. (2023). Closing the loop: Establishing reverse logistics for a circular economy, a systematic review. *Journal of Environmental Management, 328*, 117017.

Montresor, S., & Vezzani, A. (2023). Digital technologies and eco-innovation. Evidence of the twin transition from Italian firms. *Industry and Innovation*, 1–35.

Morgan, T. R., Tokman, M., Richey, R. G., & Defee, C. (2018). Resource commitment and sustainability: A reverse logistics performance process model. *International Journal of Physical Distribution & Logistics Management, 48*(2), 164–182.

Pokharel, S., & Mutha, A. (2009). Perspectives in reverse logistics: A review. *Resources, Conservation and Recycling, 53*(4), 175–182.

Ramos, T. R. P., Gomes, M. I., & Barbosa-Póvoa, A. P. (2014). Planning a sustainable reverse logistics system: Balancing costs with environmental and social concerns. *Omega, 48*, 60–74.

Rehman, S. U., Giordino, D., Zhang, Q., & Alam, G. M. (2023). Twin transitions & industry 4.0: Unpacking the relationship between digital and green factors to determine green competitive advantage. *Technology in Society, 73*, 102227.

Rogers, D. S., & Tibben-Lembke, R. S. (1999). *Going backwards: Reverse logistics trends and practices* (Vol. 2). Reverse Logistics Executive Council.

Rogers, D. S., & Tibben-Lembke, R. S. (2001). An examination of reverse logistics practices. *Journal of Business Logistics, 22*(2), 129–148.

Röllecke, F. J., Huchzermeier, A., & Schröder, D. (2018). Returning customers: The hidden strategic opportunity of returns management. *California Management Review, 60*(2), 176–203.

Sun, X., Yu, H., & Solvang, W. D. (2022). Towards the smart and sustainable transformation of reverse logistics 4.0: A conceptualization and research agenda. *Environmental Science and Pollution Research, 29*(46), 69275–69293.

Wilson, M., & Goffnett, S. (2022). Reverse logistics: Understanding end-of-life product management. *Business Horizons, 65*(5), 643–655.

Xu, X., Lu, Y., Vogel-Heuser, B., & Wang, L. (2021). Industry 4.0 and industry 5.0—Inception, conception and perception. *Journal of Manufacturing Systems, 61*, 530–535.

Chapter 6
Digital Technologies for Sustainable Development: Opportunities and Challenges in the Renewable Energy Communities Paradigm

Gianluca Solazzo, Gianluca Elia, Giuseppina Passiante, and Palmalisa Marra

Abstract Digital technologies (DTs) offer new avenues for organisations to boost business performance, innovation and agility and play a pivotal role in sustainable development by enhancing resource efficiency, reducing adverse environmental effects and supporting the shift to renewable energy. Specifically, renewable energy communities (RECs), as a socio-technical model, underscore the significance of digital technologies in facilitating energy decentralisation and efficiency while fostering community involvement and local economic growth. Extensive research highlights DTs' capacity to cut emissions and foster low-carbon economies, with specific studies on RECs focusing on digital tools for energy optimisation, renewable integration and community engagement. However, challenges such as costs, technical complexities and data security in RECs require further investigation to devise effective adoption strategies. This study aims to identify the key challenges and mitigated steps for DTs adoption in RECs through a literature review and dependency impact analysis, categorising the main opportunities and hurdles into their socio-cultural, economic and technological dimensions. The findings aim to guide decision-making for RECs, enhance digital resilience and efficiency and contribute to sustainable development goals. This work offers valuable insights for both academics and practitioners in understanding adoption barriers and the effects of DTs on renewable energy systems and the broader energy transition.

Keywords Digital technologies · Renewable energy communities (RECs) · Sustainable development · Energy efficiency · Energy transition

---

G. Solazzo (✉) · G. Elia · G. Passiante
Department of Engineering for Innovation, University of Salento, Lecce, Italy
e-mail: gianluca.solazzo@unisalento.it; gianluca.elia@unisalento.it; giuseppina.passiante@unisalento.it

P. Marra
Links Management & Technology SpA, Lecce, Italy
e-mail: palmalisa.marra@linksmt.it

G. Passiante (ed.), *Digital Innovation Management*, Applied Innovation and Technology Management, https://doi.org/10.1007/978-3-031-80426-7_6

6.1 Harnessing Digital Transformation for Renewable Energy Communities

The spread of digital technologies and devices and the vast amount of available data create new possibilities for production systems and consumer networks to enhance business performance, innovation potential and strategic and operational agility (Dąbrowska et al., 2022). Digital technologies support the societal ability to address environmental and social sustainability challenges by improving resource efficiency and the monitoring and reduction of environmental effects and streamlining the transition to renewable energy and circular economy (Mondejar et al., 2021; Ranta et al., 2021; Rosário & Dias, 2023).

Framed in this context and the European Union's challenging objectives for 2030, renewable energy communities (RECs) are an emerging socio-technical paradigm and a valuable asset in the EU strategy for energy transition (Bauwens et al., 2022). RECs promote the decentralisation of energy production, energy efficiency and the use of renewable energy while encouraging citizen participation and supporting local economies (Capellán-Pérez et al., 2018). The EU RED-II (the Renewable Energy Directive) and the Internal Energy Market (IEM) directives allow citizens to become active players in the electricity system by producing, storing and selling self-produced renewable electricity. As part of this transformation, end consumers, once passive, are encouraged to take an active role by reducing their demand or by locally generating or storing energy.

As an example of consumer empowerment and community-driven initiatives, RECs can also play a key role in social innovation, as they reflect a fundamental shift in citizens' behaviour and their consumer role (Dimitropoulos et al., 2021). REC initiatives are increasing in Europe thanks to a combination of government support, economic incentives and a growing awareness of both the need for clean energy and the opportunity offered by digital technologies (DTs) to successfully develop RECs (Reinaud et al., 2017).

The literature shows that various Industry 4.0 technologies, including blockchain, the Internet of Things (IoT), big data and artificial intelligence and cloud computing (Lyu & Liu, 2021), contribute to the transformation of the energy sector (Pandey et al., 2023). Better monitoring, operation and maintenance of renewable energy assets, more refined system operations and control closer to real-time, the implementation of new market designs and the emergence of new business models are examples of the benefits that applications based on these technologies can bring to RECs (Scharl & Praktiknjo, 2019). Nevertheless, it is relevant to study and understand the drop-offs of DT adoption to better inform RECs' stakeholders (e.g. community members, external investors and governments) of the effects and challenges deriving from any digitalisation initiative.

This work identifies the most popular DT-based tools and applications adopted in the RECs. With a dependency impact analysis (DIA), the challenges that the adoption of specific digital technologies could have on an entire system, are highlighted and grouped into six categories along three dimensions. The remainder of the chapter is structured as follows: Section 6.2 presents the background, whereas Sect. 6.3 describes the literature review and analytical process. Section 6.4 presents the findings, and Sect. 6.4 brings some discussions and conclusions.

6.2 Digitalisation in the Energy Sector: Setting the Stage

As the pace of digitalisation in the power industry has accelerated over the past few years, energy companies have heavily invested in digital technologies associated with the Industry 4.0 revolution (Nagasawa et al., 2017). The underpinning of these changes in many countries, particularly in EU member states, was important in liberalising the electricity market and introducing new renewable energy regulations (Akberdina & Osmonova, 2021). Pushed by the EU strategy for the definition of citizens' essential role in the energy transition, RECs are benefitting from global digital trends being implemented in the energy industry, such as the decentralisation of power generation, the digitalisation of infrastructure, intelligent control and engineering or the creation of new opportunities for end consumers (Verma et al., 2020).

6.2.1 Renewable Energy Communities as the Driver of a Sustainable Transition

A REC can be described as a way of enhancing democratic values and participation in the energy sector (Wierling et al., 2020). Broadly speaking, RECs are heterogeneous sets of collective actors performing one or more activities in the energy sector by exploiting renewable energy sources. As stated by Rossetto et al. (2022), actors include households, SMEs and local public bodies or non-profit organisations that have in common a place (neighbourhood) or an interest (concern for climate change issues; Moroni et al., 2019).

The described commonalities support peer organisation and community governance, which becomes democratic and horizontal rather than centralised and hierarchical. Performing one or more activities in the energy sector is a consequence of the willingness of REC actors to take direct action in the energy sector (such as the satisfaction of their energy-related needs). Collective actions support higher-scale and -scope economies and generate new sources of value in the form of relations among community members and relational goods (Verde & Rossetto, 2020). RECs can differ in terms of size (number of members) and internal homogeneity (different backgrounds and socio-demographics), motivations and goals of collective actions, types of activities performed and their geographical level of influence.

Liljenfeldt and Da Silva Soares (2020) described four characteristics of REC initiatives: (1) a set of energy-related activities, (2) a focus on the 'community', (3) an inclusive process and (4) a process of (local) benefit sharing. Energy-related activities range from power generation to demand reduction (Simcock et al., 2016) to experimentation with new technical and social innovations. Key activities typically involved in a REC are (Caramizaru & Uihlein, 2020)

- Energy generation may be centralised or decentralised, with smaller-scale power generation distributed throughout the community.
- Energy is stored during periods of high renewable energy production and used during periods of low production.
- Energy is distributed through the traditional power grid, microgrids or peer-to-peer energy trading platforms.
- Energy consumption and the sharing of renewable energy by community members are achieved through energy-efficient building design, appliances and equipment and behaviour changes, such as reducing energy consumption during peak demand periods.
- Energy management involves the monitoring and control of energy generation, storage, distribution and consumption to ensure that the community is operating efficiently and sustainably.
- There is community-building and the engagement of members in the planning, design and implementation of renewable energy projects.
- Energy service delivery includes supporting services for the delivery infrastructure.

6.2.2 Renewable Energy Communities and Digital Technology Adoption

DTs have the potential to transform grid networks into smart grids and allow for the processing, control and management of the enormous data flow (Kettunen & Mäkitalo, 2019). DTs are also used to guarantee two-way communication from smart devices to the control centre to calculate real-time consumption, load data and cost of energy (Manbachi, 2018; Wang et al., 2018). The literature has devoted particular attention to Industry 4.0 (Singh et al., 2021; Weigel & Fischedick, 2019) as the most frequently adopted DT in the energy sector. Światowiec-Szczepańska and Stępień (2022) stated that these technologies are interdependent and are largely universal, as they have been used in many applicative domains with comprehensive benefits related to the stability, efficiency and environmental sustainability of the energy sector (Nazari & Musilek, 2023). In the RECs context, studies have explored the use of digital tools and platforms for monitoring and optimising energy use, integrating renewable energy sources into the grid, developing new energy markets, engaging community members and analysing data (Broska et al., 2022; Hernandez-Matheus et al., 2022). Overall, the literature shows that RECs' dependence on DTs is increasing, and DTs have the potential to play a critical role in supporting the transition to sustainable energy systems (Ceglia et al., 2022).

New work, however, is needed to understand the challenges and limitations associated with the adoption of DTs within RECs (Boulanger et al., 2021), and this process needs to be further explored and studied with a multi-disciplinary approach.

6.3 Unveiling Challenges in Digital Technology Adoption for RECs

Framed on the above-described premises, this chapter aims at addressing the following research question: *'What are the key challenges to be faced by a REC in the process of digital technology adoption?'* To address such research curiosity, a review of the specialised literature was undertaken. To identify relevant articles for the study, a keyword-based search was performed using the query: '(Renewable Energy Communit*) and digitalization', where the term 'digitalization' refers to 'the use of digital technologies and data (digitised and natively digital) to create revenue, improve business, replace/transform business processes (not simply digitising them) and create an environment for digital business, whereby digital information is at the core' (Stark, 2020).

The query was performed in the Scopus® and Science Direct® databases, which returned 24 and 67 items, respectively. The identified records were screened, and all duplicates were deleted. Furthermore, specific criteria were adopted to define the eligibility of sources, so a list of inclusion and exclusion criteria has been applied, as shown in Table 6.1.

The study aimed to incorporate a wide range of relevant papers, and it thus did not rely solely on factors like citation count or impact factor for selection. The final number of papers analysed is 40. A comprehensive analysis of each paper was undertaken to extract qualitative findings and potential contributions to the research topic. Cross-validation was performed during ad-hoc meeting sessions, as well as with the contribution of three domain experts.

The output of the literature review was also analysed through a dependency impact analysis to detail the relationships between RECs' entities (stakeholders and processes) in changing settings (i.e. the adoption of new DTs or disruptive events to existing ones) and evaluating their effects. The DIA is a type of Impact Analysis originally used for software maintenance and evolution triggered by frequent change

Table 6.1 Inclusion and exclusion criteria for the literature review

Inclusion criteria	Exclusion criteria
1. Full access to the source	1. Grey research
2. Articles, conference papers, book chapters, reviews	2. Duplicate source
3. Source evaluating the energy, economic or environmental benefits arising from DTs adoption in RECs	3. Sources containing not relevant keywords
4. Source dealing with exploitation of at least one DT	4. Non-English source
5. Source describing the results of a simulation or case study	

requests (Lehnert, 2011). DIA focuses on detecting dependencies to evaluate the potential consequences of changes on parts of the product that must be reworked when implementing these changes. Performing a dependency impact analysis (DIA) on DTs for a REC involves four main steps:

1. Identification of stakeholders involved in the REC.
2. Analysis of the interdependencies between the DTs and the REC stakeholders.
3. Identification of the potential challenges and effects of any disruptions to the DTs or the stakeholders.
4. Development of strategies and actions to mitigate the risks and effects.

The results of the literature review highlighted several examples of DTs adopted within energy communities with the purpose of improving their energy efficiency, reducing their reliance on traditional power sources and increasing their resilience to power outages and other disruptions.

6.3.1 DTs Within REC Processes and Activities: Results of the Literature Review

Figure 6.1 summarises the applications implemented in RECs' initiatives and projects, the emerging DTs on which these applications are developed and the RECs' processes and activities as defined by the European Commission (2020) affected by the adoption of these applications.

Based on the review, *smart grids* and *microgrids* play an essential role in the transition to sustainable energy systems by enabling RECs to more efficiently and effectively manage energy production, distribution and consumption (Loggia et al., 2022; Lund, 2014; Tenti & Caldognetto, 2023). For REC members, smart grids

Digital Technologies used	DTs Application adopted	RECs' affected processes and activities
Big Data and analytics, IoT, blockchain	Smart Grids/micro-grids	Energy distribution
Big Data and analytics, machine learning	Predictive maintenance applications	Energy services
Big Data and analytics, machine learning, IoT sensors, blockchain.	Renewable Energy Production tools	Energy generation
IoT sensors, blockchain, Artificial Intelligence	Virtual power plants (VPPs)	Integration of RES into the existing energy system
Big Data and analytics , machine learning, IoT sensors, Cloud computing.	Community Energy Management Systems	Energy consumption and sharing
ICT, Cloud computing.	Citizen engagement platforms	Community engagement, education and outreach
IoT sensors, Big Data analytics, Digital Twins	Simulation and modelling tools	Energy services
IoT sensors Blockchain	P2P energy trading	Energy supply and selling

Fig. 6.1 Results of the literature review

contribute to increased information and awareness of energy use, potentially enabling energy savings. A smart grid integrates a range of Industry 4.0 DTs, such as machine learning algorithms, which are used to predict when renewable energy sources will be available and when they will need to be stored for later use (Muench et al., 2022; Świątowiec-Szczepańska & Stępień, 2022) or to predict when power demand will be high or low, adjusting the distribution of power accordingly to meet the needs of customers (Świątowiec-Szczepańska & Stępień, 2022). For RECs using microgrids—self-contained power grids that can operate independently from the main grid—DTs play a critical role in Virtual Power Plants, which are digital systems that aggregate the electricity generation and storage capacity of multiple decentralised energy resources. Within a REC, a VPP can be used to optimise the integration of renewable energy sources into the grid by providing a flexible and dynamic way to manage and balance energy supply and demand.

The analysed paper showed how the adoption of predictive maintenance tools, based on big data and machine learning algorithms and used to identify potential equipment failures before they occur, help RECs to reduce the downtime of their assets and improve the reliability of power plants. The integration with IoT sensors and monitoring equipment is crucial to managing the flow of electricity through the distribution grid, although it could turn into a complex infrastructure to deploy in small settings (Shin et al., 2021; Tavares, 2022).

DTs play a crucial role for RECs in the optimisation of the energy production process and the integration of several renewable energy sources into the power grid. Tools and applications for the latter improve grid visibility and offer enhanced coordination capabilities and learning opportunities (Cicceri et al., 2023; Nazari & Musilek, 2023; Pandey et al., 2023).

Community Energy Management Systems are tools based on big data and analytics, machine learning and IoT sensors, used to implement solutions for the monitoring and management of energy consumption patterns. Their adoption is also increasing RECs as they empower community members to actively manage energy use, providing real-time information about energy consumption and enabling community members to make informed decisions that can reduce their energy bills (Dorahaki et al., 2023). Furthermore, DTs are crucial for the diffusion of P2P energy trading in RECs. Blockchain technology can enable the direct trading of electricity among REC consumers and prosumers by removing the need for a central authority to clear transactions. Many barriers, however, still need to be addressed, such as regulatory frameworks, which are rarely adapted to accommodate direct trading between peers without the intervention of intermediaries and have unclear or prohibitive rules regarding tariffs or grid access for prosumers (Pereira et al., 2022; Zhang et al., 2019; Zhou & Lund, 2023).

Moreover, citizen engagement platforms have been exploited in many REC initiatives to promote the implementation of energy-efficient technologies, encourage behavioural changes and develop energy-saving programmes and incentives (Cavallaro et al., 2023). A wide range of ICT technologies (ranging from social media to mobile apps, from webinars and virtual events to online forums, from crowdfunding platforms to virtual reality) can be used to build public support for local renewable energy initiatives and facilitate community discussion, engage with local businesses, government and community organisations to build partnerships that support the transition to renewable energy (Huttunen et al., 2022; Shortall et al., 2022).

Finally, DTs as IoT sensors, machine learning and advanced analytics can be used for simulation and modelling, allowing integrated simulation using asset data and real-time operation data for digital twin services. They can be used to simulate a 'living model' of a REC's assets and optimise their operations (Adu-Kankam & Camarinha-Matos, 2022; Nguyen-Huu et al., 2022) or to analyse the effect of constituent assets on the grid and the well-being of community members (Byrne et al., 2022).

6.3.2 *Dependency Impact Analysis of DTs within RECs*

The performed dependency impact analysis showed that the adoption within a REC of each DT generated relevant impacts and risks to a subset of REC stakeholders. Since a REC has a wide range of stakeholders involved in the community's renewable energy and sustainability initiatives, six categories of stakeholders (Fig. 6.2) of a REC should be considered, based on the work of Heuninckx et al. (2022).

For each category of applications and tools, the challenges of adoption in a REC have been identified related to the identified stakeholders. A matrix template has been built, with the left-hand column containing the challenges identified and, in the top row, the stakeholders affected by these challenges. Three impact levels ([3]: high impact, [2]: medium impact, [1]: low impact) have been identified and used to mark the intersection between a single challenge and the concerned stakeholder.

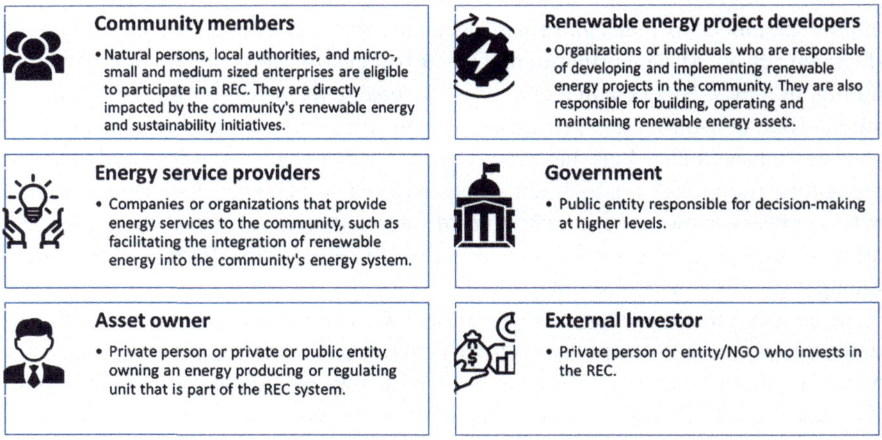

Fig. 6.2 Categories of stakeholders considered for this work

The results of the challenges associated with each of the DTs analysed are presented in Table 6.2.

Table 6.2 Results of the dependency impact analysis

Challenges	Mostly impacted stakeholders	Potential impacts of disruptions	Mitigation actions
Smart grids/micro-grids			
[COST], [TECH] High implementation costs as they require significant investments in new infrastructure and technologies [SECURITY] Data privacy and security concerns regarding data related to energy consumption and grid operations, if not adequately protected [TECH] Interoperability challenges for devices, systems and software that need to work together seamlessly [POLICY] Regulatory uncertainties regarding the legal and financial implications of smart grid adoption [SECURITY] Reliance on technologies susceptible to cyberattacks, software glitches and other technical failures, potentially leading to grid instability or power outages	[3] energy service providers [2] community members [2] RE project developers	Discontinued services due to supply disruptions or grid instability Financial losses due to increased energy costs Cybersecurity risks leading to equipment failure or energy supply disruptions	Redundancy and backup systems Cybersecurity measures
Predictive maintenance applications			
[COST], [TECH] Implementation costs, such as investments in hardware, software and training [TECH] Technical challenges related to advanced data analytics and machine learning, which can be complex and require specialised skills and expertise [TECH] Uncertainty of the predictions	[3] asset owners [3] RE project developers [2] community members	Unpredicted equipment failure Financial losses due to increased maintenance costs Safety risks Cybersecurity risks result in data breaches and compromised equipment performance	Investment in quality predictive maintenance applications designed specifically for RE equipment Cybersecurity measures

(continued)

Table 6.2 (continued)

Challenges	Mostly impacted stakeholders	Potential impacts of disruptions	Mitigation actions
Renewable energy production tools			
[SECURITY] Reliance on technologies susceptible to cyberattacks, software glitches and other technical failures, potentially leading to grid instability or power outages [TECH] Interoperability challenges for devices, systems and software that need to work together seamlessly	[3] community members [3] asset owners [1] external investors	Discontinued services due to supply disruptions Public perception and decreased support for REC Financial losses due to increased production costs	Regular maintenance and inspection Investment in education programmes for community members on how to maintain renewable energy production tools
Virtual power plants (VPPs)			
[SECURITY] Reliance on technologies susceptible to cyberattacks, software glitches and other technical failures, potentially leading to grid instability or power outages [SECURITY] Data privacy and security concerns on data related to energy production and consumption, if not adequately protected [TECH] Interoperability challenges for devices that may use different communication protocols and standards	[3] energy service providers [2] RE project developers [2] community members	Discontinued services resulting in energy shortages Financial losses due to reduced energy sold Cybersecurity risks related to data breaches	System redundancy Cybersecurity measures (i.e. encryption, multi-factor authentication and intrusion detection systems)
Community energy management systems			
[COST], [TECH] Implementation costs such as investments in hardware, software and training [SECURITY] Data privacy and security concerns related to members' energy production and consumption, if not adequately protected [TECH], [ACCESS] Technical challenges related to advanced data analytics and machine learning technologies, can be complex and require specialised skills and expertise [TECH] Interoperability challenges for devices, systems and software that need to work together seamlessly	[3] community members [3] asset owners	Discontinued services resulting in energy shortages Financial losses due to increased costs and loss of revenues The public perception that will perceive RECs as unreliable or unsafe	System redundancy Regular maintenance and testing of CEMS components Investments in training and education programmes for community members to help them understand how to use and manage the CEMS effectively

(continued)

Table 6.2 (continued)

Challenges	Mostly impacted stakeholders	Potential impacts of disruptions	Mitigation actions
Citizen engagement platforms			
[CHANGE] Limited engagement of members of the community who are less tech-savvy or have limited access to technology [COST], [ACCESS] High implementation costs, as they require significant investment resources, including time, money and expertise, which may be a barrier for some communities [CHANGE] Conflicting opinions by facilitating the expression of conflicting opinions can create tensions and disagreements within the community [CHANGE] Resistance to change from some community members who may be sceptical of the value of these tools or resistant to change in general	[3] community members [2] external investors [1] government	Decreased participation and trust Delayed decision-making related to planning and management decisions Missed opportunities to incorporate community feedback and potentially improve the REC project Cybersecurity risks related to data breaches	High-quality citizen engagement platforms designed specifically for RE initiatives Regular updates and maintenance Cybersecurity measures Backup communication channels
Simulation and modelling tools			
[SECURITY] Privacy concerns around data privacy and security, particularly if personal data is collected and stored [CHANGE], [ACCESS] Limited engagement and participation for members of the community who may not have access to or be comfortable using digital technologies [COST], [TECH] COST and complexity: Adopting these tools can require significant investment in terms of time, money and expertise, which may be a barrier for some communities	[3] RE project developers [2] community members [1] government [1] external investors	Cybersecurity risks related to data breaches Delayed decision-making related to planning and management decisions Reduced system performance Increased operational and labour costs	Regular updates and maintenance Cybersecurity measures Backup tools

(continued)

Table 6.2 (continued)

Challenges	Mostly impacted stakeholders	Potential impacts of disruptions	Mitigation actions
P2P energy trading			
[TECH] Technical challenges related to advanced Blockchain and smart contracts, can be complex and require specialised skills and expertise. [POLICY] Regulatory uncertainties related to a regulatory framework which is still evolving [COST] Market volatility is caused by volatile and fluctuating market-based pricing [SECURITY] Data privacy and security concerns, related to members' sensitive data, if not adequately protected [TECH] Interoperability challenges for devices, systems and software that need to work together seamlessly	[3] community members [2] RE project developers [2] government [1] external investors	Reduced energy independence (may not be possible to buy/sell energy) Decreased community members engagement, as they can be discouraged from participating Cybersecurity risks related to data breaches Legal and regulatory compliance after a disruption	High-quality P2P energy trading platforms Regular updates and maintenance Cybersecurity measures

Note: Categories of challenges: [COST] = costs; [TECH] = technical complexities; [DIGITAL_ACCESS] = digital infrastructure access; [RESIST_CHANGE] = resistance to change; [SECURITY] = data privacy and security; [POLICY] = policy and regulations. Impact levels: [3]: high impact; [2]: medium impact; [1]: low impact

6.4 Discussions and Conclusions: Navigating the Digital Transformation in RECs

This work has highlighted the main DT applications adopted in a REC, the set of processes and generated effects and the benefits and challenges for RECs stakeholders.

Benefits and challenges in DT adoption can be clustered into six main categories: *costs*, *technical complexities*, *data privacy and security*, *access to digital infrastructure*, *resistance to change* and *policy and regulations.*

Resistance to change relates to the 'positive and negative beliefs and attitudes that can influence DTs adoption or affect members' acceptance after a disruption event' (Ponce et al., 2016). *Access to digital infrastructure* constitutes another category of challenges, since low-income RECs may not have access to the necessary digital infrastructure. In some cases, members may not have the necessary skills or knowledge to fully use the technology effectively.

Concerning *Cost*, for many of the possible REC stakeholders, adopting tools and applications based on DTs requires high initial investments (in terms of time, money and expertise). Financial losses due to increased costs and loss of revenues due to

DT disruptions may not be sustainable for RECs already in place. From a technological perspective, challenges concern *technical complexities* and *data protection, privacy and security*. For the first category, compatibility issues and interoperability challenges may slow DT adoption in a REC. As the number of connected devices increases, standards are needed on multiple layers to lower implementation barriers for new energy business models. For the latter, as more devices are connected to the energy infrastructure and the REC is increasingly digitalised, cybersecurity risks increase as well. Risks include targeted attacks due to more connected devices, more advanced hybrid threats, human failures, outdated cyber-systems, a lack of skilled workers and the misuse of artificial intelligence (AI). Moreover, as digitalisation requires large amounts of real-time data flows, REC members might not be willing to share their energy usage data. This should represent an incentive to make data collection processes secure by introducing more sophisticated protocols to protect the privacy and ensure transparency about who can access data and how it can be used.

Finally, evolving or inconsistent *policies and regulations* may create uncertainty and make it difficult for communities to plan and invest in digital transformation initiatives. For example, the lack of policy support can slow down renewable energy development or energy efficiency improvements, so that there may be little motivation for community members to invest in DTs; there is uncertainty in regulatory frameworks related to regulations around data privacy and security; consumer protection and grid connection requirements may create barriers to DT adoption; and interference with market competition could also limit the benefits that a renewable energy community could achieve through the adoption of DTs.

The results shed light on an under-researched topic with potentially disruptive implications for all those REC initiatives and projects that rely on the adoption of applications and tools based on Industry 4.0 DTs. The results that emerged from this work are then valuable to inform decision-making around the adoption and implementation of DTs, help REC organisations be better prepared for potential disruptions, leading to more secure, resilient and efficient DT systems, and can support the overall goal of digital transformation and sustainable development.

The implications of this work reside at both the academic and practitioner levels. For researchers, it contributes to identifying the barriers and challenges to the adoption of DTs in RECs and the effect of DTs on the efficiency and reliability of renewable energy systems. For practitioners, the results of impact analysis can help to assess potential losses due to significant changes within REC projects and prepare to tackle potential problems. This work also creates new opportunities for future research. For example, extending the DIA with an extended proposition of strategies to mitigate the risks and impacts is a necessary step forward to provide REC stakeholders with a set of actions to follow. The obtained findings could be also tested with real cases of RECs to be validated.

References

Adu-Kankam, K. O., & Camarinha-Matos, L. M. (2022). A framework for the integration of IoT components into household digital twins for energy communities. In *Internet of Things. IoT through a multi-disciplinary perspective: 5th IFIP international cross-domain conference, IFIPIoT 2022, Amsterdam, The Netherlands, October 27–28, 2022, proceedings* (pp. 197–216).

Akberdina, V., & Osmonova, A. (2021). Digital transformation of energy sector companies. In *E3S web of conferences* (Vol. 250, p. 06001). EDP Sciences.

Bauwens, T., Schraven, D., Drewing, E., Radtke, J., Holstenkamp, L., Gotchev, B., & Yildiz, Ö. (2022). Conceptualizing community in energy systems: A systematic review of 183 definitions. *Renewable and Sustainable Energy Reviews, 156*, 111999.

Boulanger, S. O. M., Massari, M., Longo, D., Turillazzi, B., & Nucci, C. A. (2021). Designing collaborative energy communities: A European overview. *Energies, 14*(24), 8226.

Broska, L. H., Vögele, S., Shamon, H., & Wittenberg, I. (2022). On the future(s) of energy communities in the German energy transition: A derivation of transformation pathways. *Sustainability, 14*(6), 3169.

Byrne, N., Chassiakos, A., Karatzas, S., Sweeney, D., Lazari, V., Karameros, A., Tardioli, G., & Cabrera, A. G. (2022). A multi-level digital twin for optimizing demand response at the local level without compromising the well-being of consumers. In *ICCEPM 2022: The 9th international conference on construction engineering and Project Management, Las Vegas, Nevada, USA*.

Capellán-Pérez, I., Campos-Celador, Á., & Terés-Zubiaga, J. (2018). Renewable energy cooperatives as an instrument towards the energy transition in Spain. *Energy Policy, 123*, 215–229.

Caramizaru, A., & Uihlein, A. (2020). *Energy communities: An overview of energy and social innovation* (Vol. 30083). Publications Office of the European Union.

Cavallaro, E., Sessa, M. R., & Malandrino, O. (2023). Renewable energy communities in the energy transition context. *International Journal of Energy Economics and Policy, 13*(3), 408.

Ceglia, F., Marrasso, E., Pallotta, G., Roselli, C., & Sasso, M. (2022). The state of the art of smart energy communities: A systematic review of strengths and limits. *Energies, 15*(9), 3462.

Cicceri, G., Tricomi, G., D'Agati, L., Longo, F., Merlino, G., & Puliafito, A. (2023). A deep learning-driven self-conscious distributed cyber-physical system for renewable energy communities. *Sensors, 23*(9), 4549.

Dąbrowska, J., Almpanopoulou, A., Brem, A., Chesbrough, H., Cucino, V., Di Minin, A., & Ritala, P. (2022). Digital transformation, for better or worse: A critical multi-level research agenda. *R&D Management, 52*(5), 930–954.

Dimitropoulos, N., Sofias, N., Kapsalis, P., Mylona, Z., Marinakis, V., Primo, N., & Doukas, H. (2021). Forecasting of short-term PV production in energy communities through machine learning and deep learning algorithms. In *2021 12th international conference on Information, Intelligence, Systems & Applications (IISA)* (pp. 1–6). IEEE.

Dorahaki, S., Rashidinejad, M., Ardestani, S. F. F., Abdollahi, A., & Salehizadeh, M. R. (2023). An integrated model for citizen energy communities and renewable energy communities based on clean energy package: A two-stage risk-based approach. *Energy*, 127727.

Hernandez-Matheus, A., Löschenbrand, M., Berg, K., Fuchs, I., Aragüés-Peñalba, M., Bullich-Massagué, E., & Sumper, A. (2022). A systematic review of machine learning techniques related to local energy communities. *Renewable and Sustainable Energy Reviews, 170*, 112651.

Heuninckx, S., Te Boveldt, G., Macharis, C., & Coosemans, T. (2022). Stakeholder objectives for joining an energy community: Flemish case studies. *Energy Policy, 162*, 112808.

Huttunen, S., Ojanen, M., Ott, A., & Saarikoski, H. (2022). What about citizens? A literature review of citizen engagement in sustainability transitions research. *Energy Research & Social Science, 91*, 102714.

Kettunen, P., & Mäkitalo, N. (2019). Future smart energy software houses. *European Journal of Futures Research, 7*, 1–25.

Lehnert, S. (2011). A taxonomy for software change impact analysis. In *Proceedings of the 12th international workshop on principles of software evolution and the 7th annual ERCIM workshop on software evolution* (pp. 41–50).

Liljenfeldt, J., & Da Silva Soares, J. P. (2020). *Developing community energy initiatives: A literature review for the project local labour market in the energy transition*. Uppsala University.

Loggia, R., Flamini, A., Massaccesi, A., Capizzi, A., Moscatiello, C., & Martirano, L. (2022). Microgrids models for the aggregation of end-users in energy communities. In *2022 AEIT International Annual Conference (AEIT)* (pp. 1–6). IEEE.

Lund, H. (2014). *Renewable energy systems: A smart energy systems approach to the choice and modeling of 100% renewable solutions*. Academic.

Lyu, W., & Liu, J. (2021). Artificial intelligence and emerging digital technologies in the energy sector. *Applied Energy, 303*, 117615.

Manbachi, M. (2018). Impact of distributed energy resource penetrations on smart grid adaptive energy conservation and optimization solutions. In *Operation of distributed energy resources in smart distribution networks* (pp. 101–138). Academic.

Mondejar, M. E., Avtar, R., Diaz, H. L. B., Dubey, R. K., Esteban, J., Gómez-Morales, A., & Garcia-Segura, S. (2021). Digitalization to achieve sustainable development goals: Steps towards a smart green planet. *Science of the Total Environment, 794*, 148539.

Moroni, S., Alberti, V., Antoniucci, V., & Bisello, A. (2019). Energy communities in the transition to a low-carbon future: A taxonomical approach and some policy dilemmas. *Journal of Environmental Management, 236*, 45–53.

Muench, S., Stoermer, E., Jensen, K., Asikainen, T., Salvi, M., & Scapolo, F. (2022). *Towards a green and digital future*. Publications Office of the European Union. https://doi.org/10.2760/977331

Nagasawa, T., Pillay, C., Beier, G., Fritzsche, K., Pougel, F., Takama, T., & Bobashev, I. (2017). Accelerating clean energy through industry 4.0 manufacturing the next revolution. A report of the United Nations industrial development organization.

Nazari, Z., & Musilek, P. (2023). Impact of digital transformation on the energy sector: A review. *Algorithms, 16*(4), 211.

Nguyen-Huu, T. A., Tran, T. T., Tran, M. Q., Nguyen, P. H., & Slootweg, J. (2022). Operation orchestration of local energy communities through digital twin: A review on suitable modeling and simulation approaches. In *2022 IEEE 7th international energy conference (ENERGYCON)* (pp. 1–6). IEEE.

Pandey, V., Sircar, A., Bist, N., Solanki, K., & Yadav, K. (2023). Accelerating the renewable energy sector through industry 4.0: Optimization opportunities in the digital revolution. *International Journal of Innovation Studies, 7*(2). https://doi.org/10.1016/j.ijis.2023.03.003

Pereira, H., Gomes, L., & Vale, Z. (2022). Peer-to-peer energy trading optimization in energy communities using multi-agent deep reinforcement learning. *Energy Informatics, 5*(4), 1–18.

Ponce, P., Polasko, K., & Molina, A. (2016). End user perceptions toward smart grid technology: Acceptance, adoption, risks, and trust. *Renewable and Sustainable Energy Reviews, 60*, 587–598.

Ranta, V., Aarikka-Stenroos, L., & Väisänen, J. M. (2021). Digital technologies catalyzing business model innovation for circular economy—Multiple case study. *Resources, Conservation and Recycling, 164*, 105155.

Reinaud, J., Faraggi, P., & Clinckx, N. (2017). Accelerating energy & environmental transition in Europe through digital. *Annales des Mines—Responsabilité et Environnement, 87*, 98–104.

Rosário, A. T., & Dias, J. C. (2023). The new digital economy and sustainability: Challenges and opportunities. *Sustainability, 15*(14), 10902.

Rossetto, N., Verde, S. F., & Bauwens, T. (2022). A taxonomy of energy communities in liberalized energy systems. In *Energy communities* (pp. 3–23). Academic.

Scharl, S., & Praktiknjo, A. (2019). The role of a digital industry 4.0 in a renewable energy system. *International Journal of Energy Research, 43*(8), 3891–3904.

Shin, W., Han, J., & Rhee, W. (2021). AI-assistance for predictive maintenance of renewable energy systems. *Energy, 221*, 119775.

Shortall, R., Mengolini, A., & Gangale, F. (2022). Citizen engagement in EU collective action energy projects. *Sustainability, 14*(10), 5949.
Simcock, N., Willis, R., & Capener, P. (2016). *Cultures of community energy: International case studies*. The British Academy.
Singh, M., Jiao, J., Klobasa, M., & Frietsch, R. (2021). Emergence of digital and X-as-a-service (XAAS) platforms in German energy sectors. In J. Stark (Ed.), *Digital transformation on industry-continuing change*. Springer.
Stark, J. (2020). *Digital transformation of industry*. Springer.
Świątowiec-Szczepańska, J., & Stępień, B. (2022). Drivers of digitalization in the energy sector—The managerial perspective from the catching up economy. *Energies, 15*(4), 1437.
Tavares, T. M. M. (2022). Development and analysis of a local energy market using blockchain. *Energy Reports, 8*(1), 99–113.
Tenti, P., & Caldognetto, T. (2023). Integration of local and central control empowers cooperation among prosumers and distributors towards safe, efficient, and cost-effective operation of microgrids. *Energies, 16*(5), 2320.
Verde, S. F., & Rossetto, N. (2020). *The future of renewable energy communities in the EU: An investigation at the time of the clean energy package*. European University Institute.
Verma, P., Savickas, R., Buettner, S. M., Strüker, J., Kjeldsen, O., & Wang, X. (2020). *Digitalization: Enabling the new phase of energy efficiency*. Group of Experts on Energy Efficiency, GEEE-7, 2020-12.
Wang, Y., Chen, Q., Hong, T., & Kang, C. (2018). Review of smart meter data analytics: Applications, methodologies, and challenges. *IEEE Transactions on Smart Grid, 10*(3), 3125–3148.
Weigel, P., & Fischedick, M. (2019). Review and categorization of digital applications in the energy sector. *Applied Sciences, 9*(24), 5350.
Wierling, A., Zeiss, J. P., Hubert, W., Candelise, C., Gregg, J. S., & Schwanitz, V. J. (2020). Who participates in and drives collective action initiatives for a low carbon energy transition? In *Paradigms, models, scenarios and practices for strong sustainability* (pp. 239–256). Editions Oeconomia.
Zhang, M., Eliassen, F., Taherkordi, A., Jacobsen, H. A., Chung, H. M., & Zhang, Y. (2019). Energy trading with demand response in a community-based P2P energy market. In *2019 IEEE international conference on communications, control, and computing Technologies for Smart Grids (SmartGridComm)* (pp. 1–6). IEEE.
Zhou, Y., & Lund, P. D. (2023). Peer-to-peer energy sharing and trading of renewable energy in smart communities—trading pricing models, decision-making and agent-based collaboration. *Renewable Energy, 207*, 177–193.

Chapter 7
Artificial Intelligence Platforms Enabling Conversational Chatbots: The Case of Tiledesk.com

Gianluca Lorenzo, Gianluca Elia, and Andrea Sponziello

Abstract Artificial intelligence (AI) is changing the way businesses interact with customers. One of the most significant contributions of AI to customer service is the creation of conversational chatbots, which provide pre-built models, tools and interfaces that makes customer interaction easier and faster. Today, with natural language processing technologies and the growing use of Large Language Models, AI-powered chatbots can understand and process human language, enabling them to respond appropriately to customers' input and create unique and personalised multichannel communication experiences. To create these chatbots, businesses can either opt for custom development, which usually requires significant technical expertise and resources, or use platforms based on no-code approach. The latter provide a user-friendly interface based on pre-coded components, templates and other tools that allow, even non-technical users, to create and deploy in a faster, more accessible and cost-effective way, chatbot applications. After a brief introduction about the digital transformation of the customer engagement process, this chapter introduces the chatbot as a new tool to radically innovate interactions with customers. It describes the emerging no-code chatbot paradigm by highlighting both its functional and technological issues. Finally, the open-source tool from Tiledesk.com case is introduced, together with an example of a real application.

Keywords Artificial intelligence · Natural Language Processing · Large Language Models · Conversational chatbots · No-code development platforms · Customer service automation

---

G. Lorenzo (✉) · G. Elia
Department of Engineering for Innovation, University of Salento, Lecce, Italy
e-mail: gianluca.lorenzo@unisalento.it; gianluca.elia@unisalento.it

A. Sponziello
Tiledesk srl, Galatina (LE), Italy
e-mail: andrea@tiledesk.com

G. Passiante (ed.), *Digital Innovation Management*, Applied Innovation and Technology Management, https://doi.org/10.1007/978-3-031-80426-7_7

7.1 Introduction

The widespread popularity of messaging platforms has fuelled the rise of chatbots, making them a prominent interface for interacting with people and software services. This technology can significantly automate various aspects of company operations, streamlining processes and enhancing efficiency. A chatbot, also known as a conversational chatbot, is a software application that may enhance users' engagement in online conversations by leveraging cognitive, emotional and behavioural activities (Gupta et al., 2024). As defined by Hill et al. (2015), chatbots are 'machine conversation systems that interact with human users via natural conversational language'.

These software programs can be engaged in dialogue with users in a way that mimics human conversation, allowing people to interact with them through text or speech.

Chatbots have become increasingly popular in recent years due to advancements in natural language processing (NLP) and machine learning (ML) techniques. These advancements have enabled chatbots to better understand user inputs, interpret contexts and generate appropriate responses, thus allowing more meaningful and personalised communications (Lebeuf et al., 2018).

The key feature of a chatbot is its ability to handle a wide range of conversations and tasks, from providing customer support and answering questions to assisting with online purchases or booking appointments. Chatbots can thus be integrated into various platforms, such as websites, messaging apps and social media channels, making them highly versatile tools for businesses and organisations to engage with their customers.

Modern chatbots leverage a combination of artificial intelligence (AI) and deep learning models (Devlin et al., 2019) like recurrent neural network (RNN), sequence to sequence (Seq2Seq), long short-term memory (LSTM), bidirectional encoder representation from transformers (BERT) and generative pre-trained transformer (GPT), along with techniques like reinforcement learning and transfer learning to enhance the capabilities of algorithms and increase their performance.

While these technological advancements are impressive, the main challenge remains crafting chatbots that fully grasp the intricacies of human conversation, including context, style, emotion and character (Sun et al., 2018). Researchers are actively exploring methods to address these limitations by developing conversational AI platforms and user-friendly interfaces that may be used directly by experts in communication and businesspeople to create their own chatbots with the aim of enhancing customer experience and positively affecting the social aspects of communication with customers (Bag et al., 2022). These interfaces often use drag-and-drop functionality (the no-code paradigm), empowering individuals with limited technical expertise to leverage the power of chatbots for their business needs.

7.2 Transformation of the Customer Engagement Process Through the Chatbot

In recent years, the landscape of customer engagement has undergone a significant transformation largely driven by technological advancements and changing consumer expectations. This shift has been particularly evident in the realm of customer experience, where digital technologies compel an open-ended experience enabled by multiple interfaces (Amitrano et al., 2021), and the rise of customer relationship management systems, messaging platforms and chatbots has redefined how businesses interact with their customers. One key effect of this transformation is the emergence of chatbots to boost the engagement function. They ensure that conversations flow seamlessly, deliver relevant and valuable information and keep users interested in the platform for extended periods (Hepziba & Florence, 2020). Chatbots empower businesses to engage customers through personalised experiences, leveraging contextual information with user consent and offering convenient payment options as well. By personalising the experience through contextual information, chatbots position conversational commerce as a major force in the retail landscape (Pounder, 2016). Today, they have become drivers of a company's customer-centric operations because of their fast replies, round-the-clock assistance and ability to comprehend user inquiries (Shah, 2023).

From a business standpoint, messaging platforms have emerged as powerful tools that can improve customer experience by providing immediate and personalised answers to customer questions and increasing customer satisfaction. Users can get assistance or information without having to wait for or interact with a human operator. Moreover, chatbots can automatically handle a wide range of common requests and problems, reducing the need for human support staff and increasing operational efficiency to speed up business processes. This allows companies to save time and resources and focus on more complex and strategic tasks.

Chatbots have also the potential to understand and respond in multiple languages simply by embedding multilingual support, thus enabling companies to reach a larger and more diverse audience. During their interactions with customers, chatbots collect a huge amount of data, which can be further analysed to support the design of marketing strategies, better understand user needs and tailor product or service offerings accordingly.

Therefore, customers who appreciate easy interactions with businesses through familiar messaging interfaces are abandoning lengthy phone calls or the navigation of complex menus and prefer readily accessible touchpoints for acquiring information or seeking assistance. Customers now have the power to connect with 24/7, self-service channels through customer assistants (Hopkins & Silverman, 2016), which are becoming the dominant interface for customer interactions. Indeed, such interface is gradually evolving to become technology-dominant rather than human-driven (Larivière et al., 2017). Furthermore, advancements in AI-powered customer assistants allow them to incorporate features that simulate human characteristics, such as friendliness. These characteristics are recognised as essential elements in fostering positive service interactions (Verhagen et al., 2014).

As digitally enabled tools, chatbots can be active 24/7, thus ensuring that users can get assistance or information at any time, even outside business hours. Users' interactions also become training sets that chatbots use to enhance their performance by providing increasingly relevant and personalised responses. This personalisation can further enhance the user experience and increase the chatbot's effectiveness in providing solutions to various issues and questions posed by users. Chatbots are programmed to follow rules and provide accurate answers, significantly reducing the number of human errors. This is particularly beneficial in sensitive areas where accuracy is crucial for business goals.

Unlike the delayed nature of emails, these platforms enable immediate back-and-forth communication. Businesses can address customer concerns and inquiries promptly, building trust through a sense of responsiveness.

In addition to multilingual features, messaging platforms create a unified brand experience through multimodal communication. Customers expect a seamless experience regardless of the chosen channel. These platforms bridge the gap by offering communication across various platforms like SMS, social media apps and even directly through a business website. This empowers customers to connect on their preferred channel, ensuring a smooth and consistent interaction.

Messaging platforms offer a plethora of business advantages, which are briefly synthesised below.

Efficiency has become central in customer service interactions. Traditional methods involving numerous phone calls and lengthy email queues are being supplanted by a focus on real-time communication channels. Customer service agents can effectively manage multiple chat conversations simultaneously, leading to a significant reduction in resolution times and an overall enhancement of operational efficiency (Reddy, 2017).

Furthermore, the implementation of automated workflows alleviates the burden on customer interface operators. Repetitive and straightforward tasks can be effectively addressed by chatbots, thereby liberating valuable agent time for addressing more complex customer inquiries.

The real-time dialogue with customers through personalised messages and individualised information involves their cognitive and emotional dimensions, thus enabling more effective and responsive customer engagement (Gupta et al., 2024).

Centralised communication further streamlines operations. All customer interactions through the platform are stored in a central location. This eliminates the need to search through scattered emails or voicemails, simplifying record-keeping and providing valuable historical context for future interactions. In addition, the centralisation of customer data and interactions makes feasible the setup of comprehensive analytical functionalities that may support managers in a deeper understanding of their customer base.

While the above considerations have highlighted the advantages associated with the adoption of messaging platforms for customer service, it is equally important to acknowledge the potential shortcomings inherent to their implementation.

Security considerations necessitate the implementation of robust safeguards to ensure the protection of sensitive customer data entrusted to businesses through messaging platforms (Uma, 2023). This necessitates strict adherence to relevant data protection regulations and established industry best practices.

The efficient handling of customer inquiries necessitates a strategic resource management approach. This entails the allocation of adequate staffing levels and the provision of comprehensive training for customer service agents. Such measures are crucial for ensuring the prompt and professional resolution of customer concerns. Therefore, a complete transition towards solely self-service customer channels, particularly during the initial stages of customer engagement, might not be an optimal strategy for firms. The potential absence of a human touch during online interactions can impede the development of trust and rapport, potentially hindering sales conversions (Raymond, 2001).

7.3 The Rise of New Generations of Chatbots in the Customer Interface

Messaging platforms, such as WhatsApp, Facebook Messenger, Telegram or WeChat, have become ubiquitous in people's daily lives, offering a convenient and familiar way for consumers to communicate with businesses. As argued above, this shift towards messaging as a preferred communication channel has prompted companies to adapt their customer service strategies to be more responsive and accessible through these platforms. The immediacy and convenience of messaging have set new expectations for customer interactions, emphasising the need for businesses to be available and responsive across these channels around the clock.

Parallel to the rise of messaging platforms, the advent of chatbots has further revolutionised customer engagement. Initially, chatbots were simple rule-based systems capable of handling basic inquiries, but the introduction of generative AI technologies, such as ChatGPT, has taken chatbot capabilities to an entirely new level. These advanced AI models, by leveraging on pre-trained models based on existing datasets, generate new data and creative content that resembles existing data (Gupta et al., 2024; Kar et al., 2023). In this way, they can understand and generate human-like text, enabling them to handle a wide range of customer service inquiries with a degree of nuance and understanding that was previously unattainable. This has not only improved the efficiency of customer service operations but also significantly enhanced the quality of customer interactions, making them more personalised and engaging. Generative AI technologies have also expanded the scope of customer engagement beyond traditional customer service inquiries. They are now used in various customer touchpoints (Batat, 2022), from personalised product recommendations and content creation to interactive marketing campaigns and customer feedback analysis. This broad application of generative AI has made customer interactions more dynamic and provided businesses with deeper insights into customer needs and preferences.

The integration of generative AI into customer engagement strategies represents a paradigm shift in how businesses interact with their customers. It has enabled a more conversational, personalised and efficient customer experience, setting new standards for customer satisfaction and loyalty.

The generative AI chatbots mark a revolutionary leap in the way businesses interact with their customers. Two recent studies (Mattas, 2023; Paul et al., 2023) have investigated the capabilities of large language model (LLM)-powered chatbots in customer service interactions and providing customers with immediate responses to their inquiries, thus leading to a more efficient issue resolution compared to traditional customer service chatbots. These sophisticated AI-powered chatbots are not just tools for automating responses; they are at the forefront of radically innovating customer interactions, redefining the boundaries of what is possible in digital customer engagement by generating clear, consistent and contextually relevant content (Gupta et al., 2024).

In the evolving landscape of chatbots, two distinct types stand out for their unique approaches and capabilities:

- *Legacy chatbots*, often driven by Natural Language Understanding (NLU), which operate on an intent-based approach by identifying a user's intent (represented by the input of the communication) and responding with predefined answers.
- *No-code chatbots*, which represent a new paradigm of application development that empowers individuals with minimal or no coding experience to create various applications for managing customer relationships (Bhattacharyya & Saurabh, 2021; Lethbridge, 2021), thus combining time and cost savings with fast development life cycles and enhanced product quality (Rokis & Marite, 2022).

Legacy chatbots use predefined rules to process users' requests and provide responses. Due to their weak flexibility, AI-powered chatbots have been introduced to overcome such limitations by using machine learning techniques to understand human language and elaborate a proper answer.

No-code chatbots are more flexible in terms of application design and development, and it is easier to integrate them with advanced technologies, such as LLMs, including generative AI tools. This synergy makes no-code chatbots able to deliver more personalised, context-aware and conversational experiences that surpass the capabilities of traditional NLU-based legacy chatbots.

7.3.1 Legacy Chatbots

Legacy chatbots use predefined rules to process users' requests and provide responses. The most used legacy chatbot widely adopted in business is the rule-based chatbot. It leverages a rule-based framework for managing well-defined interactions, including frequently asked questions and basic customer service inquiries (Adamopoulou & Moussiades, 2020). Rule-based chatbots operate on a foundation of predefined decision rules, often structured as a decision tree. These systems are programmed to recognise specific user inputs, typically formulated as keywords or phrases and deliver corresponding predefined responses. During user interaction, the chatbot identifies these keywords or phrases that are present within the input by using pattern-matching techniques. The identified keywords then trigger the selection and delivery of the most relevant pre-programmed response. Due to their predictable nature, rule-based chatbots excel in scenarios characterised by a limited and clearly defined range of potential user inquiries. At the same time, however, this characteristic makes rule-based chatbots unable to comprehend contextual nuances or address queries that fall outside their pre-programmed responses.

Another typology of legacy chatbot exploits machine learning and NLP techniques (Adamopoulou & Moussiades, 2020). Unlike rule-based chatbots, NLP-based chatbots extract semantic meaning from the user's inputs, thus considering the entire conversation history and not just the user's isolated messages. In such a way, NLP-based chatbots may generate responses that are more contextually relevant. Additionally, they do not require a pre-programmed response for every conceivable user input, thus offering more flexibility (Lin et al., 2016). More specifically, NLP-based chatbots leverage NLU capabilities (McShane, 2017) to extract contextual information from unstructured users' inputs that are formulated in human language, thus inferring the user's underlying intent (Jung, 2019) to generate a tailored response. The intent classification component can be implemented by following different alternatives: using classifiers based on the support vector machine (SVM) algorithm; adopting several kinds of neural networks, such as recurrent neural networks [e.g. long short-term memory (LSTM) or gated recurrent unit (GRU)] or employing pre-trained models (based on the manual annotation of entities) that could be further customised through fine-tuning on a domain-specific dataset labelled with intents (Hien et al., 2018). NLP-based chatbots are limited, however, by their dependence on a fixed set of intents and responses, making them less adaptable to handle more complex and nuanced human conversations.

To overcome such limits, modern chatbots, particularly those that leverage advanced NLP techniques, can dynamically generate text based on the ongoing conversation and the user's inferred intent. A significant challenge within the field of Natural Language Generation (NLG), however, lies in effectively translating these internal representations and capturing the nuances of human language. LLMs have emerged as a prominent paradigm within NLP, demonstrating exceptional capabilities in chatbot development and NLG tasks.

Thus, generative AI chatbots have arisen; they perform particularly well since they can understand and generate human-like text responses. This ability allows them to engage in meaningful conversations with customers, addressing a wide array of inquiries with remarkable accuracy and a semblance of empathy (George & George, 2023). Unlike their rule-based predecessors, generative AI chatbots can handle complex and nuanced customer queries, providing tailored and contextually relevant responses. This level of interaction was once the sole domain of human-based customer service, but today it can be achieved at scale with AI.

Moreover, these advanced chatbots can learn from interactions, continuously improving their responses and adapting to new types of inquiries over time. This ability to learn and evolve makes them an invaluable asset for businesses in the aim or enhancing the efficiency and effectiveness of the customer service function (Aggarwal et al., 2023). Generative AI chatbots can provide immediate, 24/7 support across multiple channels, ensuring that customers receive timely assistance whenever they need it.

LLMs, built by using deep learning models, such as BERT, GPT, PaLM 2 or LLaMa 2, are based on transformer architecture (Vaswani et al., 2017). Such architecture is characterised by its use of stacked encoder and/or decoder blocks. Each of these blocks incorporates multi-head attention and feed-forward neural network layers. The sequential stacking of these blocks progressively enhances the model's representational capacity. This increased capacity empowers the model to learn intricate patterns and relationships within the training data.

The strategic deployment of generative AI chatbots can transform customer service from a cost centre into a valuable touchpoint for building customer relationships and loyalty (Batat, 2022). By delivering personalised experiences and engaging customers in meaningful conversations, these chatbots can significantly enhance customer satisfaction and retention. Furthermore, by handling routine inquiries, they free up human agents to tackle more complex and sensitive issues, thereby optimising resource allocation and enhancing the overall quality of customer service. In essence, generative AI-powered chatbots represent a new era in customer engagement, where the synergy between human intelligence and artificial intelligence can create unparalleled customer experiences. As these technologies continue to advance, their potential to innovate and enhance customer interactions is boundless, heralding a future where businesses can foster deeper and more meaningful connections with their customers.

7.3.2 No-Code Chatbots

Recent advancements in software development have witnessed the emergence of no-code and low-code solutions. These solutions empower individuals with minimal or no coding experience to create various applications (Bhattacharyya & Saurabh, 2021; Lethbridge, 2021). The adoption of no-code and low-code solutions presents several potential advantages for enterprises. These solutions can lead to time and cost savings while simultaneously accelerating development life cycles and enhancing product quality (Rokis & Marite, 2022). Mirroring the broader trends within software development, the chatbot development landscape is witnessing a surge in low-code and no-code solutions. This is evident in the proliferation of offerings from various market players, enabling the creation of chatbots even when one has minimal to no coding expertise.

The no-code chatbot paradigm represents a significant leap forward in chatbot development and integration. This approach allows for the creation and deployment of chatbots without the need for extensive coding, making it accessible to a broader range of users, including those that lack a technical background. No-code chatbots are characterised by their flexibility and ease of integration with advanced technologies, such as LLMs, including generative AI like ChatGPT. This synergy enables no-code chatbots to deliver more personalised, context-aware and conversational experiences that surpass the capabilities of traditional NLU-based chatbots. The no-code paradigm facilitates rapid development and iteration, allowing businesses to quickly adapt their chatbots to changing customer needs and preferences. The shift from the NLU chatbot to the no-code paradigm signifies a broader trend in AI and customer engagement technologies towards more accessible, flexible and powerful solutions. This transition enables businesses to harness the full potential of AI to create engaging, intelligent and conversational applications that meet the demands of today's dynamic digital landscapes. Some examples of a no-code or low-code platform for creating chatbots are

- DialogFlow: A bot-building platform that facilitates the development of conversational agents, including chatbots and voice applications. It leverages NLP techniques to enable these agents to interact with users in a natural and engaging manner. Additionally, the platform offers integration with various marketing channels.
- BotCore: A conversational AI development platform that leverages artificial intelligence, machine learning and NLP technologies to facilitate the creation of chatbots.
- Botsonic AI: A no-code chatbot development tool that uses GPT-4 to facilitate the creation of chatbots without the necessity for programming expertise. Notably, the platform allows users to leverage their own data for chatbot training, potentially leading to improved customisation and domain-specific performance.
- Landbot AI: A platform for creating chatbots designed to engage customers and enhance user experience within a business context. Landbot AI simplifies the chatbot development process by offering an intuitive user interface and readily available pre-built conversational elements.
- Botsify: A platform for building chatbots that prioritises user-friendliness and caters to businesses seeking solutions for customer engagement and support automation.
- Tiledesk: A platform enabling the creation of conversational applications powered by LLMs. It prioritises user-friendliness by employing a visual, block-based design approach, empowering individuals with limited coding experience, often referred to as *citizen developers*, to construct intricate chatbot functionalities.

7.4 Opportunities and Challenges for Chatbot Adoption

The integration of LLM-powered chatbots and conversational apps into company operations presents a spectrum of opportunities and challenges that are reshaping the landscape of business applications. This new paradigm, which emphasises chat-based interactions over traditional standalone applications, offers compelling advantages in terms of the efficiency, accessibility and democratisation of technology (Sundberg & Holmström, 2023).

No-code chatbot development platforms democratises access to AI for organisations. These platforms address the challenges faced by organisations with limited resources or technical expertise in AI development. By providing user-friendly interfaces and pre-built functionalities, such platforms empower users to develop and deploy AI models and tools without requiring in-depth knowledge of complex algorithms. Furthermore, the cloud-based nature of these platforms eliminates critical issues regarding installation, maintenance and management, thus simplifying the overall chatbot development process (Sundberg & Holmström, 2023).

Organisations are increasingly turning to low-code and no-code development platforms to meet the growing demands for speedy application delivery and highly customised automation workflows by equipping non-IT business professionals with the digital competencies and skills required from the modern agile environment. Chatbots perfectly fit these requirements and conditions, and organisations are shaping new business technologists and citizen technologists to develop lightweight solutions to achieve enhanced productivity, efficiency and agility (Gartner Forecasts Worldwide, 2023).

The increasing diffusion of low-code and no-code chatbot development tools allows organisations to achieve the following key opportunities (Sufi, 2023):

- Strictly align with business and IT requirements.
- Address resource scarcity, especially time and cost.
- Minimise the training time for using the platform services.
- Quickly develop and test prototypes and demos without huge investment.
- Favour the comparison of multiple AI algorithms used to develop chatbot services.
- Ensure cybersecurity by design.
- Outsource infrastructure maintenance through cloud-based services.

At the same time, low-code and no-code platforms are unlikely to eliminate the need for manual coding in the future, suggesting an evolutionary rather than revolutionary effect on research practices (Bock & Frank, 2021). This is fundamentally due to the following challenges that such platforms continue to face:

- Limited customisation.
- Lack of flexibility and on-premise support.
- Integration difficulties.
- Platform dependence and migration problems.
- Scaling complications.

7.5 The Case of Tiledesk's No-Code Chatbot

Within the field of no-code development platforms, this case study investigates the Tiledesk platform (https://tiledesk.com/) by showing the value it can generate to address the automation of business operations.

Tiledesk is an emerging prominent framework in the no-code development landscape, especially for creating LLM-enabled conversational applications. It is an open-source platform (with MIT licence), thus promoting community contributions and offering flexibility for customisation and installation in private cloud or data centres.

It is designed to empower businesspeople and individuals who lack extensive coding skills to build complex chatbot functionalities by providing them with a visual and block-based design approach. This shift from intent-based to block-based logic enables users to visually assemble chatbot conversations and workflows, making the process more intuitive and accessible.

As shown in Fig. 7.1, the platform has integrated LLMs like ChatGPT to enhance chatbot responses and decision-making capabilities. This integration allows blocks within the chatbot flow to analyse user input and make decisions, thus enhancing the dynamism and intelligence of the entire conversational application.

Tiledesk is equipped with a proper design studio that enables a visual and no-code design of applications without relying on third-party libraries, thus ensuring a wide range of accessibility and customisation options. The platform aims to simplify the development of conversational apps by enabling a drag-and-drop interface

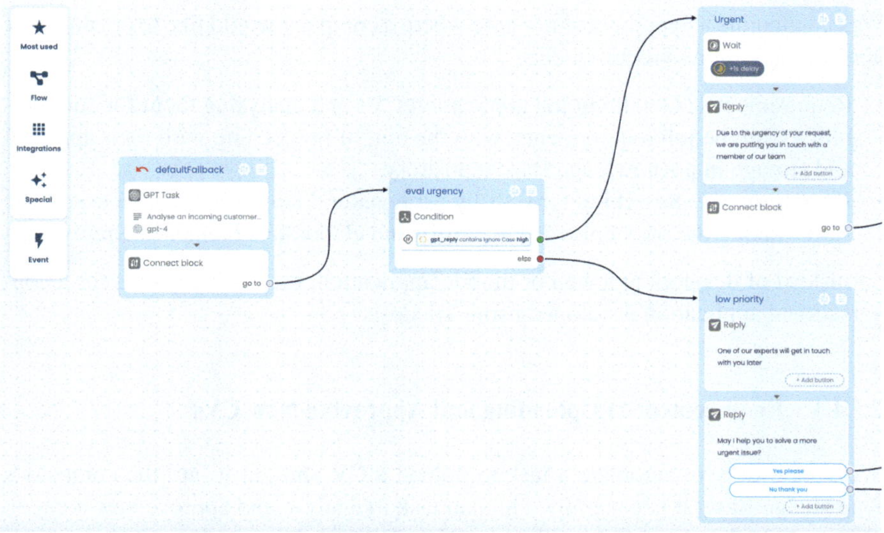

Fig. 7.1 Integration of Tiledesk with LLMs

for connecting logical blocks, including those powered by AI, to design complex conversational flows without writing any lines of code.

Tiledesk offers user-friendly interfaces and pre-built functionalities that empower users to deploy AI models and develop chatbot applications, thus eliminating the need for in-depth knowledge of complex algorithms and integration of complex technological architectures. Additionally, the cloud-based nature of this platform eliminates concerns regarding its installation, maintenance and management, thus significantly simplifying the overall chatbot development process.

The application development process proposed by Tiledesk consists of assembling pre-built AI components that are visualised as modular blocks. These blocks are chained together in a user-defined sequence, and a specific input format is defined for each of them (e.g. CSV extension) for generating a definite output (e.g. a CSV or image) that serves as the input for the next block. Once the chatbot application is deployed, it can be accessed through a conversational interface, such as WhatsApp. This triggers the execution of the defined workflow, where each block performs its designated function according to the user's profile.

This methodological approach realises a paradigm shift in application development since it eliminates the need for traditional programming languages by offering an intuitive and potentially more accessible method of building applications. This approach ushers in a new era of conversational applications, where user interaction and application functionalities are seamlessly integrated within a conversational interface.

7.5.1 A Demo Scenario

We can imagine a hypothetical use case where a company would like to create a new application with two requirements:

- Requirement 1: Obtaining job application CVs and analysing them for compatibility with the job requirements, with the aim of proceeding with their approval and storage in a Knowledge Base repository.
- Requirement 2: Searching for CVs by using natural language to indicate specific skills among the ones uploaded to certify and elaborate a human-like reply.

Instead of developing a web or mobile application, the company opts for a conversational application developed using Tiledesk.

7.5.1.1 Requirement 1: Uploading and Approving New CVs

While it is easy to automate a task to upload a CV and put it into the company's Knowledge Base, it is generally a human task to analyse and approve new content. This task is delegated to an AI task. With Tiledesk Visual Flow Designer, it is

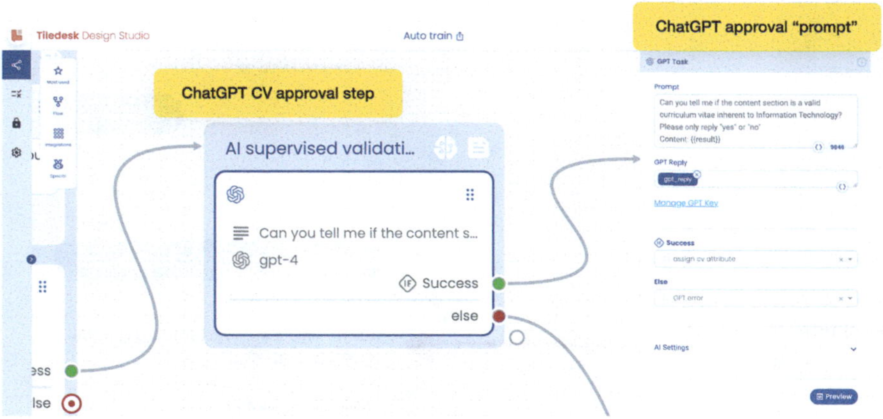

Fig. 7.2 Setting up a ChatGPT action block in Tiledesk

possible to create an OpenAI task to approve new CVs. Figure 7.2 shows how to setup a ChatGPT action block.

A GPT task action block is embedded in the flow. It receives the uploaded CV and analyses it through a specific prompt as follows:

> ChatGPT prompt: 'Can you tell me if the content section is a valid curriculum vitae inherent to Information Technology? Please only reply yes or no'.

ChatGPT receives the CV content and replies after analysing it accordingly to the prompt. The output (yes or no) will be used to move on within the flow accordingly.

With a simple 'drag and drop' operation and the right 'prompt' configuration, Tiledesk just replaced a human task with an automated one, and the task is executed in real time. Figure 7.3 shows the flow of interactions between the chatbot and the user for CV upload and validation.

7.5.1.2 Requirement 2: Search for a CV Using Natural Language

To implement this requirement, a special trend in chatbot design is used, such as retrieval-augmented generation (RAG). RAG is a sophisticated process that enriches the inputs to a Large Language Model like ChatGPT with additional information, typically by accessing a knowledge base. This approach allows RAG chatbots to use the advanced linguistic understanding of models like ChatGPT while extending their knowledge infinitely. Essentially, a RAG chatbot acts as a bridge between retrieval-based models, which search databases for the most relevant answers, and generative models, which dynamically create responses. Such a combination provides three main advantages: using advanced language understanding without the need to train an LLM from scratch, expanding the chatbot's knowledge base and making content searches interactive and intuitive.

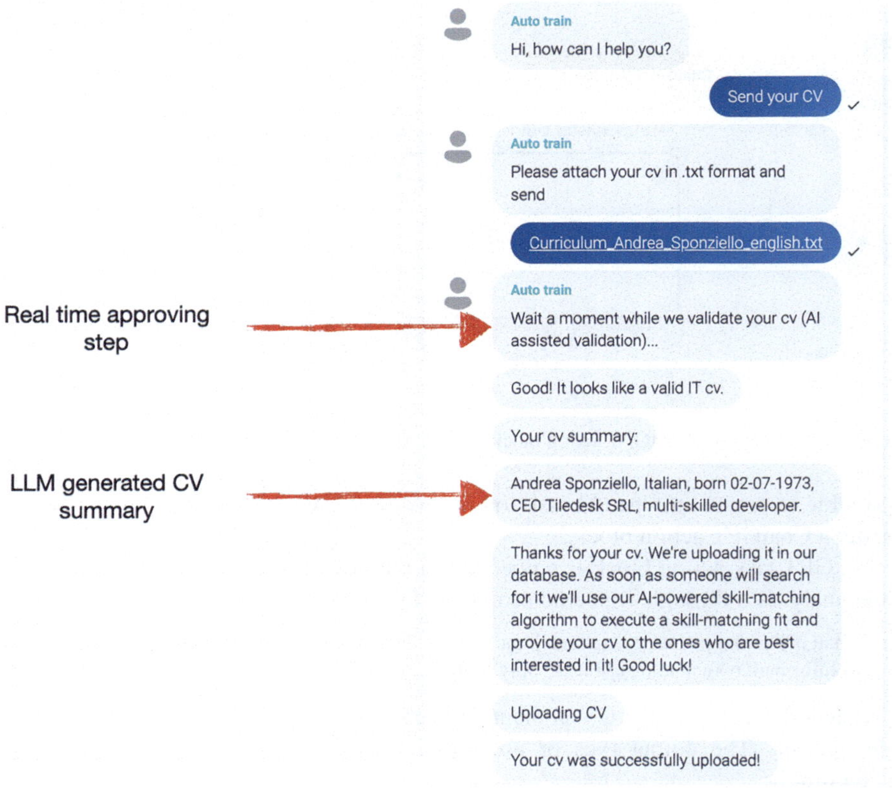

Fig. 7.3 Flow of interactions between the chatbot and the user for CV upload and validation

During the approval task, the CV is submitted and approved by a special engine that indexes the contents through a RAG indexing engine.

Afterwards, without using coding skills, it is possible to simply drag and drop on the stage an 'Ask the Knowledge Base' action. This is a special action able to query previously indexed contents by using a vector data store and OpenAI, mixing the two to find the content and generating an appropriate human-like reply for the end user, as shown in Fig. 7.4.

Much logic is involved in this task, but Visual Designer hides its complexity and makes this automation accessible to anyone, even those with no coding skill. Figure 7.5 shows a demo session of a chatbot–user interaction.

The RAG chatbot can correctly understand the human query, replying in a human-like way. The total time-to-market of this application was about 2 h. A visual approach to AI-application composition boosted the application development, together with the choice to develop a conversational application rather than a traditional UI-based application.

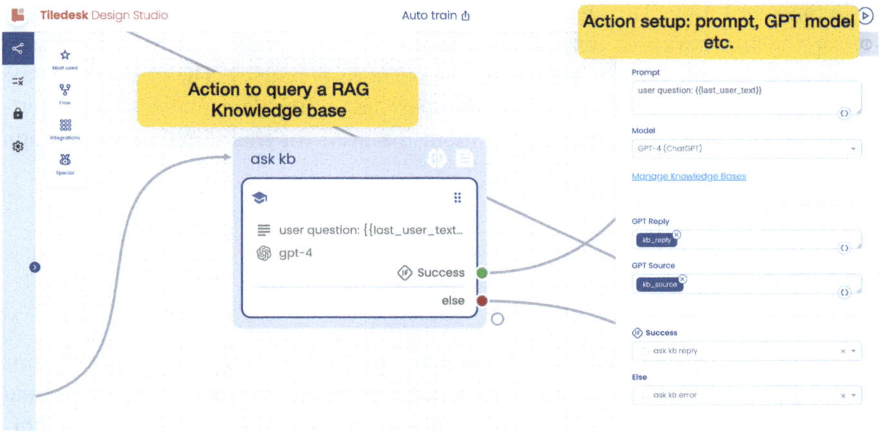

Fig. 7.4 Combination of a vector data store and OpenAI to find contents and generate proper human-like replies

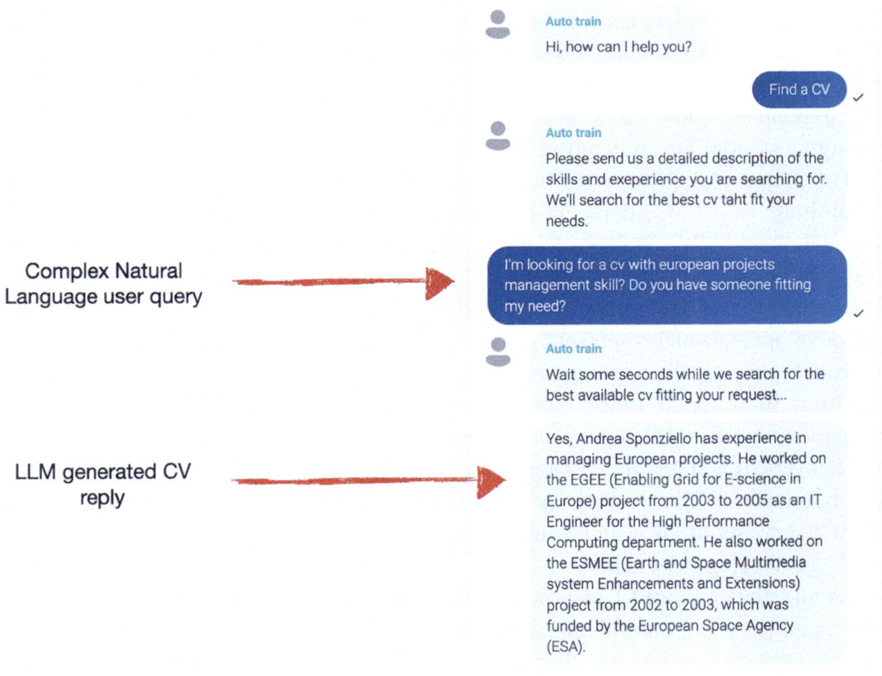

Fig. 7.5 User interface: AI Chatbot powered by vector data store and OpenAI, displaying generated responses

In the near future, Tiledesk plans to extend its capabilities beyond customer service applications to more general business-use cases, leveraging LLM technologies to automate repetitive tasks and streamline business processes. The goal is to create conversational apps that can perform complex tasks, like data analysis and reporting, through simple dialogues and without the need for traditional coding or app development processes.

7.6 Conclusions

Conversational chatbots represent a research topic that crosses four distinct streams of literature: human behaviour, interactions between information systems and humans, communication, and personal information disclosure and anthropomorphism (Bălan, 2023). They denote the current frontier of human–machine interaction that leverages the power of AI to create a more intuitive and engaging user experience, enabling interactions to flow naturally within a chat interface. By leveraging natural language processing and AI algorithms, they can 'understand and produce natural language, learn from experience and portray emotions' (Bălan, 2023; Hoyer et al., 2020). Indeed, conversational chatbots significantly reduce the learning adoption curve for non-IT users as they leverage the familiar format of messaging, making complex tasks more approachable and less daunting than navigating through a standalone application.

The increasing diffusion of no-code development platforms, augmented by the capabilities of LLMs, democratises the creation of sophisticated conversational applications which contribute to bridge the gap between business and information technology experts (Masili, 2023). By eliminating the need for extensive coding, companies can save significant time and bypass the high costs associated with hiring developers, which represent today a scarce and very expensive resource. This approach not only lowers expenses but also accelerates the development process, resulting in a much lower time-to-market for new applications and features. Moreover, the Visual Designer tools integrated into no-code platforms make chatbot and conversational tool development accessible to a wider range of personnel within an organisation. This inclusivity fosters a culture of innovation and allows for a more diverse set of ideas and solutions to emerge from various departments, not just the IT or development teams.

Finally, the usage of LLM-powered chatbots within organisations to provide customers with a more natural and attractive user experience creates also the opportunity for the organisation to collect, process and analyse vast amounts of data rapidly, thus providing valuable insights and reports. This function can significantly enhance decision-making processes for management, offering fast, data-driven analysis that supports strategic planning and operational efficiency.

Despite these opportunities, however, the integration of LLM-powered chatbots and conversational apps is not without any risks or challenges. For example, ensuring data privacy and security within these conversational interfaces is paramount, as they often handle sensitive customer data and company information (Uma, 2023). Additionally, maintaining the accuracy and relevance of the AI's responses requires ongoing monitoring and updating to reflect changes to a company's policies, products, services and communication strategy. Finally, ensuring that these AI systems can understand and appropriately respond to the nuances and complexities of human language and intent may represent a critical issue to manage.

In conclusion, the transition towards LLM-powered chatbots and conversational apps represents a significant shift in how businesses approach application development and customer engagement. By prioritising conversational interactions, companies can leverage the benefits of reduced costs, increased accessibility and rapid deployment, all while facing and addressing the challenges inherent in adopting cutting-edge AI technologies. This approach not only streamlines operations but also opens up new avenues for innovation and customer interaction.

Acknowledgement This chapter was partially developed with the financial support of Apulia region (Italy) in the framework of P.O. FESR 2014-2020—TECNONIDI, and Invitalia in the framework of Cultura Crea 2.0—Asse Prioritario II PON 'Cultura e Sviluppo' 2014–2020.

References

Adamopoulou, E., & Moussiades, L. (2020). Chatbots: History, technology, and applications. *Machine Learning with Applications, 2*.

Aggarwal, L., Vasisht, U., Kanwar, R., Kumar, A., & Goswami, P. (2023). *Analyzing Chatgpt based on large language model from industrial perspective*. Available at SSRN 4563696.

Amitrano, C. C., Russo Spena, T., & Bifulco, F. (2021). Digital engagement and customer experience. Digital transformation in the cultural heritage sector: Challenges to marketing in the new digital era, 119–136.

Bag, S., Srivastava, G., Bashir, M. M. A., Kumari, S., Giannakis, M., & Chowdhury, A. H. (2022). Journey of customers in this digital era: Understanding the role of artificial intelligence technologies in user engagement and conversion. *Benchmarking: An International Journal, 29*(7), 2074–2098.

Bălan, C. (2023). Chatbots and voice assistants: Digital transformers of the company-customer interface—A systematic review of the business research literature. *Journal of Theoretical and Applied Electronic Commerce Research, 18*(2), 995–1019.

Batat, W. (2022). When customer experience encounters digital technologies. In *Strategies for the digital customer experience* (pp. 49–77). Edward Elgar Publishing.

Bhattacharyya, S. S., & Saurabh, K. (2021). Study of deployment of "low code no code" applications toward improving digitization of supply chain management. *Journal of Science and Technology Policy Management, 14*(2), 271–287.

Bock, A. C., & Frank, U. (2021). Low-code platform. *Business Information Systems Engineering, 63*, 733–740.

Devlin, J., Chang, M. W., Lee, K., & Toutanova, K. (2019). BERT: Pre-training of deep bidirectional transformers for language understanding. In *Proceedings of the 2019 conference of the North American chapter of the Association for Computational Linguistics: Human language technologies, NAACL-HLT 2019. 1* (pp. 4171–4186). Minneapolis, MN, USA: Association for Computational Linguistics.

Gartner Forecasts Worldwide Low-Code Development Technologies Market to Grow 20% in 2023. https://www.gartner.com/en/newsroom/press-releases/2022-12-13-gartner-forecasts-worldwide-low-code-development-technologies-market-to-grow-20-percent-in-2023

George, A. S., & George, A. H. (2023). A review of ChatGPT AI's impact on several business sectors. *Partners Universal International Innovation Journal, 1*(1), 9–23.

Gupta, R., Nair, K., Mishra, M., Ibrahim, B., & Bhardwaj, S. (2024). Adoption and impacts of generative artificial intelligence: Theoretical underpinnings and research agenda. *International Journal of Information Management Data Insights, 4*(1), 100232.

Hepziba, E., & Florence, J. (2020). Role of chat-bots in customer engagement valence. *Psychology & Education, 57*(9), 2181–2186.

Hien, H. T., Cuong, P.-N., Nam, L. N. H., Nhung, H. L. T. K., & Thang, L. D. (2018). Intelligent assistants in higher-education environments: The FIT-EBot, a chatbot for administrative and learning support. In *Proceedings of the ninth international symposium on information and communication technology* (pp. 69–76). ACM.

Hill, J., Ford, W. R., & Farreras, I. G. (2015). Real conversations with artificial intelligence: A comparison between human–human online conversations and human–Chatbot conversations. *Computers in Human Behavior, 49*, 245–250.

Hopkins, B., & Silverman, A. (2016). *The top emerging technologies to watch: 2017 to 2021*. https://www.forrester.com/report/The+Top+Emerging+Technologies+To+Watch+2017+To+2021/-/E-RES133144

Hoyer, W. D., Kroschke, M., Schmitt, B., Kraume, K., & Shankar, V. (2020). Transforming the customer experience through new technologies. *Journal of Interactive Marketing, 51*(1), 57–71.

Jung, S. (2019). Semantic vector learning for natural language understanding. *Computer Speech & Language, 56*, 130–145.

Kar, A. K., Varsha, P. S., & Rajan, S. (2023). Unravelling the impact of generative artificial intelligence (GAI) in industrial applications: A review of scientific and grey literature. *Global Journal of Flexible Systems Management, 24*(4), 659–689.

Larivière, B., Bowen, D., Andreassen, T. W., Kunz, W., Sirianni, N. J., Voss, C., et al. (2017). Service encounter 2.0: An investigation into the roles of technology, employees and customers. *Journal of Business Research, 79*, 238–246.

Lebeuf, C., Storey, M., & Zagalsky, A. (2018). Software bots. *IEEE Software, 35*(1), 18–23.

Lethbridge, T. C. (2021). *Low-code is often high-code, so we must design low-code platforms to enable proper software engineering. Leveraging applications of formal methods, verification and validation: 10th international symposium on leveraging applications of formal methods, ISoLA 2021, Rhodes, Greece, October 17–29, 2021, proceedings 10*. Springer.

Lin, L., D'Haro, L., & Banchs, R. (2016). *A web-based platform for collection of human-chatbot interactions* (pp. 363–366). https://doi.org/10.1145/2974804.2980500

Masili, G. (2023). No-code development platforms: Breaking the boundaries between IT and business experts. *International Journal of Economic Behavior (IJEB), 13*(1), 33–49.

Mattas, P. S. (2023). *ChatGPT: A study of AI language processing and its implications*. Journal homepage: www.ijrpr.com ISSN 2582 (2023): 7421.

McShane, M. (2017). Natural language understanding (NL, unot NLP) in cognitive systems. *AI Magazine, 38*(4), 43–56.

Paul, J., Ueno, A., & Dennis, C. (2023). ChatGPT and consumers: Benefits, pitfalls and future research agenda. *International Journal of Consumer Studies, 47*(4), 1213–1225. https://doi.org/10.1111/ijcs.12928

Pounder, J. (2016). *Huddle—Humanity in the machine*. Mindshare. https://www.mindshareworld.com/sites/default/files/mindshare_Huddle_humanity_machine_2016_0.pdf

Raymond, J. (2001). No more shoppus interruptus. *American Demographics, 23*(5), 39–40.

Reddy, T. (2017). *How chatbots can help reduce customer service costs by 30%*. https://www.ibm.com/blogs/watson/2017/10/how-chatbots-reduce-customer-service-costs-by-30-percent/

Rokis, K., & Marite, K. (2022). *Challenges of low-code/no-code software development: A literature review. International conference on business informatics research*. Springer.

Shah, S. J. H. (2023). Chatbots for business and customer support. In *Trends, applications, and challenges of Chatbot technology* (pp. 212–221). IGI Global.

Sufi, F. (2023). Algorithms in low-code-no-code for research applications: A practical review. *Algorithms, 16*, 108.

Sun, X., Chen, X., Pei, Z., & Ren, F. (2018). Emotional human machine conversation generation based on SeqGAN. In *Proceedings of the 2018 first Asian conference on Affective Computing and Intelligent Interaction (ACII Asia), Beijing, China, 20–22 May 2018* (pp. 1–6).

Sundberg, L., & Holmström, J. (2023). Democratizing artificial intelligence: How no-code AI can leverage machine learning operations. *Business Horizons, 66*(6), 777–788.

Uma, S. (2023). Conversational AI Chatbots in digital engagement: Privacy and security concerns. In *Trends, applications, and challenges of Chatbot technology* (pp. 274–317). IGI Global.

Vaswani, A., et al. (2017). Attention is all you need. *Advances in Neural Information Processing Systems, 30.*

Verhagen, T., Van Nes, J., Feldberg, F., & Van Dolen, W. (2014). Virtual customer service agents: Using social presence and personalization to shape online service encounters. *Journal of Computer-Mediated Communication, 19*(3), 529–545.

Chapter 8
The Smart City as a Model of Digital Innovation for Urban Development

Gianmarco Girardo, Alessandro Bartolini, and Giuseppina Passiante

Abstract The chapter deals with the development of smart cities as a model of digital innovation for urban development. The main factors that characterise smart cities are analysed, including innovation, environmental sustainability, intelligent mobility, human and social capital, and participatory governance. The integration of the Internet of Things (IoT) is identified as a crucial element for connecting the physical and virtual world, optimising urban resources and improving public services. The role of low power wide area networks (LPWAN) in supporting IoT applications, essential for the creation of smart cities, is also explored. Finally, the chapter examines the main application areas of smart cities, including intelligent buildings, energy management, environmental monitoring, urban mobility and territorial security, underlining how these technologies can improve the quality of life of citizens and promote sustainability. It is therefore analysed how the A2A group, a leading company in digital transformation and sustainability, implements technological solutions for the purpose of creating smart cities.

Keywords Smart city · Digital innovation · Sustainability · Internet of Things (IoT) · Low power wide area networks (LPWAN) · Intelligent mobility · Smart governance · Environmental monitoring

G. Girardo (✉) · A. Bartolini
A2A Smart City – A2A Group, Milan, Italy
e-mail: gianmarco.girardo@a2asmartcity.it; alessandro.bartolini@a2asmartcity.it

G. Passiante
Department of Engineering for Innovation, University of Salento, Lecce, Italy
e-mail: giusppina.passiante@unisalento.it

G. Passiante (ed.), *Digital Innovation Management*, Applied Innovation and Technology Management, https://doi.org/10.1007/978-3-031-80426-7_8

8.1 Introduction

A wide array of studies has focused on the new competitive space generated by the digital economy, which is changing the urban economy's behaviour and boosting the development of urban innovation processes (Shy et al., 2023).

As a result of these processes, innovation communities are emerging: complex arrangement of innovation technologies, methodologies, applications, organisations and institutional contexts (Ciasullo et al., 2020). In these innovation communities, each enterprise adds one or more distinct aspects of a product/service for the end consumer by exchanging digital knowledge with other members. Four key factors characterise smart communities in the world of innovation: an increasing number of players, an increasing level of connectivity among the players, space and the time independence of their relations (Passiante et al., 1999). These four factors, taken in isolation, are not new, but their combined effect represents a major discontinuity in the world of innovation and suggests the need to re-think the dynamics of urban innovation ecosystems.

An urban innovation ecosystem here must be conceived not in terms of a set of organisations or actors (e.g. citizens, innovations, institutions) but as the network of its interactions, which develop according to a variable geometry, also using digital technologies. Individual actors interact incessantly with each other, and this interaction determines, at a meso-level, a particular configuration of the urban innovation ecosystem related to its specific intellectual capital resources (human capital, structural capital and social capital), as well as its development and its evolutionary path.

According to this perspective, the concept of a *smart city* represents a modern urban model that seeks to enhance and streamline the lives of its inhabitants and the broader urban environment. The development of smart cities is currently, following an initial phase in 2012–2013, in its second phase of growth marked by the integration of the Internet of Things (IoT). The foundation for these advancements is the significant urbanisation trend, where urban populations are surpassing rural ones, necessitating a focus on sustainability.

In Italy, the progression of smart cities has been shaped by smart metering legislation. The 'Autorità per l'Energia Elettrica, il Gas e l'Acqua' enforced the ARG/GAS 155/08 regulation in October 2008, mandating the installation of 17.5 million smart gas meters by 2018. To comply, gas utilities had to establish the requisite technological infrastructure. Given the substantial investments required for these implementations, it was possible to consider a multi-service approach to expedite investment returns (Di Castelnuovo & Fumagalli, 2013).

Regarding technology, various solutions exist, but this chapter will concentrate on low power wide area networks (LPWANs), the latest generation among enabling technologies, addressing the four critical consumption criteria: low power, long range, low traffic and low cost. The most viable options within this category are SigFox and LoRaWAN, which differ in respects like communication requirements, security and certification. Despite these differences, both LoRa and SigFox provide cost-effective and energy-efficient solutions for Internet of Things (IoT) and machine-to-machine (M2M) applications.

Lastly, it is essential to outline the potential application areas for smart city initiatives. These include building, entertainment, environmental monitoring, inclusion, lighting, metering, mobility management, territory monitoring, public transport, security, smart waste management and smart water grid.

8.2 The Urban Revolution: A Journey Through Smart Cities

Most definitions of smart cities identify such cities as those where technology is used to improve the services provided to the community and its residents. Therefore, a smart city can be described as the use of advanced information technology to make infrastructure elements and critical services, including administration, education, health, public safety, real estate, transport and utilities more intelligent, interconnected and efficient.

The challenges of climate change, population growth, urbanisation and resource depletion mean that the world's major cities must adapt to ensure their survival and prosperity. Cities, in fact, occupy only 2% of the earth's surface but emit nearly 80% of global carbon dioxide and significant amounts of other greenhouse gases, so rethinking the city model from a smart city perspective is necessary in this scenario.

Smart cities can be identified according to six main attributes (Somayya & Romaswamy, 2014):

- Smart economy: innovation and competitiveness.
- Smart mobility: infrastructure and transport.
- Smart environment: resource efficiency and sustainability.
- Smart people: creativity and social capital.
- Smart living: evolving lifestyles.
- Smart governance: citizen participation and empowerment.

8.2.1 Smart Economy: Innovation and Competitiveness

Before outlining its characteristics, it is appropriate to provide a broader definition of economics. The economy is the system that regulates the production, distribution, trade and consumption of limited goods and services between two or more actors, which may be individuals, enterprises, organisations or governments.

The special features of the smart economy mainly include a focus on a high-quality education system, publicly funded scientific research, favourable tax incentives for business, excellent infrastructure, high-quality national and international connections, widespread broadband deployment and the presence of excellent public services, including, by way of example, healthcare.

8.2.2 Smart Mobility: Infrastructure and Transport

The central objective of smart mobility is to promote climate change and energy-efficiency goals. This encompasses real-time traffic management, passenger transport control, parking regulation, tolling, support for electric vehicles and the implementation of tracking and logistics applications, as well as the adoption of bike- or car-sharing services and more.

Several solutions contribute to the implementation of smart mobility. These include video surveillance and AI-based analysis of images and videos for constant traffic monitoring and number plate recognition. In addition, integrated information systems are becoming increasingly common in vehicles. With passengers and drivers enjoying increasing access to the network on board various means of transport, such as buses, trains, boats and planes, the possibility of accessing vehicle-generated data opens up. This makes it possible to monitor the vehicle and share environmental information acquired through RFID, computers, sensors, CCTV or embedded cameras.

8.2.3 Smart Environment: Resource Efficiency and Sustainability

The smart environment is a context enriched with sensors, actuators and IT components capable of sensing, calculating, communicating and managing the interactions between individuals and the spaces in which they reside. For example, building doors, domestic lighting, water taps, heating or ventilation systems in offices are just some of the elements that can be designed to adapt to people's needs, as well as constantly monitor environmental parameters.

8.2.4 Smart People: Creativity and Social Capital

The assessment of a smart city is not only limited to the availability and quality of the information and communications technology infrastructure (ICT). The essential role of human capital, represented by citizens and education in urban development, is paramount. Numerous studies indicate that cities with a high percentage of an educated workforce and citizens with a high sense of citizenship achieve the highest urban growth rates.

The acceptance and inclusion of citizens are crucial to the success of the technological and political ambitions of smart cities. After all, citizens are the main reason for the existence of the city and its policies. In the context of smart people, several factors, such as social and ethnic plurality, flexibility, creativity, cosmopolitanism and active participation in public life, emerge as key elements. From the smart people perspective, citizen participation in citizen science projects emerges as a decisive lever for their transformation into smart citizens.

8.2.5 Smart Living: Evolving Living

The concept of *smart living* is articulated through the reality of 'smart people' in cities and 'smart environments', with the home serving as the fundamental environment.

From a smart living perspective, the smart home is configured as a place with appliances connected in a pervasive network, facilitating communication between them and with the owner or inhabitants. The objective is to monitor and optimise the use of electricity and general energy, as well as to control indoor air quality to mitigate possible health problems.

Automation through IoT technology and devices enables the creation of a system aimed at

- Detecting users and social connections between them.
- Accessing user data.
- Determining the social context based on network topology, user preferences and characteristics.
- Setting social objectives according to the social context and user profile.
- Coordinating user behaviour by raising awareness of environmental and energy issues.
- Providing an output based on the analysed context.

8.2.6 Smart Governance: Innovation for the City of the Future

Governance constitutes the manifestation of political, economic and administrative authority in managing the socio-cultural and economic environment of a country. It represents the set of mechanisms, processes and institutions through which citizens and groups express their interests, exercise their legal rights and duties and resolve their differences.

From this governance perspective, smart governance can be defined as the set of future-oriented practices of public services in cities. The main objective is to achieve greater efficiency, community leadership, working flexibility, sound infrastructure and continuous improvement through innovation.

Technology is at the heart of this process, facilitating and supporting decision-making processes in metropolitan cities, reforming how public services are delivered and moving towards greater efficiency, effectiveness and transparency.

Smart city governance incorporates the use of electronic devices in government offices, video conferencing systems, surveillance and tracking networks, such as

RFID tags, smart cards, sensors and actuators. It also makes use of communication channels, such as television, radio, newspapers and social media, to provide information and services to citizens in cities.

IoT technologies offer the possibility of uniting the physical and virtual worlds through the identification of objects, collection, analysis and communication of information. IoT technology is fundamental for building smart cities for several reasons. Firstly, it enables the efficient management of urban resources, improving the quality of public services, such as lighting, waste management and public transportation. Additionally, IoT allows real-time monitoring of various environmental parameters, contributing to greater sustainability and safety. The collection and analysis of data, made possible by IoT, provide a solid basis for making informed and timely decisions, optimising the operation of urban infrastructures and enhancing the quality of life for citizens. In the next section, we will delve further into the reasons IoT is so crucial for the development of smart cities.

8.3 The Internet of Things: Connecting the Physical and Virtual Worlds

The IoT paradigm is not bound to a single technology; on the contrary, depending on the project or sector context, different communication networks are suggested to meet specific needs.

IoT devices vary considerably in size, cost and autonomy but share a common three-tier architecture: interface with the physical world, mediation and a control centre. This structure allows a harmonious connection between objects in the real world and their control in the virtual world, providing flexibility and adaptability to different contexts and sectors.

8.3.1 First Level: Interface with the Physical World

The first level includes sensors and tags, both of which are characterised by wide pervasiveness and deployment. These devices interact with their surroundings, providing a unique identifier in the form of a code and acquiring data from the field or issuing commands to an actuator. There are two categories of nodes: passive tags, which have no power supply, and battery-powered tags, which have limited processing power and memory. The cost varies depending on the application, ranging from a few eurocents up to 30–150 euros. Service life depends on usage, being naturally longer for passive tags, which can last up to 10 years.

8.3.2 *Second Level: Communication Hub in the IoT Ecosystem*

The second level consists of gateways, RFID readers, translators and repeaters, which are responsible for collecting data from the first level of sensors. Their main task is to aggregate this data and then transmit it to the central processing system. These devices are characterised by their higher processing and storage capacity, different communication interfaces and variable cost.

8.3.3 *Third Level: SAC and Information Systems in IoT Data Integration*

The third level houses the SAC (Centralized Acquisition System), which stands for central acquisition systems, together with information systems and operational infrastructures dedicated to data management. The responsibilities of this level include the collection of information from the previous level, the management of the architecture, the storage and processing of data and finally the availability of the information obtained. The cost of these devices varies widely, depending on the specific characteristics of the information system.

8.3.4 *LPWA: The Internet of Things Revolution*

Low power wide area (LPWA) technology presents itself as the leader, fulfilling all the necessary requirements to overcome the limitations of WiFi, Bluetooth and traditional 2G, 3G and 4G networks.

Designed to meet the four 'Ls'—*low power, long range, low traffic* and *low cost*—LPWA adopts a scheme that prioritises energy conservation over data rate. This optimisation makes it ideal for machine-to-machine and IoT applications, where low power consumption and limited data transmission are crucial. At the same time, LPWA ensures wide coverage, potentially exceeding that of a traditional mobile phone cell.

Unlike other approaches, LPWA does not require expensive licences to allocate radio spectrum bands. The cost of setting up public wireless infrastructure, however, is significant, and the time required to achieve adequate coverage for a wide audience is considerable.

In the LPWA network landscape, the main technology is currently long-range wide area network (LoRaWAN), developed by Semtech, a semiconductor manufacturer. LoRaWAN, with bands of 868 and 915 MHz and a bandwidth of less than 500 KHz, is a non-proprietary technology supported by the LoRa Alliance. Founded in

December 2014, this association includes companies such as Semtech, Microchip, Link Labs and Embit.

8.4 Smart City Application Areas

The smart city brings with it different and numerous areas of application. This section summarises the functionalities of each and presents the technologies that foster the IoT paradigm.

8.4.1 Intelligent Construction: Transforming Building Habits

This system is designed to bring intelligence to buildings, offering services beyond the capabilities of traditional buildings, such as tracking energy costs over time. Accessible through web interfaces or smartphone apps, a variety of services are available:

- Security: This includes the monitoring of potential gas leaks, the structural integrity of buildings and the presence of unwanted individuals.
- Preventive maintenance: The application of sensors at critical points allows the monitoring of the wear and tear on specific installations, optimising maintenance management to detect and resolve problems promptly, thus extending service life.
- Energy management: Recognising that the building sector contributes significantly to global energy consumption, this system focuses on efficient energy management. Buildings, responsible for one-third of total energy-related CO_2 emissions, require targeted action. Energy policy instruments, evolving since the 1990s, have been extended to include new non-residential buildings and existing buildings during renovations.

Existing public buildings can consume considerable amounts of energy due to their inefficient building envelopes, outdated installations and lack of management systems. Targeted policies are essential to reducing the carbon footprint and energy consumption of existing buildings.

8.4.2 Framework for the Enhancement of Cultural Heritage

This framework aims to support and promote cultural and artistic heritage through the implementation of advanced technologies. Commonly, use is made of chips associated with near-field communication (NFC) technology or QR codes, placed near monuments or other places of interest. These elements interact with visitors' handheld devices, enabling the exchange of contextual information to enrich the visitor experience. While NFC technology is often used, QR codes offer a viable alternative, although they are not directly part of the IoT paradigm.

8.4.3 Environmental Monitoring: A Sustainable City

Through a widespread network of sensors scattered throughout the territory, several parameters essential for environmental monitoring can be monitored. The main aspects subject to monitoring include

- Air pollution: By measuring the concentration of elements like fine dust and carbon dioxide, it is possible to assess the air quality in different areas of the city. This data enables rapid corrective action to be taken, such as limiting vehicle access if pre-determined thresholds are exceeded.
- Water pollution: Like air, monitoring extends to the concentration of elements such as heavy metals, chemical waste and fertilisers. This approach aims to preserve various aquatic ecosystems.
- Wastewater monitoring: This area involves monitoring pollution levels in rivers or areas close to the sea. The objective is to make informed decisions on discharge permits and authorisations, helping to promote the city's overall environmental sustainability.

8.4.4 Smart Lighting for a Sustainable City

Public lighting, which accounts for a significant portion of total energy consumption, offers vast potential for energy savings through efficient lighting systems based on electronic control. The energy consumption associated with streetlights comes mainly from inefficient systems that require large amounts of energy. Furthermore, in life cycle terms, the main costs associated with conventional lighting come from their operation, including energy and maintenance, rather than from the initial investment costs.

Estimates indicate that Europe could save up to three billion euros by switching from a conventional system to one based on new street lighting technologies. The adoption of solid-state light-emitting diodes (LEDs), driven by significant financial and technological forces, has revolutionised the lighting industry. LEDs offer longer system life, lower energy consumption and less environmental damage than conventional solutions.

Through intelligent control, LEDs have ushered in a new generation of intelligent lighting, integrating sensors and controls with various connectivity interfaces. In street lighting, intelligent LED lighting networks enable dimming, occupancy control and optimal lighting operations. This not only reduces energy consumption but also prolongs service life and decreases the need for maintenance, reducing the overall system costs (Castro et al., 2013).

8.4.5 Smart Metering: Energy Optimisation for a Sustainable Future

The innovative *smart metering* technology revolutionises energy efficiency, enabling the precise control of consumption and measurement of potential savings in various areas. Founded on a control system based on a network of sensors for real-time monitoring, smart metering offers the possibility of accurate billing and setting tariffs more suitable for users, eliminating the need for periodic checks by operators (Krishnamurti et al., 2012).

Key features include

- Real-time monitoring: enables the real-time monitoring of energy consumption, ensuring more efficient management and greater consumer awareness of consumption.
- Precise billing: eliminates billing errors through accurate consumption tracking.
- Anomaly detection: allows the control and timely verification of any anomalies in the system.

This approach offers significant advantages, including the ability to explore new commercial opportunities through the detailed mapping of users' energy behaviour. In addition, it allows the creation of new commercial proposals and the instantaneous adjustment of prices according to supply and demand dynamics, optimising the entire commercial chain.

The four main types of smart metering include

- Smart electric metering.
- Smart water metering.
- Smart gas metering.
- Smart heat metering.

This versatile system aims to shape a sustainable energy future by providing targeted solutions to specific monitoring and metering needs.

8.4.6 Optimising Urban Mobility Through Smart Cities

Mobility management stands out as one of the most relevant areas of smart cities, promising significant benefits and savings for citizens and the community both in terms of time and emission reductions.

In large cities, the traffic problem is an urgent issue to be addressed, as moving millions of people every day requires adequate infrastructure. IoT technology presents itself as a key solution, generating benefits in three main areas: traffic monitoring and management, information mobility and parking management.

Using sensors and traffic light technologies, real-time traffic information can be collected. This data is used to optimise the flow of public transport, ambulances and emergency vehicles, reducing road congestion: for example, by dynamically adjusting traffic lights to improve the flow of intersections.

Closely related to traffic monitoring, this area aims to make the information collected available to citizens. Using sensors that detect abnormal situations, such as accidents, it is possible to suggest optimal routes to destinations, avoiding critical areas.

Furthermore, a significant percentage of traffic is due to drivers seeking parking, a problem that can be addressed with innovative solutions. Sensors placed on asphalt, surveillance cameras or sensors on lampposts detect the availability of parking spaces and communicate this information to citizens. Smartphone apps guide users through optimal routes to the available parking spaces, reducing the search time and air pollution (Cheng et al., 2012).

These advances, which can also be used through digital panels and apps, promise to revolutionise urban mobility, bringing direct benefits to citizens and helping to build more sustainable communities.

8.5 IoT Technologies for Territorial Security and Environmental Prevention

From this perspective, strategically located sensors assume a key role in monitoring different situations, focusing mainly on citizen safety, natural disaster prevention and critical emergency preparedness.

The main objectives of these technologies are

- Flood prevention and monitoring.
- Fire prevention and monitoring.
- Temperature detection in forest areas for the early detection of forest fire outbreaks.
- Landslide prevention and monitoring.
- Dam safety and monitoring.
- Earthquake monitoring.
- Monitoring environmental parameters for landfill management.

These technological approaches, using advanced sensors, aim to ensure territorial security and mitigate the effects of environmental disasters, contributing to a more efficient management of emergencies and safeguarding the well-being of local communities.

8.5.1 Public Transport: Efficiency and Timely Information

The issue of public transport is intrinsically linked to the one explored above. Public transport systems not only contribute to urban traffic but are also subject to the negative effects of traffic jams or accidents, generating inconvenience not only for passengers but for the entire community. This sector can be divided into three key sub-areas: location and route planning, monitoring the flow of travellers and information mobility.

The first area sub-area concerns public transport vehicles equipped with GPS or other communication technologies to enable the real-time monitoring of their location. Systems like cameras and sensors along the route contribute to route monitoring.

Technologies like automatic vehicle monitoring (AVM) integrate GPS tracking and advanced diagnostics, facilitating the central control and management of alternative routes in the event of accidents or mechanical problems. They enable direct communication with citizens via apps or websites accessible from any device connected to the network.

The monitoring of the flow of travellers is carried out through dedicated sensors that monitor the flow of people in transit or waiting in real time. Continuous analysis enables the timely dispatch of additional vehicles when demand exceeds expectations.

Lastly, a better passenger experience is ensured through transport vehicles that communicate with predefined stops, providing real-time information on their location and waiting times and the availability of free seats. Information is communicated through variable panels near stops, dedicated websites and mobile apps.

These solutions aim to improve efficiency and the passenger experience by providing timely information and facilitating more dynamic route management in response to community needs.

8.5.2 Urban Security: Intelligent Technologies for Citizen Protection

Citizen safety is a crucial priority for any city that aspires to call itself 'smart'. Dealing with urban crime, managing disasters and responding to emergencies and incidents typically require the implementation of video surveillance technology. The use of cameras with night vision and fast zoom enables the effective monitoring of critical areas, transmitting real-time images to operations centres via advanced wireless technologies. Innovative software can identify dangerous situations, providing law enforcement with the ability to intervene quickly when necessary. In addition to security, smart cameras can support various functionalities, such as parking management and information mobility. The three main sub-areas include crowd monitoring, the identification and management of events and the localisation of people.

Examples of technologies used for these purposes are dedicated devices for monitoring crowds at resonant events, such as conferences, trade fairs or sporting events; the identification of suspicious behaviour to counter petty crime phenomena; and the configuration of software capable of recognising unexpected situations, such as traffic accidents or assaults that immediate alert to the relevant authorities for a prompt response. Finally, the localisation of people is performed through cameras for real-time communication or analysis of past logs using specific software for the detection of persons wanted by the police or missing persons.

These smart solutions not only improve the overall security of the city but also provide flexible tools to tackle everyday challenges, helping to create a more protected urban environment that is responsive to the needs of citizens.

8.5.3 Smart Waste Management: Innovations for a More Sustainable City

The topic of waste management efficiency offers a wide range of benefits, helping to implement more effective recycling policies, optimise collection services and improve the overall quality of the urban environment. The three sub-areas identified include personalised identification of bins and rubbish bags, monitoring of container filling and vehicle localisation.

The introduction of personal electronic cards, for example, with RFID tags, to allow access to dry bins and detailed profiling of specific areas improve the efficiency of the collection service, associating each rubbish bag with its owner by means of RFID tags for more accurate pricing based on actual waste production.

Moreover, the use of sensors to monitor the height or weight of the waste inside the containers with the aim of automatic signalling when bins reach a certain capacity optimises emptying operations. The calculation of optimal routes based on actual needs helps avoid unnecessary stops near half-empty bins.

Finally, the implementation of GPS systems on collection vehicles guarantees constant monitoring of their position and distance travelled. The timely detection of vehicle breakdowns enables near-real-time maintenance and ensures a continuous and efficient service.

These innovations promote smarter waste management, contributing to a more sustainable city and improving the overall quality of urban life (Elia et al., 2016).

8.5.4 *Modernisation of Water Networks: Introduction to Smart Water Networks*

In the context of smart grids, the focus of the transformation is the installation of smart meters. Among the main applications, we consider the intelligent water grid, focusing on this innovative solution.

Today's extensive and complex water infrastructures are progressively ageing and deteriorating. Consisting of different elements, such as pipe segments, pumps and valves, these networks are heterogeneous in terms of age and material. Difficult access to these structures can make it difficult for some municipalities to maintain a complete inventory of their assets or identify leaks in water systems. Economic challenges impose significant funding constraints, relegating water infrastructure to low positions on the priority scale. Delaying proper maintenance, however, can cause significant failures and breakdowns, generating further damage and disruptions.

In this context, the implementation of intelligent water networks emerges as a key solution for the efficient management of water distribution networks. This two-way system is equipped with advanced sensors, precise measurements and control devices integrated into the network. Through remote and continuous monitoring, the intelligent water network detects and diagnoses problems at an early stage. This approach provides utilities with real-time data on the status of the system, contributing to the immediate detection of leaks in the network.

The implementation of intelligent water networks not only offers an effective management tool but also promotes water and energy savings, addressing the challenges of obsolete water infrastructure in an innovative and sustainable way.

8.6 A2A Group: A Partner for Municipalities and Public Administration

A concrete initiative aimed at the creation of a smart city is offered by the Italian A2A Group that deals with energy, water and the environment. A2A has launched an ambitious integrated multi-service and multi-company project, aiming to connect a wide range of sensors and devices through the LoRa network.

This innovative project covers several Italian cities, with a particular focus on cities in Lombardy, including Milan, Bergamo and Brescia. A2A's initiative represents a significant step towards the creation of functional and connected smart cities capable of improving the quality of urban life and optimising public services using advanced technologies and smart grids.

8.6.1 The Evolution of A2A: A Model for Buildings

To make public buildings and schools smarter, the installation of sensors is essential. These devices monitor energy consumption and improve security. For example, a control sensor for lighting, heating and air conditioning, together with a volumetric security sensor, helps optimise energy efficiency and ensure a safe environment.

8.6.1.1 Intelligent Lighting

Intelligent lighting is realised using energy-efficient LED lamps and sensors that allow remote control. The municipality can monitor the energy consumption of groups of lamps in real time, intervening promptly in the case of anomalies. This approach not only saves energy but also enables more efficient management of lighting resources.

8.6.1.2 Smart Parking

In the planned future, each parking space will be equipped with a sensor that provides information on occupancy and recognises specific cars. A dedicated app will allow drivers to locate free spaces, while the municipality will have real-time data on payment status. This solution improves the parking experience for citizens and offers the municipality new opportunities for effective management and monitoring.

8.6.1.3 Smart Waste Management

Public litter bins are equipped with sensors that send real-time alerts on their fill level. Specialised software helps the municipality optimally plan the waste collection route, improving efficiency and ensuring a tidier city and lower CO_2 emissions.

8.6.1.4 Intelligent Water Network

By implementing sensors along the water network, the municipality can obtain real-time information on water flow. This advanced system allows for the immediate detection of leaks, enabling the municipality to take prompt action to preserve water resources and prevent wastage.

In short, these smart solutions not only improve the efficiency of public services but also promote sustainable resource management, helping to create a smarter, future-oriented city.

8.6.1.5 Smart Districts and the Technological Revolution in Urban Planning

In the context of urban evolution and digital transformation, the emergence of smart districts represents a fundamental chapter in the story of smart cities. A *smart district* is a portion of the urban fabric where advanced technologies and the IoT converge to improve quality of life, service efficiency and environmental sustainability. Through the integration of innovative solutions, these smart districts position themselves as cutting-edge urbanisation models, redefining the very concept of living and working in an urban environment.

8.6.1.6 IoT Technologies and LoRaWAN Network

At the heart of every smart district are the IoT technologies seen above, which enable connection and communication between devices and systems. In particular, the LoRaWAN plays a crucial role, offering extensive coverage and low power consumption, ideal for transmitting data between connected objects over a geographical area as large as an entire urban district. Thanks to this infrastructure, smart districts can deploy a wide range of smart sensors and devices, collecting data in real time and enabling proactive resource management.

8.6.2 Contribution of Smart Districts to Smart Cities

In conclusion, smart districts are not only places of technological innovation but form the foundation of the smart cities of the future. Through the implementation of advanced IoT technologies and the use of networks like LoRaWAN, these districts contribute significantly to the creation of smart cities, providing crucial data for resource optimisation, improving the quality of life of citizens and promoting the sustainable management of urban resources. The experience gained in smart districts like the one in Milan represents a step forward in building smart and resilient cities, projecting our concept of urban life towards new horizons of innovation and progress.

8.7 Smart Cities and the Challenges for Sustainability: Innovation for a Green Future

The technologies mentioned here and the creation of smart urban contexts are crucial in addressing environmental challenges by leveraging advanced technologies to optimise resource usage and reduce environmental effect. Through the implementation of intelligent energy, waste and transportation management systems, smart cities can significantly reduce greenhouse gas emissions and pollution. For example, smart grids enable more efficient energy distribution, reducing waste and integrating renewable sources, such as solar and wind energy.

Public lighting using LED technology controlled by motion sensors can reduce energy consumption by turning on lights only when needed. Advanced waste management systems, such as smart bins equipped with sensors, optimise collection routes and promote recycling. Furthermore, the integration of sensors and data platforms enables the continuous monitoring of air and water quality, allowing for timely and targeted interventions. This real-time data can be used to alert citizens and allow immediate measures to be taken to reduce pollution.

Green infrastructure, such as green roofs, green walls and urban parks, enhances biodiversity, absorbs CO_2 and helps regulate the urban microclimate, reducing the heat-island effect. Additionally, smart cities promote sustainable mobility using electric public transport, bike lanes and bike-sharing systems, reducing reliance on private cars and thus lowering CO_2 emissions.

In summary, smart cities represent a sustainable model of urban development that can play a crucial role in safeguarding the environment for future generations while simultaneously improving citizens' quality of life through a healthier environment and more efficient services.

References

Castro, M., Jara, J., & Skarmeta, F. (2013). Smart lightining solutions for smart cities. In *27th international conference on Advanced information networking and applications workshops*. Barcelona: WAINA.

Cheng, J., Wang, L., Shu, L., & Feng, Y. (2012). A fairness-aware smart parking scheme aided by parking lots. In *Communication software services and multimedia applications symposium*. IEEE International Conference on Communications.

Ciasullo, M. V., Troisi, O., & Grimaldi, M. (2020). Multi-level governance for sustainable innovation in smart communities: An ecosystem approach. *International Entrepreneurship and Management Journal, 16*, 1167–1195.

Di Castelnuovo, M., & Fumagalli, E. (2013). An assessment of the italian smart gas metering program. *Energy Policy*.

Elia, V., Gnoni, M., & Tornese, F. (2016). Assessing the efficiency of a PSS soluion for waste collection: A simulation based approach. *Procedia CIRP, 47*, 252–257.

Krishnamurti, T., Schwarts, D., Davis, A., Fischoff, B., Bruine-de-Bruinm, W., Lave, L., & Wang, J. (2012). Preparing for smart grid technologies: A behavioral decision research approach to understanding consumer expectations about smart meters. *Energy Policy, 41*, 790–797.

Passiante, G., Romano, A., & Elia, V. (1999). The web economy: Towards a new spatial context for learning and innovation processes in the business environment. In *139th congress of the European Regional Science Association*. Dublin.

Shy, Y., Zhang, T., & Jiang, Y. (2023). Digital economy, technological innovation and urban resilience. *Sustainability, 15*(12), 9250.

Somayya, M., & Romaswamy, R. (2014). Smart cities—Six dimensions. *A scholarstical articles review*.

Chapter 9
Digital Innovation Ecosystems for the Sustainable Growth: Analysis of the Italian Circular Economy Platform and Networks

Gioconda Mele, Pasquale Del Vecchio, and Marco De Maggio

Abstract The chapter aims to help advance the debate on digital innovation ecosystems as suitable environments supporting the achievement of circular economy (CE) goals. Coherently with the institutional debate on Twin Transition, this chapter offers an overview of the state of the theory and a comprehensive reading of political frameworks supporting the creation of digital innovation ecosystems for the CE transitions of both regions and firms. Empirically, the study provides evidence of a comparative analysis of the initiatives registered by the European Circular Economy Stakeholders Platform as good practices of digital innovation ecosystems promoting circular and sustainable achievements. By confirming the actuality of the issue in academic, institutional and societal contexts, the research offers a starting point for future studies and experiments.

Keywords Digital innovation ecosystem · Circular economy platforms · Network · Sustainability

---

G. Mele (✉)
Department of Engineering for Innovation, University of Salento, Lecce, Italy
e-mail: gioconda.mele@unisalento.it

P. Del Vecchio
Department of Engineering, LUM University, Casamassima, Italy
e-mail: delvecchio@lum.it

M. De Maggio
Presidency of the Council of Ministers of the Italian Government, Rome, Italy
e-mail: m.demaggio@governo.it

G. Passiante (ed.), *Digital Innovation Management*, Applied Innovation and Technology Management, https://doi.org/10.1007/978-3-031-80426-7_9

9.1 Introduction

Digital technologies are transforming innovation processes and outcomes in all sectors, affecting the lives of people, organisations and institutions (Van Veldhoven & Vanthienen, 2022). Their relevance is largely recognised as an opportunity for the achievement of sustainable growth (Popkova et al., 2022), even if not all actors can make the efforts required for the digital transition for sustainability (Caputo et al., 2023). From this perspective, governments and supranational institutions have recently launched programmes for promoting actions to sustain the digital ecological transition (Secundo et al., 2020). Focusing on the European and Italian contexts, such relevant challenges have recently been associated with specific political frameworks, such as the EU Next Generation or the Italian National Plan for Recovery and Resilience (PNRR), which represent for countries and regions an opportunity to promote and sustain digital transformation and sustainable growth. Those goals, also known as areas of missions, are strictly connected since there can be no process of digital transformation that is not also sustainable, just as there not be sustainable growth that ignores the opportunities offered by the digital technologies. In both cases, the change required assumes the profile of a paradigm shift, affecting the market and society. Its results are based on the adoption of technologies as well as on the collaboration of a plurality of stakeholders (Del Vecchio et al., 2021). In the same vein, the paradigm of Twin Transition has been recently brought to the attention of scholars and practitioners (Chen et al., 2023). Coherently with the non-linear innovation models and the neo-Schumpeterian view of technological innovation (Romano et al., 2014), the debate on such important changes highlights the importance of innovation ecosystems as a lens for shaping the complexity of the phenomena associated with Carayannis and Campbell (2011). Framed in the above premises, this chapter aims to explore the current landscape of strategies and initiatives implemented at the European and Italian levels to support the processes of digital transformation and sustainable growth. Specifically, the chapter aims to address the following research question: *What are specific innovation policy strategies and initiatives in place to support the creation of digital innovation ecosystems for sustainable growth?*

Starting with the pillars and objectives of the different initiatives, the chapter presents a qualitative review of the literature on the topics of digital innovation ecosystems and the circular economy (CE); Sect. 9.2 offers a synthetic overview of the main political frameworks undertaken at the national and European levels to support the creation of digital innovation ecosystems, supporting the circular transition. In Sect. 9.3, a comparative analysis of some good practices registered by the European Circular Economy Stakeholders Platform (ECESP) is presented. Finally, the chapter will present some implications for the political agendas of institutions and researchers.

9.2 State of the Art of the Digital Innovation Ecosystem for Sustainability

Digital innovation ecosystems have become central in the debate of scholars, practitioners and policymakers. From the academic point of view, they have recalled contributions, including regional development and open innovation (Dedehayir et al., 2018; Oh et al., 2016) and more recently studies focused on sustainability (Del Vecchio et al., 2021; Secundo et al., 2022). Digital innovation ecosystems are grounded in the evidence that digital technologies have amplified the opportunities for innovation emerging from the interrelation and integration of a plurality of actors operating as sources and providers of knowledge (Romano et al., 2014). The systemic view behind the digital innovation ecosystems recalls the need to approach innovation as a not-yet-linear process nurturing collaborative and networked environments (Powell et al., 1996; Zajac & Olsen, 1993). Furthermore, digital innovation ecosystems highlight the evidence that, in the current turbulent market environment, the process of sustainable value creation requires participation and the embrace of approaches to ensuring user-centrality by switching from competitive to collaborative strategies (Parker et al., 2016). In a recent study on digital business ecosystems, Aksoy (2023) refers to them as dynamic environments characterised by adaptability, scalability and resilience. If digital technologies and platforms increase the opportunities of connection and orchestration for delivering sustainable value, their complex nature makes it necessary to reconfigure firms' business strategies and market rules (Nambisan et al., 2017). As institutional environments activating virtuous and knowledge-intensive knowledge flows (Asheim & Gertler, 2006; Romano et al., 2014), digital innovation ecosystems are interested in the recent debate on sustainable growth (Del Vecchio et al., 2021). It is from this perspective that the inbound and outbound purposive knowledge flows emerging in these ecosystems can be addressed towards the creation of sustainable value and well-being. By focusing on the knowledge-based dimension emerging from the systemic approaches to innovation issues, it is possible to refer to the Quintuple Helix model of Carayannis and Campbell (2011) for mapping and managing the dynamics undertaken in such contexts. In an evolutionary line starting from the Triple Helix model (Etzkowitz & Zhou, 2006; Garner & Ternouth, 2011; Leydesdorff & Etzkowitz, 1998), the Quintuple Helix model is grounded in the primary three helix of academia, industry and public institution and the fourth helix of a media-based and culture-based public (as an evolution of the Quadruple Helix of Carayannis & Campbell, 2009) within the natural environment by highlighting the need for major attention to the sustainability issues. The environmental dimension characterising the Quintuple Helix model is coherent with other approaches to innovation, such as ecological economics (Rau et al., 2018), industrial ecology (Nielsen, 2007) and more recently the CE (Urbinati et al., 2017). Focusing on the CE, the issue of the digital innovation ecosystem can provide interesting speculations in terms of value co-creation processes, enablers and contextual features (Centobelli et al., 2020).

The debate on the CE has recently recalled contributions from different fields. As a branch of sustainability science and a lever for the achievement of the Sustainable Development Goals (SDGs) of the United Nations' Agenda 2030 (Geissdoerfer et al., 2018), the CE focuses on the opportunity to maintain resources longer in the loop associated with economic systems, with the aim of minimising waste, emission and costs (MacArthur, 2013; Ranta et al., 2018). The CE is also associated with the shift from the linear to circular configuration of production and consumption structures (Nußholz, 2018) As socio-technical paradigm resulting from the combination of know-how related to technological, market and social dimensions, the debate on the CE finds inspiration in the digital innovation ecosystems. The plurality of stakeholders involved in the results is crucial to the creation of social, economic and environmental value (Evans et al., 2017; Geissdoerfer et al., 2018). The effective implementation of a CE paradigm shift relies on environmental, political and social implications, recalling the active involvement of users (Urbinati et al., 2017) because of the knowledge-intensive nature of their interactions. Accordingly, the advancement of the debate on the CE suggests the adoption of a systemic view for the full understanding of its organisational and strategic implications.

9.3 Public Policies and Institutional Framework Supporting the Creation of Digital Innovation Ecosystems for the Circular Economy

The creation of digital innovation ecosystems supporting the transition of firms, communities and regions towards the CE has received increasing attention within the institutional and political debate. This section has the objectives of providing an overview of the main frameworks developed at the European, Italian and Apulian levels by demonstrating the coherence and scalability of such levels.

At the European level, the issue of the digital innovation ecosystem finds important references to the model of governance inspired by the Triple, Quadruple and Quintuple Helix, as mentioned. The well-known 'knowledge triangle' that is assumed as the basis of the governance of the European Institute of Innovation and Technology (EIT) has inspired several political actions and frameworks.

By focusing on the most recent documents, the topic of digital innovation ecosystem has been integrated into the areas of action promoted by Horizon Europe, as a funding programme for research and innovation. With a financial budget of 95.5 billion euros, Horizon Europe aims to boost competitiveness and growth by reserving a particular attention to the climate changes and the societal challenges of the United Nations (i.e. the 17 Sustainable Development Goals; UN_SDGs).

In identifying research and innovation as levers for development and cohesion among European countries, Horizon Europe aims to create and spread the diffusion of excellent knowledge and technologies.

Horizon Europe identifies innovation ecosystems as suitable environments supporting national, regional and local territories in the achievement of green, digital and social transitions, reinforcing networking and connectivity to accelerate business growth and social value as well as the competitiveness of SMEs, also through the effective usage of the European Regional Development Funds.

Conceived for supporting European countries in facing the challenges and limitations due to Covid-19, the Plan Next Generation Europe is the most important programme of public funds promoted at the European level. In its long agenda of actions, Next Generation Europe identifies the digital and green transitions as the primary objectives for the creation of a resilient and innovative European community.

Within the framework of Next Generation Europe, each European country has been invited to develop a national agenda for the management of the funds approved. In coherence with the strategic goals of the European Plan, the Italian government has developed the National Plan for Recovery and Resilience (*Piano Nazionale di Ripresa e Resilienza* (PNRR)), which identifies the topics of digital transformation and green transition as relevant areas of actions with meaningful financial support. The relevant resources of the PNRR have drawn the attention of the Italian government to the issues of sustainable growth and the CE by integrating the areas of intervention already identified in the Italian Sustainable Development Strategy and the Italian Circular Economy Strategy and to reinforce the effort towards the digital transition already begun in the National Plan for Digital Italy (Piano per l'Italia Digitale).

Further evidence can be identified in the agendas of the Italian regions that, within the framework of European programmes and strategies, such as the Smart Specialisation Strategy (S3), are called to design and implement their own regional strategies for supporting intelligent, inclusive and sustainable growth. This process of regional planning started in 2014 with the previous European frameworks of 'Horizon 2020' and the Cohesion Policy. The Apulian Regional Strategy of Smart Specialisation (Puglia 2030) has required an updating of its territorial analysis, technological specialisation and mainly regional objectives of growth. In July 2022, the final version of Puglia 2030 had been approved by the European Commission. In its premises, the Apulian Strategy sees digital technologies as enablers of smart growth and notes their positive effect on the creation of innovation ecosystems. Such a pattern of intelligent growth must converge towards the achievement of the environmental and societal goals also defined within the Apulian Regional Strategy for Sustainable Development.

In the richness of perspectives and opportunities offered, all these political agendas and frameworks reveal a wide range of challenges that are still open and require synergic and systemic actions.

9.4 Italian Circular Economy Stakeholder Platform Analysis

This section reveals the findings of a desk analysis conducted on Italian digital platforms and ecosystems with a specific focus on the CE, as catalogued by the European Circular Economy Stakeholder Platform (ECESP). Prior to delving into the analysis of these platforms, it is essential to provide a concise introduction to ECESP.

ECESP was created in March 2017 as a collaborative effort between the European Commission and the European Economic and Social Committee. Its primary aim is to serve as a central hub for stakeholders with an interest in advancing the circular economy agenda in Europe. Functioning as a network of networks, the platform was conceived to facilitate the transition towards a CE and support the implementation of the EU Action Plan for the CE. Oversight of the platform is entrusted to a coordination group comprising 24 members, including various stakeholders, such as business networks, institutions, civil society representatives and workers, with ENEA representing Italy. ECESP offers an online platform where stakeholders can access and exchange information on best practices related to the CE. These include valuable insights, knowledge resources and specific information on legislation, regulations and ongoing projects at the EU level pertaining to circular economy initiatives. The overarching goal of the platform is to gather and disseminate experiences and successful practices related to the CE across Europe, with the intention of enabling members to replicate these initiatives effectively.

Since its foundation, ECESP has dedicated itself to fostering the exchange of best practices and has consequently advocated the establishment of a collection of Circular Economy Good Practices to facilitate the dissemination of knowledge related to the CE (Cappellaro et al., 2020).

The desk analysis focused on the entries listed by ECESP. From this dataset, the sample was narrowed down to include only platforms and projects developed in Italy.

The sample analysed includes 14 Italian platforms focused on promoting circular economy practices:

- Circular Economy Lab.
- Circular Economy Platform of Ports (LOOP-Ports).
- DigiCirc: Digital Innovations for the Circular Economy.
- ENEA Platform for Industrial Symbiosis.
- European Regions Towards Circular Economy.
- Forest Sharing, an innovative platform for responsible forestry.
- Italian Circular Economy Stakeholder Platform.
- Italian Phosphorus Platform.
- Network Economia Circolare.
- Osservatorio Innovazione Packaging.
- R-PVC Hub.

- Taranto Circolare.
- The Economy of Francesco.
- Tondo.

The following section presents the main results of the desk analysis.

9.5 Circular Economy Lab

9.5.1 Aim and Mission

The Circular Economy Lab is an innovation initiative resulting from the partnership between Cariplo Factory and Intesa Sanpaolo Innovation Centre aimed at advancing the Italian economic system and promoting new models of value creation for the collective benefit, thus accelerating the transition towards circular economy models. The mission of the Circular Economy Lab is to experiment with and disseminate new models of value creation that combine the development of businesses and organisations with the protection and enhancement of human, natural, social and economic capital.

9.5.2 Activities and Network Created

With a focus on open and inclusive innovation, the Circular Economy Lab seeks to engage major corporations and transformative entities, including start-ups, innovative SMEs, universities, research centres and technology transfer centres. Leveraging its expertise and capabilities, the Circular Economy Lab aims to promote circular economy principles and methodologies through educational programmes and by facilitating networking opportunities among participants in the innovative ecosystem.

Encouraging companies to transition towards a circular model involves tailoring the approach to each company's unique circumstances, including its level of maturity regarding CE concepts, technologies and models. This process can be facilitated through the design of a *circular journey framework*, wherein companies can embark on a tailored intervention path. This path typically begins by acquiring skills in and awareness of the circular field, progresses to identifying innovative pathways through targeted projects and ongoing support and involves maintaining active engagement with stakeholders and the circular innovation ecosystem. The *circular economy lab model* is built upon this approach and identifies three essential pillars: *circular connection*, *circular innovation* and *circular education*.

9.5.3 Achievements

Many projects and open challenges have been organised by the laboratory in various fields and sectors, such as Circular Water 4 Healthcare. This initiative aims to establish a scalable and replicable best practice for water recovery, specifically targeting contrast liquids and the management of hospital wastewater. The goal is to implement processes that can serve as innovative models for the Italian and international healthcare sectors. Other examples include the Iren Startup Award, which focuses on circular products and materials, and Call4Energy, for mobility evolution.

9.6 Circular Economy Platform of Ports (LOOP-Ports)

9.6.1 Aim and Mission

The primary objective of the LOOP-Ports project is to streamline the shift towards a CE within the port industry. This involves maximising the retention of products, materials and resources within the economy for as long as feasible while minimising waste generation.

LOOP-Ports aims to aid the European economy's transition towards closed-loop systems by establishing a network of ports dedicated to circular economy principles. This network will foster an innovation ecosystem centred around port activities and encourage the implementation of circular economy initiatives within ports.

9.6.2 Activities and Network Created

The network will enable the sharing of experiences and best practices, offer policy suggestions and promote training and the development of new business prospects, both within port clusters and in other sectors associated with this domain.

The LOOP-Ports network concentrates on high-emission materials, notably metals, plastics, cements and biomaterials. It has commenced the following activities:

- Compiling a broad spectrum of examples of circular economy initiatives already implemented in the EU port sector, along with additional best practices worldwide.
- Analysing the primary drivers (e.g. legal, policy, financial or market structures) to identify intervention opportunities and formulate specific recommendations to enhance circular economy endeavours in port ecosystems.
- Creating customised training materials and piloting training programmes to enhance skills, knowledge and innovation capacities within and among various port clusters.

- Establishing a comprehensive database containing information collected from EU ports, focusing on relevant variables for mapping EU ports concerning the CE.
- Developing a web tool for the CE to showcase project outcomes and facilitate information exchange among network members, stakeholders and the public.
- Establishing a pan-EU network of ports dedicated to circular economy activities, including workshops and roundtables with stakeholders to gather interests, viewpoints and expectations.
- Designing business models for real-use cases selected during the project, analysing their replication.

LOOP-Ports comprises 13 partners from six EU Member States (Spain, Italy, France, Germany, Denmark and the Netherlands) and ran for a little over 2 years, concluding in November 2020.

9.6.3 Achievements

LOOP-Ports project analysed more than 450 ports, developing seven business models and three training pilots. Moreover, one web tool has been developed, as well as more than 30 international workshops on the CE.

9.7 DigiCirc: Digital Innovations for the Circular Economy

9.7.1 Aim and Mission

Digital Innovations for the Circular Economy (DigiCirc) primarily functions as an innovation ecosystem. It aims to connect companies, both small and large, alongside public entities and researchers, to collaborate on addressing a crucial objective: enhancing the sustainability of the economy. The strategy involves transitioning to a CE, which entails using materials and energy more efficiently over extended periods and ensuring that any remaining leftovers or waste serve as inputs for other processes.

9.7.2 Activities and Network Created

DigiCirc supports the use of new digital technologies as valuable resources for monitoring and communicating the status, location and quality of materials, particularly those categorised as by-products or waste. This facilitates improved collaboration among organisations and the development of operations that are both efficient and circular.

Moreover, DigiCirc arranges three business acceleration programmes, both online and in physical settings, aimed at aiding SMEs/start-ups in innovating within the circular economy sector by leveraging digital technologies. These programmes will concentrate on three specific thematic areas: circular cities, bioeconomy and the blue economy.

9.7.3 Achievements

Several circular economy initiatives have been created throughout Europe, spearheaded by clusters within the DigiCirc ecosystem, such as *Greater Green* (Europe's first cross-border network for environmental technology), *RES_TMO* (Concepts for an Integrated, Efficient and Sustainable Energy Supply and Storage), *Smart Meter Inclusif* (AI to support the proactive management of energy consumption by end users), *Transition Zero* (the large-scale deployment of guaranteed zero-energy renovations) and many others.

9.8 ENEA Platform for Industrial Symbiosis

9.8.1 Aim and Mission

ENEA has developed Italy's first platform that aims to streamline the process of *industrial symbiosis*: the exchange of resources between two or more dissimilar industries. *Resources* includes not only materials (by-products or waste) but also energy residues, services and expertise.

9.8.2 Activities and Network Created

This methodology adopts a horizontal network approach, fostering synergies and closing the loop between resource supply and demand.

The platform comprises.

- An expert structure identifying potential industrial symbiosis solutions.
- A comprehensive, georeferenced information structure detailing the territory, its infrastructure, stakeholders and available resources.
- A network connecting various stakeholders.
- A user-friendly web interface.

Among its services, the platform generates individual reports for companies, highlighting potential matches of interest. Additionally, it is working on operational manuals for industrial symbiosis.

9.8.3 *Achievements*

The tool enables a comprehensive analysis of a company's resource management system, covering materials, energy by-products, water, services and expertise. This analysis aims to achieve both internal efficiency (optimisation and enhancement within the company) and external efficiency (assessment of collaborative and exchange approaches, implementation of industrial symbiosis initiatives in the region). In total, 250 companies participate in the network, with 2646 resources and 1946 cases of symbiosis identified.

9.9 European Regions Towards Circular Economy (CircE)

9.9.1 *Aim and Mission*

The CircE Project (European regions towards Circular Economy) seeks to enhance the adoption of CE practices in Europe in alignment with the European Commission's Circular Economy Package (2015). Its primary objective is to assist the participating partners in enhancing the effectiveness of their policy instruments to promote a circular economic model. This is achieved through exchanging knowledge and experiences among partners, actively engaging stakeholders and conducting in-depth analyses of the economic system.

Circe project engages eight partners at both the regional and local levels, encompassing representatives from diverse European social and economic contexts.

The objective of the Interreg Europe Project CircE is to develop action plans that, steering specific policy instruments (plans and programmes), support and improve the transition to a CE in specific business sectors.

9.9.2 *Activities and Network Created*

In terms of activities, the project has organised a total of 78 policy learning events. It has also identified 48 good practices, produced seven action plans and led to the increased capacity of 63 people. In terms of results, the project has succeeded in improving nine regional development policies.

9.9.3 Achievements

The method developed within the project, known as the CircE Toolbox, is regarded, along with the action plans, as a significant accomplishment of the project. It serves as a foundation for establishing a support system for strategic decision-making regarding the implementation of CE policies within European regions.

9.10 Forest Sharing: An Innovative Platform Taking Care of Woods

9.10.1 Aim and Mission

Forest Sharing proposes a new way to manage forests based on a circular and shared approach. Forest Sharing is a digital platform launched in 2020 where forest owners connect with each other, as well as with businesses and professionals, to form a community aimed at creating shared value from abandoned or unmanaged forests. The Forest Sharing project, initiated by the startup Bluebiloba, targets those who are unable to independently manage their forests, offering them a community that can assist in revitalising and adding value to their properties.

9.10.2 Activities and Network Created

The platform operates as follows. The forest owner enters the data of their forest and selects the management options (e.g. timber harvesting, recreational tourism development, maintenance), which can be managed individually or combined. Forest Sharing technicians analyse the forest properties and, together with the owners, choose the best solutions. The management forms (timber harvesting, recreational tourism development, maintenance) can be managed individually or combined.

Forest Sharing applies CE principles to the forestry sector by recognising that wood and non-wood forest products are just one aspect of a range of activities and services that can occur in forests. Through the community fostered by the Forest Sharing platform, it becomes feasible to integrate fire prevention efforts, such as road planning, with tourism development, such as using roads for recreational activities like hiking, trekking and horseback riding. Additionally, the platform enables the integration of revenue from timber harvesting with the expenses associated with protecting rare plant species using monitoring systems. This integration is facilitated by the implementation of multi-objective forest management plans that involve forests owned by different individuals, allowing for the sharing of economic and environmental benefits among neighbouring or adjacent forests, as has been done historically.

9.10.3 Achievements

Over 18,000 hectares of forest have been brought together in 2 years, with approximately 750 owners nationwide joining the Forest Sharing community. Additionally, the project has been recognised through national and international initiatives, receiving mentions and awards for its sustainability efforts.

9.11 Italian Circular Economy Stakeholder Platform (ICESP)

9.11.1 Aim and Mission

The Italian Platform of Actors for the Circular Economy (ICESP), promoted by ENEA (the Italian National Agency for New Technologies, Energy and Sustainable Economic Development), was launched in 2018 and is structured as a network with the goal of establishing a national focal point for initiatives, experiences, challenges, perspectives and expectations regarding the CE. It aims to present Italy's perspective on the CE in Europe with a unified voice to promote the Italian approach to CE through dedicated actions.

9.11.2 Activities and Network Created

ICESP is structured as a network aimed at creating a national convergence point on initiatives, experiences, challenges, prospects and expectations regarding the CE that Italy wants to represent in Europe with a unified voice, promoting the Italian way of conducting the CE through dedicated actions. The platform has adopted a statement of intent: a manifesto of intents and purposes and regulations that allows the involved organisations to share their commitment to achieving common objectives in Italy regarding the CE.

Its main objectives are to.

- Promote the dissemination of knowledge.
- Foster dialogue and possible synergies among Italian actors of initiatives.
- Map Italian best practices.
- Promote the integration of initiatives at the Italian level.
- Establish a permanent operational tool to promote and facilitate dialogue and cross-sector interactions.
- Spread Italian accomplishments and the Italian way of conducting CE, starting from the traditions and unique aspects of Italy and its related cultural, social and entrepreneurial models.

The initiatives of the platform are directed towards a variety of stakeholders, including public administration, businesses, research institutions and civil society. Currently, ICESP consists of 309 participating organisations, of which 150 are signatories to the statement of intent.

The activities of the platform are also carried out through working groups (WGs) and cross-cutting groups (CCG) open to the participation of all interested parties, even non-members of the platform itself, as experts in the field, to foster debate and results. These groups work on the topics most relevant to the CE, selected based on the analysis of the main priorities and issues that require assessment of intervention solutions, as well as suggestions from platform members, through the main documents available at the national level (from public and private institutions).

9.11.3 Achievements

To date, ICESP has established six working groups and three cross-cutting groups:

1. WG1: Research and Eco-Innovation, Knowledge Dissemination and Training.
2. WG2: Political and Economic Tools.
3. WG3: Tools for Measuring the Circular Economy.
4. WG4: Sustainable and Circular Value Chains.
5. WG5: Circular Cities and Territories.
6. WG6: Best Practices and Integrated Approaches.
7. CCG1: Ecodesign and Circular Business Models.
8. CCG2: Market for Recycled, Recovered and By-Products.
9. CCG3: Committee for the Review of Best Practices.

The annual conference of the ICESP represents the institutional moment during which the main results of the work carried out by the platform's working groups are presented, serving as an expert contribution to CE issues.

9.12 Italian Phosphorus Platform (IPP)

9.12.1 Aim and Mission

In 2019, the Ministry for Environment and Energy Security initiated the establishment of the National Phosphorus Platform, with ENEA appointed as the managing body. The primary goal is to attain national self-sufficiency in the phosphorus cycle and ensure alignment with European policies. This platform comprises various stakeholders involved in the phosphorus cycle, including research institutions, academic bodies, public and private entities, companies, associations and civil society. Phosphorus is identified as a critical and strategic raw material for Europe, given its high dependency on imports from non-European countries and negligible recycling rates from end-of-life products.

9.12.2 Activities and Network Created

The platform brings together companies, institutions, research bodies, citizens and associations with the aim of achieving self-sufficiency for phosphorus, a critical raw material for Europe, at the national level, while also coordinating with European policies.

The platform operates under the principles of the CE, focusing on closing the loop across the entire value chain, from primary production to recovery from secondary sources. It is structured into four working groups (WP), each addressing the issue from a different perspective:

1. WP1—Management and Coordination.
2. WP2—Technologies and Best Practices.
3. WP3—Legislation.
4. WP4—Market.

Additionally, the Platform collaborates with the ICESP, particularly regarding the Agrifood subgroup within the 4th Working Group (WG1) focusing on 'Circular and Sustainable Value Chains'.

9.12.3 Achievements

The National Phosphorus Platform organises many events, seminars and workshops in the field and lists the best practices for circular phosphorus management and technology readiness levels in its reporting, with the objective of developing a proposal to remove the obstacles to circular phosphorus management.

9.13 Circular Economy Network

9.13.1 Aim and Mission

The Foundation for Sustainable Development, supported by a group of companies and organisations from various economic sectors, has established the Circular Economy Network as a tool to promote the development of the CE in Italy. The Circular Economy Network's work is based on several key pillars:

- Promoting, collecting and disseminating studies, research and analyses on the CE.
- Defining key circularity indicators and analysing national performance.
- Analysing major challenges and barriers to be addressed while proposing potential solutions.
- Developing strategies, policies and measures to be presented to policymakers, fostering positive dialogue between the business world and institutions.
- Valuing and contributing to the dissemination of best practices and cutting-edge techniques.

9.13.2 Activities and Network Created

With the aim of serving as a reference point for the strategies necessary to develop the CE, the Circular Economy Network brings together all stakeholders involved in this process to strengthen a common action through collaborative dynamics.

The network welcomes participation from businesses, associations, research institutes and other entities interested in promoting the CE and sharing the initiative's objectives as members.

In the last annual report on the CE in Italy (2023), the network proposed several actions for the implementation of the national strategy for the CE, such as

- Comply with the time schedule and timely transpose the European Union measures.
- Strengthen support for business investment.
- Provide for ecological taxation measures in the enabling act, develop the CE of critical raw materials.
- Guarantee the development of the systems envisaged by PNRR.
- Fully implement the National Waste Management Programme.
- Establish new EPR systems.
- Accelerate and simplify end-of-waste regulations,;
- Develop industrial symbiosis and promote waste prevention and reduction.

9.13.3 Achievements

The network focuses on three core activities:

- Yearly conference on the CE.
- Annual report outlining the state of the CE.
- Sustainable Development Prize for journalists and creatives.

9.14 Observatory for Innovative Packaging

9.14.1 Aim and Mission

The Observatory for Innovative Packaging project, coordinated by the University of Bologna, aims to be a reference point and connection for the packaging system community, gathering and reprocessing knowledge, seeking best practices in a predictive logic and blending project and research skills among universities, students and companies, with the goal of triggering and multiplying innovation.

9.14.2 Activities and Network Created

The observatory

- Builds a database of case studies to compare and extract common dynamics and predictive elements.
- Observes the phenomena leading to innovation within companies in the sector.
- Implements a process of hybridisation of project skills, involving research, students and companies.
- Consolidates the network of stakeholders and enables greater connections among them, following an integrated system approach.

The Packaging Innovation Observatory works to narrate, interpret and act on the phenomenon of packaging as an expression of contemporary cultural complexity, triggering innovation and supporting companies in the ecological transition, with a collaborative, holistic and quintuple-helix approach.

9.14.3 Achievements

The Packaging Innovation Observatory offers its expertise by providing Hybrid Design services among research, students and companies:

- Through the Talent Lab.
- By participating in Competitive Projects.

The platform includes more than 500 best practices in the field of circular packaging and more than 350 companies.

In addition, the platform provides insights into innovation in the packaging sector through selected articles, podcasts, reports, books, videos and papers.

9.15 R-PVC Hub

9.15.1 Aim and Mission

R-PVC Hub is a cutting-edge online platform linked to the PVC Forum Italia website, facilitating the exchange of recycled PVC by connecting supply and demand. At the core of this service is an Internet-based platform where manufacturing companies, processors and recyclers can discover new business prospects.

R-PVC HUB's aim is to establish a platform for collaboration among all stakeholders involved in PVC recycling: waste collectors, waste processors and manufacturers of recycled products.

9.15.2 Activities and Network Created

The association PVC Forum Italia, in collaboration with VinylPlus, AGPU and Recovinyl, seeks to educate interested parties by providing information on national and European regulations concerning PVC waste, as well as advancements in waste-sorting and -management technologies and the classification of by-products, waste and secondary raw materials (end-of-waste criteria).

The Datasheet section of the platform identifies what type of PVC (rigid or plasticised) is produced by registered companies.

9.15.3 Achievements

As an integral part of the VinylPlus programme, in particular for the achievement of Challenge 1 ('Controlled Life Cycle Management') of PVC, the R-PVC HUB is not an e-commerce space; it does not discuss costs or the value of the materials made available but intends to be an important meeting and sharing point among all stakeholders interested in recycling or having PVC recycled.

9.16 Taranto Circolare

9.16.1 Aim and Mission

Taranto Circolare is a platform designed to bring together businesses, projects and funding opportunities to support and promote innovative and sustainable initiatives within the region.

The goal of Taranto Circolare is to facilitate the ecological transformation of Taranto, particularly in the Città Vecchia area, by providing support and resources. This platform serves as a launchpad for projects, businesses and services by offering insights and an understanding of the local area.

9.16.2 Activities and Network Created

The initiative centres on establishing a platform where companies, authorities and organisations can engage in a network dedicated to implementing circular projects. The platform offers tailored tools and assistance to help stakeholders assess the circularity of their services and products.

Furthermore, by gathering and analysing data, the project aims to quantify material and energy flows within the city.

The platform describes several initiatives, such as, among others:

- REENLIFE4SEAS project (GREEN ENgineering solutions: a new LIFE for SEdiments And Shells).
- Jonian Dolphin Conservation (a scientific research association for the study of cetaceans in the Gulf of Taranto in the Northern Ionian Sea).
- Masseria Fruttirossi (established in 2014 with the aim of creating an agricultural pole where tradition and innovation can be integrated).
- Urban Farmer (an innovative start-up comprising an ecosystem of sustainable initiatives related to the protection of land and the environment in general).
- The REMEDIA Life project (REmediation of Marine Environment and Development of Innovative Aquaculture: exploitation of edible/not edible biomass).

9.16.3 Achievements

The Taranto Circolare platform offers measurement tools that employ internationally and nationally recognised methodologies to assess and quantify the circularity of companies, entities and organisations. With these tools, it is feasible to evaluate circularity at both the product and company levels.

9.17 The Economy of Francesco (EoF)

9.17.1 Aim and Mission

The Economy of Francesco (EoF) is an initiative prompted by Pope Francis, inviting young entrepreneurs, researchers and economists to collaborate in reshaping the current economy to combat waste culture and advocate social justice.

The initial call garnered more than 3000 applications from 120 countries, indicating widespread interest in the initiative. Annual events adhere to the principles of the Economy of Francesco, emphasising reduced environmental effects.

9.17.2 Activities and Network Created

EoF offers a continuous series of activities organised at the regional or local level, including workshops, labs, seminars, conferences, roundtables, calls for action and other engagements aimed at.

- *Doing business*, with the ambition to reconcile profit motives and strategies that prioritise individuals, generate value for the region and ensure sustainable environmental effects.
- *Young people and employment*, observing local realities while trying to bridge the gap between the business world and the demand for employment.
- *Territory and sustainability*: embracing the goals of the 2030 agenda and the methods for working to connect environmental protection and economic development.

9.17.3 Achievements

EoF was included as a best practice in the ICESP in 2023 and as best practice in the ECESP.

9.18 Tondo

9.18.1 Aim and Mission

Tondo serves as a hub for organisations committed to promoting the CE, aiming to establish an ecosystem where universities, start-ups, businesses, organisations and individuals collaborate to encourage innovation, entrepreneurship and circular practices.

Besides providing a platform for entrepreneurs, innovators, change-makers and designers to incubate new CE projects, Tondo also aims to spread awareness and knowledge on CE subjects. It supports the establishment of new companies operating under circular principles and assists existing businesses in transitioning towards a CE model.

9.18.2 Activities and Network Created

The Tondo community welcomes both businesses and individuals interested in learning about, participating in and contributing to CE initiatives.

Companies, as members, receive exclusive benefits for Tondo activities, such as access to tailored measurement tools and knowledge resources, as well as opportunities for visibility and participation in Tondo's events. Additionally, they have.

- Access to Tondo's circularity measurement tools.
- The ability to participate in Tondo's CE workshops.
- Discounts and priority access to Tondo's events and activities.

The registration fee begins at 1500 euros based on the size of the company.

People passionate about sustainability issues can join the community, have access to a flow of innovative ideas and fresh knowledge and participate in webinars and meetings to understand the basic principles of the CE. The registration fee for students is 20 euros, for researchers 35 euros and for all others 50 euros.

Moreover, Tondo offers two main services to its community:

- Tondo Lab for designing circular solutions.
- Measurement tools for assessing circularity.

9.18.3 Achievements

Tondo organises the *Re-think Circular Economy* forum, an annual event structure created to showcase a perspective on the overarching trends, potential developmental trajectories and key initiatives within the CE. It actively engages companies, start-ups and research institutions, aiming to provide a platform and resources for exploring the emerging frontiers of CE practices.

Lastly, Tondo hosts hackathons to breathe life into and actualise projects that advance the adoption of the CE. These events engage students, recent graduates and PhD candidates from different universities in the region, providing them with the chance to formulate concrete ideas and address various challenges in collaboration with partner companies.

Table 9.1 summarises all the discussed platforms and networks presented based on characteristics like type, main area and sector.

The table presents a range of networks and platforms focused on advancing the CE across various sectors and regions.

- Circular Economy Lab: This interdisciplinary platform fosters knowledge exchange and innovation in the CE. It focuses on investment, digital solutions and startups aimed at achieving climate neutrality. It serves as a business incubator offering B2B services to promote awareness and circular action.

Table 9.1 Italian circular economy platforms and networks

Network/platform	Type	Key area	Sector	Website
Circular Economy Lab	Interdisciplinary exchange, knowledge community	Innovation and investments	Awareness raising, B2B services, business incubators, startups, circular action for climate neutrality, digital solutions, innovation and investment	https://www.circulareconomylab.it/
Circular Economy Platform of Ports (LOOP-Ports)	Educational or training platform, interest group, research and innovation, sectoral	Production, consumption, waste management, secondary raw materials, innovation and investments	Bioeconomy and biomimicry, cement, steel, chemicals, education and skills, plastics, polymers and rubber	Network of Ports—LOOP-Ports project
DigiCirc: Digital innovations for the Circular Economy	Interdisciplinary exchange, knowledge community, research and innovation	Production, consumption, waste management, secondary raw materials, innovation and investments	Bioeconomy and biomimicry, business incubators, startups, digital solutions, industrial symbiosis, other (blue economy, circular cities)	DigiCirc—accelerator for circular economy
ENEA Platform for Industrial Symbiosis	National or regional	Production, waste management, secondary raw materials	Agriculture, fertilisers and forestry, bioeconomy and biomimicry, food, water and nutrients, mining, metals and minerals, packaging, plastics, polymers and rubber, recycling	Symbiosis - Home (industrialsymbiosis.it)
European Regions towards Circular Economy	Sectoral	Consumption, waste management, innovation and investments	Agriculture, fertilisers and forestry, food, water and nutrients, mining, metals and minerals, power and utilities, recycling, textiles, apparel and leather, housing and urban development	CircE | Interreg Europe
Forest Sharing	Interest group, sectoral	Innovation and investments	Circular action for climate neutrality	HOME - forestsharing.it

Italian Circular Economy Stakeholder Platform	National or regional	Production, consumption, waste management, secondary raw materials, innovation and investments		Home I Icesp
Italian Phosphorus Platform	National or regional	Waste management, secondary raw materials	Recycling	Home (piattaformaitalianafosforo.it)
Network Economia Circolare	CSO, interest group, knowledge community, national or regional	Production, consumption, waste management, secondary raw materials, innovation and investments		Home - Circular Economy Network
Osservatorio Innovazione Packaging	Knowledge community, research and innovation, sectoral	Innovation and investments	Circular design, packaging	Osservatorio sull'Innovazione del Packaging (unibo.it)
R-PVC Hub	Sectoral	Secondary raw materials	B2B services, plastics, polymers and rubber	R-PVC Hub (pvcforum.it)
Taranto Circolare	Research and innovation	Innovation and investments	Measuring circularity	Taranto Circolare
The economy of Francesco	Interest group	Consumption, waste management, secondary raw materials	Awareness raising	Alternative EoF Board I The Economy of Francesco (francescoeconomy.org)
Tondo	Knowledge community	Secondary raw materials, innovation and investments	Awareness raising, behavioural incentives, business incubators, startups, circular design, education and skills, research	https://www.tondo.tech/en/

- Circular Economy Platform of Ports (LOOP-Ports): As an educational and training platform, LOOP-Ports emphasises research and innovation in sectors like bioeconomy, cement, steel and chemicals. It aims to enhance production, consumption, waste management and the use of secondary raw materials.
- Digital Innovations for the Circular Economy (DigiCirc): This initiative supports interdisciplinary knowledge exchange and innovation. It targets various areas, such as bioeconomy, industrial symbiosis and digital solutions, providing support to startups and promoting the blue economy and circular cities.
- ENEA Platform for Industrial Symbiosis: Operating on a national or regional scale, this platform addresses production, waste management and the use of secondary raw materials in sectors including agriculture, bioeconomy and packaging. It aims to facilitate recycling and efficient resource use.
- European Regions Towards Circular Economy: This sectoral initiative focuses on consumption, waste management and innovation in agriculture, mining, power and utilities. It aims to foster recycling and sustainable urban development across European regions.
- Forest Sharing: An innovative platform dedicated to woodland care, focusing on investments in circular actions for climate neutrality. It supports sectoral interests and promotes sustainable forestry practices.
- Italian Circular Economy Stakeholder Platform: A national initiative encompassing production, consumption, waste management and secondary raw materials. It focuses on innovation and investments to advance the CE in Italy.
- Italian Phosphorus Platform: This regional platform concentrates on the waste management and recycling of phosphorus, a critical secondary raw material, promoting sustainable recycling practices.
- Network Economia Circolare: An interest group and knowledge community at the national level, focusing on production, consumption, waste management and secondary raw materials, it emphasises innovation and investments to drive the CE.
- Osservatorio Innovazione Packaging: This research and innovation-focused platform operates sectorally to promote innovation in packaging design and circular practices within the packaging industry.
- R-PVC Hub: Dedicated to secondary raw materials, this sectoral hub provides B2B services focusing on plastics, polymers and rubber. It aims to support the recycling and sustainable use of PVC.
- Taranto Circolare: A research and innovation initiative emphasising investments in measuring circularity, it aims to enhance CE practices through comprehensive metrics and evaluations.
- The Economy of Francesco: This interest group focuses on consumption, waste management and secondary raw materials. It raises awareness and promotes alternative economic models aligned with CE principles.
- Tondo: A knowledge community that emphasises secondary raw materials and innovation investments. It promotes awareness, behavioural incentives, education and support for start-ups, focusing on circular design and research.

Each of these platforms plays a crucial role in fostering the CE through diverse strategies, including research, innovation, education and practical applications across various sectors. Their collective efforts contribute significantly to sustainable development and the efficient use of resources.

9.19 Conclusion

The debate on digital innovation ecosystems for the circular economy has been vibrant during the last several years. Its relevance in both academic and institutional debate has been associated with several implications emerging for people, markets and society. It also presents elements of coherence with the recent topic of the Twin Transition, an emerging paradigm focused on digital transformation for the achievement of sustainable growth.

The conception and implementation of strategies supporting the transitions of firms and territories towards a CE configuration can benefit from the multi-stakeholders' interactions enabled by digital ecosystems as well as by their knowledge flows and contributions. In this direction, the analysis of the political framework has allowed us to verify that the topics of digital innovation ecosystems and CE are widely debated and that a plurality of opportunities at the European, national and regional levels can be identified to support territories and communities in affording the challenges of digital and green transitions.

The previous sections regarding the analysis of the Italian CE platforms and networks listed by the ECESP presented its commitment to promoting the exchange of best practices within the CE domain. Through its advocacy of the creation of a collection of Circular Economy Good Practices, ECESP has aimed to streamline the dissemination of valuable knowledge and insights across the relevant stakeholders. The identification of 14 Italian platforms dedicated to advancing CE practices further underscores the growing momentum and interest surrounding this sustainable approach. Most of the platforms are categorised as research and innovation platforms for in-depth exploration of CE issues, such as ICEP or Taranto Circolare. Others, instead, are sector-specific, such as R-PVC Hub or the Italian Phosphorus Platform.

The detailed analysis of the table in the report reveals a broad and diverse spectrum of initiatives. Each platform addresses unique aspects of the CE, from interdisciplinary exchange and knowledge communities to sector-specific innovations and national or regional efforts. The Circular Economy Lab, for instance, focuses on innovation and investments to drive digital solutions and start-ups towards climate neutrality. LOOP-Ports emphasises educational and sectoral innovations in production and waste management, while DigiCirc promotes digital innovations for industrial symbiosis and circular cities.

The ENEA Platform for Industrial Symbiosis and the Italian Circular Economy Stakeholder Platform highlight national efforts in waste management and recycling across various sectors. Platforms like Forest Sharing and The Economy of Francesco focus on specific interests, such as woodland care and alternative economic models, respectively.

Moving forward, continued collaboration and knowledge-sharing efforts facilitated by the ECESP and similar platforms will be instrumental in driving the widespread adoption of CE principles and fostering a more sustainable future for all. The integration of digital innovation ecosystems with CE initiatives not only supports sustainable growth but also enhances the resilience and adaptability of businesses and communities in the face of global challenges.

References

Aksoy, C. (2023). Digital business ecosystems: An environment of collaboration, innovation, and value creation in the digital age. *Journal of Business and Trade, 4*(2), 156–180.

Asheim, B. T., & Gertler, M. S. (2006). The geography of innovation: Regional innovation systems. In J. Fagerberg & D. C. Mowery (Eds.), The Oxford handbook of innovation (2006; online edn, Oxford Academic, 2 Sept. 2009). https://doi.org/10.1093/oxfordhb/9780199286805.003.0011

Caputo, F., Magliocca, P., Canestrino, R., & Rescigno, E. (2023). Rethinking the role of technology for citizens' engagement and sustainable development in smart cities. *Sustainability, 15*(13), 10400.

Cappellaro, F., Fantin, V., Barberio, G., & Cutaia, L. (2020). CIRCULAR ECONOMY GOOD PRACTICES SUPPORTING WASTE PREVENTION: THE CASE OF EMILIA-ROMAGNA REGION. *Environmental Engineering & Management Journal (EEMJ), 19*(10).

Carayannis, E. G., & Campbell, D. F. (2009). 'Mode 3' and 'Quadruple Helix': Toward a 21st century fractal innovation ecosystem. *International Journal of Technology Management, 46*(3–4), 201–234.

Carayannis, E. G., & Campbell, D. F. (2011). Open innovation diplomacy and a 21st century fractal research, education and innovation (FREIE) ecosystem: Building on the quadruple and quintuple helix innovation concepts and the "mode 3" knowledge production system. *Journal of the Knowledge Economy, 2*, 327–372.

Centobelli, P., Cerchione, R., Chiaroni, D., Del Vecchio, P., & Urbinati, A. (2020). Designing business models in circular economy: A systematic literature review and research agenda. *Business Strategy and the Environment, 29*(4), 1734–1749.

Chen, X., Kurdve, M., Johansson, B., & Despeisse, M. (2023). Enabling the twin transitions: Digital technologies support environmental sustainability through lean principles. *Sustainable Production and Consumption, 38*, 13–27.

Dedehayir, O., Mäkinen, S. J., & Ortt, J. R. (2018). Roles during innovation ecosystem genesis: A literature review. *Technological Forecasting and Social Change, 136*, 18–29.

Del Vecchio, P., Passiante, G., Barberio, G., & Innella, C. (2021). Digital innovation ecosystems for circular economy: The case of ICESP, the Italian circular economy stakeholder platform. *International Journal of Innovation and Technology Management, 18*(01), 2050053.

Etzkowitz, H., & Zhou, C. (2006). Triple helix twins: Innovation and sustainability. *Science and Public Policy, 33*(1), 77–83.

Evans, S., Vladimirova, D., Holgado, M., Van Fossen, K., Yang, M., Silva, E. A., & Barlow, C. Y. (2017). Business model innovation for sustainability: Towards a unified perspective for creation of sustainable business models. *Business Strategy and the Environment, 26*(5), 597–608.

Garner, C., & Ternouth, P. (2011). Absorptive capacity and innovation in the triple helix model. *International Journal of Knowledge-Based Development, 2*(4), 357–371.

Geissdoerfer, M., Morioka, S. N., de Carvalho, M. M., & Evans, S. (2018). Business models and supply chains for the circular economy. *Journal of Cleaner Production, 190*, 712–721.

Leydesdorff, L., & Etzkowitz, H. (1998). The triple helix as a model for innovation studies. *Science and Public Policy, 25*(3), 195–203.

MacArthur, E. (2013). Towards the circular economy. *Journal of Industrial Ecology, 2*(1), 23–44.

Nambisan, S., Lyytinen, K., Majchrzak, A., & Song, M. (2017). Digital innovation management. *MIS Quarterly, 41*(1), 223–238.

Nielsen, S. N. (2007). What has modern ecosystem theory to offer to cleaner production, industrial ecology and society? The views of an ecologist. *Journal of Cleaner Production, 15*(17), 1639–1653.

Nussholz, J. L. (2018). A circular business model mapping tool for creating value from prolonged product lifetime and closed material loops. *Journal of Cleaner Production, 197*, 185–194.

Oh, D. S., Phillips, F., Park, S., & Lee, E. (2016). Innovation ecosystems: A critical examination. *Technovation, 54*, 1–6.

Parker, G. G., Van Alstyne, M. W., & Choudary, S. P. (2016). *Platform revolution: How networked markets are transforming the economy and how to make them work for you*. WW Norton & Company.

Popkova, E. G., De Bernardi, P., Tyurina, Y. G., & Sergi, B. S. (2022). A theory of digital technology advancement to address the grand challenges of sustainable development. *Technology in Society, 68*, 101831.

Powell, W. W., Koput, K. W., & Smith-Doerr, L. (1996). Interorganizational collaboration and the locus of innovation: Networks of learning in biotechnology. *Administrative Science Quarterly*, 116–145.

Ranta, V., Aarikka-Stenroos, L., Ritala, P., & Mäkinen, S. J. (2018). Exploring institutional drivers and barriers of the circular economy: A cross-regional comparison of China, the US, and Europe. *Resources, Conservation and Recycling, 135*, 70–82.

Rau, A. L., von Wehrden, H., & Abson, D. J. (2018). Temporal dynamics of ecosystem services. *Ecological Economics, 151*, 122–130.

Romano, A., Passiante, G., Del Vecchio, P., & Secundo, G. (2014). The innovation ecosystem as booster for the innovative entrepreneurship in the smart specialisation strategy. *International Journal of Knowledge-Based Development, 5*(3), 271–288.

Secundo, G., Ndou, V., Del Vecchio, P., & De Pascale, G. (2020). Sustainable development, intellectual capital and technology policies: A structured literature review and future research agenda. *Technological Forecasting and Social Change, 153*, 119917.

Secundo, G., Schena, R., Russo, A., Schiavone, F., & Shams, R. (2022). The impact of digital technologies on the achievement of the Sustainable Development Goals: Evidence from the agri-food sector. *Total Quality Management & Business Excellence*, 1–17. https://doi.org/10.1080/14783363.2022.2065981

Urbinati, A., Chiaroni, D., & Chiesa, V. (2017). Towards a new taxonomy of circular economy business models. *Journal of Cleaner Production, 168*, 487–498.

Van Veldhoven, Z., & Vanthienen, J. (2022). Digital transformation as an interaction-driven perspective between business, society, and technology. *Electronic Markets, 32*(2), 629–644.

Zajac, E. J., & Olsen, C. P. (1993). From transaction cost to transactional value analysis: Implications for the study of interorganizational strategies. *Journal of Management Studies, 30*(1), 131–145.

Chapter 10
Digital Transformation in International Education

Claudio Petti, Antonella Longo, and Antonio Ficarella

Abstract The chapter starts with a reflection on the nature and effects of the digital acceleration of higher education imposed by the Covid-19 pandemic outbreak. The first part examines the various forms and experiences of virtual internationalisation brought to the fore by the health emergency. This is done using an illustrative case of the experience of the Department of Engineering for Innovation at the University of Salento (Lecce, Italy). Then the reflection shifts to the need to distinguish between the short-term and long-term effects of the ongoing digital transformation in higher education. This distinction cannot and will not be addressed in isolation from the effects on the entire higher education sector.

From this perspective, the final part of the chapter will be devoted to considering whether and to what extent this transition responds to the objectives of the new European planning in terms of international education mobility: specifically, concerning the potential benefits and challenges of the massive diffusion of digital technologies regarding inclusion (of both individuals and territories) and the effects in terms of the environment and sustainability.

Keywords Digital transformation · e-learning · Higher education · Internationalisation · Sustainability

C. Petti (✉) · A. Longo · A. Ficarella
Department of Engineering for Innovation, University of Salento, Lecce, Italy
e-mail: claudio.petti@unisalento.it; antonella.longo@unisalento.it; antonio.ficarella@unisalento.it

G. Passiante (ed.), *Digital Innovation Management*, Applied Innovation and Technology Management, https://doi.org/10.1007/978-3-031-80426-7_10

10.1 Introduction

The Covid-19 pandemic changed everything, including the use of digital tools in international higher education—or rather, the approach to the use of digital tools in the field. As a matter of fact, while in terms of goods, industries and politics, the pandemic encouraged the pressures towards decentralisation and regionalisation, on the other hand it laid down the foundations for a globalisation of intangible flows, first and foremost of competencies and skills. This latter effect has much to do with digitalisation. The Covid-19 pandemic in fact exploded in a period of strong diffusion of digital technologies and, providentially, of sufficient bandwidth to allow many more activities to be carried out productively online—many more than imagined. This meant that, although people essentially remained stuck in their homes, their skills were not. Conversely knowledge, competencies and skills experienced an unprecedented circulation and diffusion.

Thus, whereas, on the one hand, digital networks guaranteed the continuity of work, life and society continuity by breaking down the pandemic's barriers to mobility, on the other hand, the very same pandemic barriers allowed many people to overcome the psychological barriers to the use of digital technologies (Petti, 2021). This combination of the explosion of Covid-19 and the acceleration of digitalisation has meant that in a very short time many of the activities that were thought of as confined to physical places and personal relationships have been projected into a potentially global arena, exponentially increasing the opportunities, but also the challenges. This is true both in the field of production, in which these phenomena are well documented, and in the higher education world, on which this work focuses.

More specifically, this chapter focuses on how digital transformation, particularly its acceleration imposed by the pandemic's outbreak, is changing a specific aspect of higher education and universities' mission: their internationalisation activities. This will be done by discussing the activities and the experiences of the Department of Engineering for Innovation at the University of Salento, Italy (DEfI) in these regards. The case is particularly illustrative since, first, DEfI has had 'virtual internationalisation' as an objective in its key actions since autumn 2019, before the explosion of the pandemic, and, second, because for more than 20 years DEfI has developed several scientific competencies about digital education and the virtualisation of education activities. Therefore, it is a privileged context to depict the sudden change in the approach to the use of digital technologies in higher education and its strong acceleration created by the pandemic. The illustration will also offer the chance, in the concluding section, for some considerations about the benefits and challenges of mass digitisation for the new European planning in terms of international mobility.

In the next section, the reflection starts from the challenge that a greater decoupling of people, places and skills, in many cases only accelerated by the pandemic, poses in a context of an information and knowledge economy where network dynamics mean that the *winner takes all* (Shapiro & Varian, 1999).

10.2 New Globalisation, the Covid-19 Pandemic and the Internationalisation of Higher Education

It is interesting to observe that, since before the Covid-19 pandemic outbreak, the internationalisation activities of universities were already suffering from the repercussions of commercial conflict and its geo-strategic derivations, such as the non-renewal or restrictions of visas for students in some countries. Similarly, the internationalisation of higher education was, along with tourism and entertainment industries, an area among those most affected by the pandemic emergency since its outset, at least in logistical terms. One might consider the multitudes of students stranded in their residences and the not-so-easy dilemmas between personal and family safety that many of them faced (Petti, 2020).

In an area that makes mobility its *raison d'être*, the constraints and restrictions on the movement of people, both physical and psychological, were particularly disruptive. The magnitude and seriousness of the effects were evident in the results of a survey by the *European Association for International Education*, carried out in autumn 2020 (EAIE, 2021), when more than half of the respondents recorded a significant decrease in incoming and outgoing student mobility for the entire academic year (2020/21[1]), with a not-too-dissimilar picture between intra- and extra-European mobility. In the first, darkest moments of the pandemic, a return to normality really looked difficult, and many questioned how—and some even whether—the internationalisation of higher education could survive Covid-19.

Another, and even more interesting, insight from the surveys above, however, were two revealing aspects of how the internationalisation of higher education was conceived (Petti, 2021). 'Revealing' because they provide useful elements to identify the possible evolutions of the internationalisation of higher education brought using digital tools.

First, there was a strong awareness of the institutes interviewed towards the forms of virtual mobility as the most recommended alternative remedy compared to the postponement of mobility (29% vs 21%, respectively) and other modalities. Only a small percentage, however, reported the forms of virtual mobility as being the first choice of students to cope with obstacles to mobility (between 7% and 10%). Although this study already reported an evolution (in just 6 months) compared to the EAIE survey completed in early March 2020 (Rumbley, 2020), in which virtual mobility was cited by percentages of less than 10%, it is still just an incremental evolution in the wake of a conceptualisation of *digital modalities as an emergency tool*. In that survey, both in the preventive responses and remedies implemented with respect to curbing the spread of Covid-19, areas related to travel and mobility (together, of course, with information and measures on health and safety) were mostly cited, with reference to their cancellation, diversion or postponement. Far less prevalent were the provision of practical information regarding how to organise and study from home or the use of remedies related to alternative forms of

[1] Based on 424 questionnaires administered in member universities from 41 countries.

mobility, such as virtual mobility, facilitated by digital technologies, with percentages of less than 5% and 10%, respectively (see Petti, 2020). The use of digital tools to facilitate alternative forms of mobility was therefore conceived as a valuable alternative to cope with exceptional circumstances—just a temporary solution to be used while waiting for a return, as soon as possible, to 'normality' characterised by physical mobility. Indeed, everywhere digital technologies were cited in terms of ensuring the continuity of teaching and administrative and institutional activities, and at best as a remedy to enable stranded students to be able to continue their activities. Indeed, reinforcing was the evidence (also from our university) about a surprisingly high number of students who carried out their usual mobility activities in 2020–2021 eventually. Indeed, the first of the two studies cited reported a high proportion of respondents who, in autumn 2020 did not expect any change in their exchange flows (40–50%).

What does the longed-for 'normality' mean, however? The question is anything but rhetorical and brings us to the second revealing aspect of the current conceptualisation of higher education's internationalisation: that is the fact that internationalisation means different things to universities and their students. Well before the EAIE surveys cited, this difference in perspectives was already clear in a joint study that, in 2017, had compared the survey made on the students of 56 American higher education institutions by Indiana University and another survey made by the American Council on Education (ACE) on the higher education institutions. The comparison of the two surveys highlights a divergence in the priorities between the universities and their students. For students, the motivators to internationalise their learning experience were not the increase in outgoing or incoming mobility and international partnerships (i.e. the priorities of their institutions) but the internationalisation of curricula, joint curricula and the involvement of teachers. That means curricula with global focuses, objectives and content and foreign languages, as well as a relevant importance attached to teachers' involvement and motivation in their own and students' international training.

10.3 Internationalisation: From Outwards to Inwards and Online

The internationalisation of curricula, as understood above, is incidentally a pillar of the *internationalisation at home* movement. Defined as the targeted integration of the international and intercultural dimensions into the formal and informal curricula of all students (Beelen & Jones, 2015), internationalisation at home focuses on the internationalisation of learning objectives through specific teaching, learning and assessment modalities aimed at incorporating a global and inter-cultural perspective into domestic curricula (Leask, 2015). On the other hand, *virtual mobility* has been a component of the Bologna Process for several years, along with *virtual exchanges*, a pillar of the Erasmus+ Programme. Collaborative online learning projects or *collaborative online international learning* (*COILs*), that is, the joint development of a course module by two or more teachers from different countries totally or partially *online,* were already concrete realities before the pandemic. These three examples are offered just to emphasise that the Covid-19 pandemic did not create new forms of mobility enabled by digital technologies but simply brought to the fore, by necessity, forms of mobility that had been discussed and developed, in some cases, for almost 30 years. Therefore, what the pandemic did was to shift the debate from a mainstream 'outward' perspective of internationalisation as 'going abroad' to an 'inwards' and, by then, academic perspective of 'internationalisation at or from home'. This latter, being more pervasive and deeper than mere physical mobility, integrated and modified the very same concept of internationalisation from something that is done only outside one's own university premises and country to something that can be done 'at home' and 'from home', that is, *online*, via the fundamental help of digital technologies.

All these phenomena preceded Covid and transcend digital technologies, since they originated from the need to spread and diffuse the educational benefits of international experiences by making them more inclusive. The tools and methods of distance learning and, more specifically, the possibilities and uses offered by digital technologies, were only the most common media by which those experiences were enabled, but inclusion was the core. For instance, *virtual exchanges* refer to a set of teaching, apprenticeship or learning activities supported by digital technologies, including e-learning, that carry out or facilitate international collaborative experiences in an online or mixed mode. Understood as a particular instance of *virtual mobility*, with a more marked orientation on integrating intercultural experiences into the formal and informal educational path of young people, *virtual exchanges* are a prominent example of the pervasiveness and inclusiveness potential of the 'inwards', 'online' and, in the authors' view, comprehensive and genuine perspective of internationalisation. In fact, not all students participate or can participate in mobility activities. This includes not only those students who cannot participate due to conditions of physical, psychological or societal vulnerability but also those students not interested in international experiences. This explains why international mobility, which is what internationalisation usually means and how it is practised, still involves a minority not only of students but also of faculty members.

The aim of alternative forms of mobility, being a *virtual mobility* or a *COIL*, is therefore to extend the benefits of an international perspective and experience from a minority of a university community to most beneficiaries, including not only university students and their teachers but also local communities (e.g. with *virtual exchanges*). Therefore, although it may seem like a post-pandemic debate, it should be clear by now that 'virtual' forms of mobility and exchanges were already widespread in many contexts. This is true not only in the developed global 'North' but also in the developing and underdeveloped 'South'. In the 'North', these forms gained momentum well before the pandemic due to an increasing awareness of the environmental effects of mobility[2] and aspects of societal inclusion and, in the 'South', by real needs fuelled by logistical difficulties, migration and the effects of conflicts. These latter, unfortunately and in contrast with the Covid-19 pandemic, are a tragic actuality and no longer just in the distant, underdeveloped and unstable 'South'. What the restrictions due to the pandemic did, therefore, was to put us in front of a new-but-old form of internationalisation of higher education. In fact, although it is necessary to continue to invest in the creation of mobility opportunities abroad, as requested by the students themselves, it is no longer possible to ignore the identification and implementation of ways to extend the opportunities to acquire international knowledge and experiences to all students and the wider academic community (see the provisions for EU funding in these regards and the new short-term/blended forms of mobility) as well as to develop the skills, competencies and relationships that are now essential for the modern world of work.

So, what if digital forms of mobility and internationalisation were not the tiring but necessary parentheses of a pandemic or (for some) conflict period but instead became an equally valid alternative to higher education's internationalisation—part of the internationalisation toolbox of each university internationalisation strategy? What if the use of these tools becomes so 'normal' that it redefines even its priorities and the concept of internationalisation itself? What if the use of digital tools eventually helps bring internationalisation back to its inner nature of encounters with new cultures, personal enrichment and the enhancement of diversity through knowledge sharing and dialogue? Is physical mobility the only way to accomplish this?

These are the questions that we asked ourselves in our department and set forth in our pandemic and post-pandemic digital push to our internationalisation activities, as illustrated by DEfI's strategic activities and initiatives in the overall virtual internationalisation actions described in the next section.

10.4 The Virtual Internationalisation Activities of DEfI

During the pandemic, DEfI, thanks to its pre-pandemic reflections and strategising of its participation in the international higher education community, events and, eventually, the presence of long-established competencies in distance and digital education in some of its research groups, used and engaged with several virtual internationalisation initiatives and projects.

These initiatives and projects were not only deployed and implemented to face Covid-19 as a mere emergency response. Instead, they were, since their inception, deployed and implemented as an experiment and with a sustainability approach: meaning with the intention and the additional necessary systematisation work to make the planned initiatives and tools replicable, shareable among colleagues and,

[2] See, for example, the study by Arsenault et al. (2019) on the annual per capita effect in terms of CO_2 of the University of Montreal's (mainly international) student mobility.

it was hoped, able to become embedded in DEfI's teaching and education activities. This is what has been called the *digital repository of international higher education*, which is not only a collection of virtual resources made available to each interested faculty but also a network of experiences and experienced fellow contacts available to shadow and help with the use of such practices and tools.

More specifically, the activities undertaken and now part of the *repository* can be categorised into two main categories (see Fig. 10.1):

- 'Practices', that is, internationalisation@home, COIL modules, virtual mobilities (for studies and internships) and virtual exchanges
- 'Tools and resources', that is, virtual, remote and augmented labs, e-learning, Massive Open Online Courses (MOOCs), Massive Open Online Labs (MOOLs) and, in general, distance-education resources.

Concerning the 'practices' side, internationalisation@home has been and is being promoted by the invitation to the department's colleagues with international collaborations and contacts to host interventions of colleagues from abroad in their courses or to organise specific seminars, as well as to hold joint lectures. Particularly relevant in these regards was the sensitisation and diffusion of information about the internal procedures and regulations, if any, for doing so. This mainly happened in the English-language courses at the master's level, but not exclusively. Another initiative in these regards was to open some introductory doctoral courses (e.g. research methods) and seminars to international partners' students. This meant not only allowing access to the platform and course, in one case to more than 20 Iranian students, but also co-organising the experience with local tutors. The aim was to minimise the extra work of DEfI's PhD in Engineering of Complex Systems programme's faculty members to try making their online courses scalable to more students. The key role of local tutors was to make the increased number of students 'neutral' in relation to DEfI faculties' planned activities, but also for DEfI's curricular PhD students' experience and learning.

Eventually, in terms of internationalisation@home, content that is more international was introduced in some programmes, like the Course in Technological Entrepreneurship offered by faculty members attached to the Management Science and Engineering Laboratory (MSE Lab), where an international entrepreneurship module was introduced. In this module, each year a specific country was introduced as the focus of teaching content and activities. Local colleagues and field experts, for example about China, introduced the enterprising business in that country.

In the same Technological Entrepreneurship Course, collaborative online international learning experiences were organised by customising another module, the business plan module, to allow several students from DEfI's and MSE Lab's partnerships network to attend business-plan lectures and work in mixed groups on projects about generating entrepreneurial ideas.

The key to the success and diffusion of the above practices was to maximise the experience while minimising the procedural and coordination burden on curricular or organising faculty. That meant adding not only the participation and involvement of local colleagues and tutors from international partners to follow and follow up

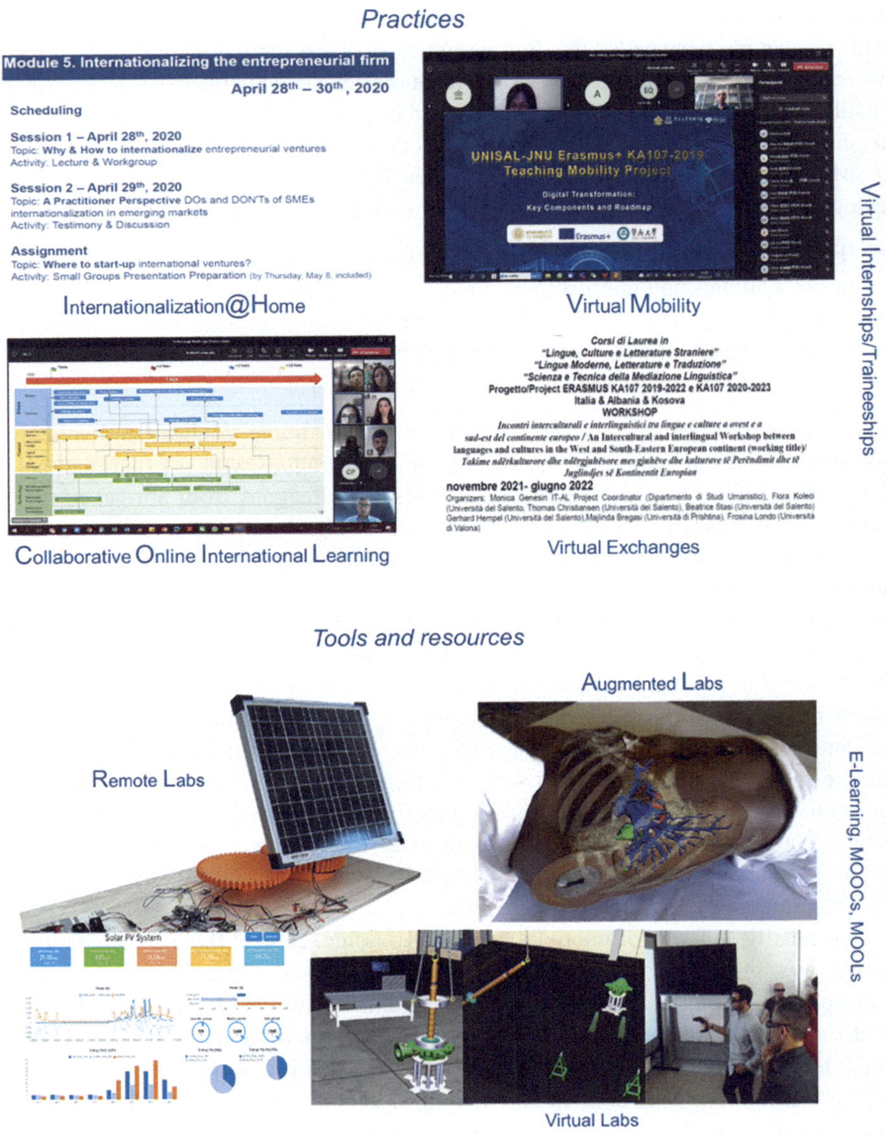

Fig. 10.1 DEfI virtual repository for higher international education

with their own students and help with possible difficulties and needs arising during the project work (in the same vein as the PhD) but also to make these experiences embedded as alternative paths within reciprocal curricular courses. This latter has proven to be not only the least 'invasive' modality for faculty and administrative personnel but also the most inclusive, not adding extra work hours and credits to students' path while at the same time offering them choice and flexibility. In fact, the key in these COILs is the collaboration of at least two faculty members, instructors in similar courses in our department and in the partner institution in which the COIL and related activities and evaluations were embedded. In this approach the evaluation is made separately by each faculty member for his or her own students, and the non-compulsory nature of the COIL is granted by treating the COIL as an alternative to the project work to which part of the final grade is usually attached. This COIL's non-compulsory nature is particularly relevant when they are organised in bachelor's degree courses or courses in Italian. This is in fact another advantage of COIL: it is a tool to internationalise the experience of students enrolled in native language courses (for both or all the institutions involved respectively in bilateral or multilateral COILs). This is almost the same way as many Erasmus blended intensive programmes (BIPs) are now organised, although at the time we were not familiar with BIPs that were still in the development and approval process of Erasmus planning. In the same vein, 'forced' virtual mobilities of Erasmus projects were organised, like a KA107 with Albania, Kazakhstan and China due to the pandemic, but also due to the post-pandemic policies of some countries: for instance, with China, in which two reciprocal mobilities were organised respectively, the first as a COIL with seminars and practical applications on technology road-mapping held by a Chinese faculty member within our Technological Entrepreneurship Course and his own Management Engineering course, and the second as a practical hands-on one-week module on Digital Business held by one of our faculty members (from the MSE Lab) to a class of Chinese students.

Concerning 'tools and resources', talking about the former, a parallel project of several laboratories (e.g. 3D printing, Pelton Turbines, Dynamometer of compression ignition engines, Jet Flame, Green Engine Combustion, Centrifugal Pumps, Photovoltaic Panel and Remote Lab for the production of solar energy) to migrate from physical to virtual spaces has been undertaken to create extended classroom laboratories. By *extended classrooms and laboratories* we mean specifically

- New spaces and new opportunities for study and encounters enabling the activities of physical and distributed working groups.
- Augmented lectures based on augmented and virtual reality technologies.
- Context-aware simulations.
- Digital twins of physical labs (i.e. *virtual labs*), *remote labs* (i.e. labs that can be used by several users physically present or at a distance through digi-tronic equipment).
- Shared platforms (see Fig. 10.2).

These new spaces are an ideal companion for transforming local physical classes into international blended classes with a high level of involvement of local and international students and faculty members. They can facilitate and make more effective virtual mobilities and extend the opportunities and benefits of intercultural exchanges and social inclusion.

Concerning resources, *Massive Open Online Courses* (*MOOCs*) have been created, also through participation in European Consortia and Erasmus+ Projects. An example is Project EUSecure, through which an interdisciplinary free online course

Fig. 10.2 DEfI extended classroom and laboratories

with a certificate in EU Security, Resilience and Sustainability has been developed in collaboration with four EU Universities (from Greece, Portugal and Hungary, the coordinator). This MOOC was not just about content but represented a truly new paradigm for the use of MOOCs that now inspires DEfI MOOCs' production and endeavours: that is, to integrate within traditional MOOCs laboratory and practical content (thanks to and integrated because of the extended laboratories described above) aimed at enabling non-formal STEM education. This breaks down the barriers between virtual and physical access to formal/theoretical and non-formal/practical content, respectively. This makes distance/blended STEM learning not only more effective but also, again, more inclusive. In fact, *virtual and remote labs*, from simulations to digital twins, make experiments accessible to a wide audience, overcoming geographic distances as well as safety and access constraints on the use physical spaces and reducing the cost of consumables. Both *virtual and remote labs*, integrated with and within MOOCs, create seamless spaces of tools and resources to enable remote international collaborative learning and work through collaborative *remote labs* aimed at making laboratory resources available at a distance, with the result of making experimental activity more effective through pooling lab resources and reducing the cost of accessing precious and expensive resources. By 'cost' we mean not only the individual institutional cost but also the societal cost. This is because of the possibility of reducing redundancy in labs and equipment by exploiting the possibility of sharing access. An example is the chance to share with technical schools Defi's 3D printer at the Rapid Prototyping lab through remote access to the printer.

Fig. 10.3 From open labs to the local territory as a lab for outdoor education

Eventually, realising the mission of internationalisation not only at and from home but 'for all', the concept of *Massive Online Open Labs (MOOLs)* arose, which are being experimented to take science outside the labs to local surroundings and citizens. A MOOL provides digital infrastructure for collecting and analysing data, openly available for scientific experiments in a shared ecosystem of educational institutions. For example, in urban contexts, thanks to the approaches of citizen science and citizen engagement experiences, students can be involved in collecting environmental and pollution data that are then shared within a local school network. This approach complements the benefit of outdoor education and citizen science, exploiting the new technologies of big data and cloud computing. At DEfI, several experiments have been run to collect data about, for instance, urban noise or air quality, visualising data from different experiments on maps along different time windows as shown in Fig. 10.3.

10.4.1 From the Emergency to a New Normal: Tracing the Long-Term Effects of Digital Transformation in Higher Education's Internationalisation

The solutions we found and are finding, as well as the replies to the questions we asked ourselves about the digitalisation of our department's internationalisation activities, are themselves the results of a reflection on the contingent against the structural nature of the transformations we have and are encountering. One underlying question triggered all our pandemic and post-pandemic reflections about the use of digital tools. Was the use of digital tools in international higher education all about Covid-19? Could it just be an emergency toolkit to activate as needed for (although we hoped not) similar emergencies?

Obviously, we did not and do not believe that, since the use of digital tools is about and can facilitate continuous inclusion (e.g. of vulnerable students) and increase its academic and societal influence by reducing the difficulties and increasing the learning quality of remote students and faculties, whatever their conditions (e.g. young students, student workers, student parents, caregivers). This applies to their communities as well, in terms of revitalising or preserving distant areas—all by controlling for environmental effects, which, as we will see in our final reflections, even digitalisation, if not used responsibly, could eliminate.

It is our belief that we are now in the third and final phase of Covid's effects on the digital transformation of higher education (see Table 10.1): the organisational restructuring following the massive use and diffusion of digital tools triggered by the Covid-19 emergency.

It is not necessary to comment on the first two phases, which were very likely a common experience to most readers, whether faculty members, administrative personnel, students or just ordinary people suddenly experiencing the digitalisation of almost every aspect of their lives.

It is in the third phase that the effects of new conceptions and forms of academic internationalisation on the evolution of higher education are produced. This discovery and, at the same time, rediscovery of digital education, in all its forms, implies a rethinking of university internationalisation, in its priorities and paradigms, with the consolidation of those forms of virtual and mixed mobility experienced in the

Table 10.1 Covid-19 and digital acceleration: from tech-conjuncture to organisational restructuring

Phase 1—The emergency: Everything online	The break-in at digital repositories and the band key. The fall of psychological barriers, the 'novelty effect'. The de-materialisation of competencies and higher education. Waiting for 'normality' and the perceptions' divide between students and their universities[a]
Phase 2—The *new* normality: From extraordinary to ordinary (and a little bit of digital fatigue)	The fading of the 'novelty effect' within the 'nostalgia effect'. From virtual mobility to the (vigorous) re-start and demand of physical mobility. Back to class and the pain and gains of blended teaching. The recognition of short-term, blended and virtual mobility.
Phase 3– What does 'new' mean?	Conjuncture against structure and the need for time and data. Organisational and administrative innovation. Recognition, collaboration schemes, regulations, competencies upgrade, MINDSET. Curricula innovation and the rethinking of international higher education. Integrated, diversified, blended, shorter, focussed, tailored, worldly, closer, @home, safe. Decoupling among people, places and competencies.

[a]See NSSE-ACE, 2017 study cited

pandemic period as well as in the development of international programmes, initiatives and courses that overcome the need for long periods of mobility. To this end, it will probably be necessary to re-orient this offer by integrating it with forms of face-to-face mobility, calibrating it to the needs of specific groups of users or types of agreements and programmes. After all, this is the line drawn by the new Erasmus+2021–27 Programme, which encourages new forms of short-term mobility and a shortening of physical mobility through the virtual component and, more generally, promotes access, inclusion and diversity, in their broadest sense, from individual to territorial fragility.

This internationalisation will be increasingly *from home* and, for this reason, more inclusive and incisive, but accompanied by the need to adapt the programs and the educational offer to the needs of students who are less and less 'local'. These include not only international students but also students from more or less neighbouring areas—those who are conceived of, especially by universities with strong ties to the territory, as with their catchment area. This new breed of 'international' students is one of the long-term effects that will bear most of the effects and trigger most of the changes, as discussed in the following concluding section.

10.4.2 Implications for Inclusion and the Environment

The main effect of a new breed of 'international' students and consequent evolution of higher education (see Petti, 2020 for more detail) is by definition a matter for universities and their relations with the territories in which they operate. Students who are digital natives may immediately grasp that the possibility of taking courses at their university *online*, doing experiments and even carrying out entire internships remotely, as some of our students did at DEfI, may be done potentially everywhere. Some more conscious may also consider that the savings that come from not having to physically move to and settle at one's own university, at least for long periods, could be invested in supporting the payment of tuition fees for courses at prestigious universities, even in other countries, or following a *blended* career path, with one cycle being done online and the following in person, and both far from their home base. This scenario prospects a possible future in which even the concept of an *international student* may dematerialise or at least become more vague, detaching itself from the place of origin and/or study to become a category, and eventually a state of mind, in an economy increasingly characterised by paradigms and those logics of the network for which the 'winner takes all'. This represents a strong push towards polarisation, a polarisation that the 'network effect'[3] can make even more dramatic.

[3] The effect by which a network has and acquires more value and attractiveness is the number of participants in that network and vice versa. See Shapiro and Varian (1999).

It is in fact undeniable that a digitalisation of mobility and training offers something that is potentially more inclusive, advantageous and, in the immediate future, necessary, but it can only be truly so if digital infrastructure and skills allow for it. In fact, a digital transition is not only a question of infrastructure but also of access: access in its broadest sense, which includes the use of skills, organisational models and equal opportunities. In this period of post-pandemic and digital structural adjustment, the needle of the scales unequivocally leans towards the universities that are more digitally and organisationally infrastructure and, one might say, better placed from a reputational perspective, another fundamental element in an information and network economy. This latter aspect clarifies the extent to what the issue concerns all universities, from small- and medium-sized to large ones and polytechnics, which measure themselves against large American and British powerhouses, which have had digital platforms, massive open online content and programmes for years.

Only a traditional conceptualisation of globalisation, however, understood as homogenisation with respect to a dominant model that is standardised by nature, could lead to the laying down of arms, perhaps interspersed with attempts of assimilation. This is, however, a model of globalisation that is not even reflected in its precursors and champions. Even McDonald's has strongly adapted to local tastes and realities. For the same reason, how can we be sure that the same teaching material, the same case studies or the same theories that underlie them will be applicable in all realities? If, on the other hand, this concept of homogenising globalisation, exacerbated by a deviant vision of diversity, were to be contrasted with the aspects of connectivity, of the possibility of encountering new cultures and of dialogue that instead enhance diversity, making it a common heritage, we could perhaps glimpse not only challenges but also opportunities for the territorial rooting of universities. From this perspective, opportunities may come from seeing the acceleration of the digital transition as a springboard and the potentially global access that it can guarantee as a stage to which to bring one's own peculiarities, without distorting them, but rather making them a distinctive element for the territory. This is not intended to downsize the role of face-to-face teaching, much less that of the local language or local specificities, but rather to enhance them for the creation of a unique training offer, recognised as an expression of the excellence of that territory, not opposing but supporting the dematerialisation of skills through new patterns of thought, by defining and conveying educational offers that are an expression of the history, culture, lifestyle and physical characteristics of the territories: a sort of reinterpretation of the concept of *terroir*[4] applied to higher education and skills. In fact, INDIRE 2019 data—the Italian Erasmus National Agency—show that the country, the city and the culture matter more than the education offer, ranking or services (90% vs. 50–75%) in Erasmus students' choices. Social life (with 76%) is also more important (Silvestri, 2019).

[4] A concept borrowed from oenology that defines the relationship that binds a vine to the microclimate and mineral characteristics of the soil in which it is grown, determining the character and uniqueness of the wine that is produced there.

This is an opportunity that, moreover, does not end with the attraction and training of new 'international' talents, but takes the form of a third mission in the service of the local community and the local economy, becoming itself a springboard onto the global stage, breaking down the physical barriers to encounters with different cultures, situations and points of view, but also breaking down the digital isolation created by the algorithms of social networks and local digital circles: for example, by promoting and animating intercultural experiences and informal and collaborative educational paths with tools like *virtual exchanges* or by increasingly promoting and spreading digital access to the local production and entrepreneurial offer.

Turning to environment and sustainability, one might recall that environmental consciousness was a key trigger of the diffusion of digital models into internationalisation. The promotion of green travel is in fact now a provision and a set of incentives within European and Erasmus programmes, and it is not a fad. In fact, in a study of academic mobility at the University of Montreal, Arsenault et al. (2019) calculated the per-capita annual effect of (purely international) mobility to be 3.85 tons of CO_2 per student, most of which (85%) is generated by air and international travel. It is not only international travel, but all the needs related to physical mobility and settlement that should be considered, not only because is relevant for the environment and our shared future but also because it is something to which modern students, our students, attach great importance.

Nonetheless, a final consideration is to be given to the fact that digitalisation does not come entirely environmentally free. It is sufficient to think that technology contributes to 4% of CO_2 emissions, about double that of global aviation, and that digital infrastructure and electronic equipment may arrive to equal all the emissions of circulating light vehicles in 2025—that is just next year. This is not surprising if we think that a one-hour video-conference would produce 150 grams of CO_2 and a real-time video stream 450 grams[5]: not as much as the pollution produced by a litre of fuel, but if multiplied by hundreds of millions (e.g. daily hours streaming YouTube and Netflix video), the content consumption ceases to be negligible. Therefore, in the same vein in which the potential for inclusiveness must be considered along with polarisation, *winner take all* and access effects, in order to be consistent with the greener priority of new European planning in terms of international education mobility, digitalisation objectives need to consider the issue of techno-pollution in the new techno-organisational model of international mobility. This, however, is another story and may be—in fact, should be—a matter for further study.

References

ACE. (2017). *Mapping internationalization on U.S. campuses*. American Council on Education.

Arsenault, J., Talbot, J., Boustani, L., Gonzalès, L., & Manaugh, K. (2019). The environmental footprint of academic and student mobility in a large research-oriented university. *Environmental Research Letters, 14*(9), 1–9.

[5] Source: the Shift Project cited in HDBlog—April 17th, 2021.

Beelen, J., & Jones, E. (2015). Redefining internationalization at home. In A. Curaj, L. Matei, R. Pricopie, J. Salmi, & P. Scott (Eds.), *The European higher education area* (pp. 67–80). Springer.

EAIE. (2021). *Snapshot on exchange mobility 2020/21*. European Association for International Education.

Leask, B. (2015). *Internationalizing the curriculum*. Routledge.

Petti, C. (2020). La globalizzazione immateriale: Verso la trasformazione dell'internazionalizzazione accademica. *L'Industria: Rivista di Economia e Politica Industriale, 3*(3), 403–416.

Petti, C. (2021). Università fra digitalizzazione e territori: Sfide e opportunità per l'internazionalizzazione dopo la pandemia. *Economia e Società Regionale, 1*(1), 107–116.

Rumbley, L. (2020). *Coping with COVID-19: International higher education in Europe*. European Association for International Education.

Shapiro, C., & Varian, H. (1999). *Information rules: A strategic guide to the network economy*. Harvard Business School Press.

Silvestri, L. (2019). *Gli studenti Erasmus in Italia. Analisi della mobilità in entrata*. INDIRE – Agenzia Nazionale Erasmus+.

The manufacturer's authorised representative in the EU is Springer Nature Customer Service Centre GmbH, Europaplatz 3, 69115 Heidelberg, Germany. If you have any concerns regarding our products, please contact ProductSafety@springernature.com

Printed and bound by CPI Group (UK) Ltd, Croydon, CR0 4YY
30/09/2026
02225569-0002